Praise
Shining in Spotl

At last a method of consecration to Our Lady as the Immaculate Conception! I have waited a long time for a book of this kind. Saint Stanislaus Papczyński and St. Maximilian Kolbe, saints particularly devoted to the Immaculate Conception, must be rejoicing in Heaven that my confrère, Fr. Thaddaeus Lancton, MIC, has developed this consecration program. I highly recommend this book and will be sharing it with everyone I know. All for the Immaculata!

— **Very Rev. Donald Calloway, MIC**
Vicar Provincial, Marian Fathers of the Immaculate Conception,
and author of *Consecration to St. Joseph: The Wonders of Our Spiritual Father*

With his typical precision and deep spirituality, Fr. Thaddaeus Lancton has graced us with an excellent and expansive treatise and meditation on the Immaculate Conception with all its implications for our daily lives. Laid out in an easy-to-access 40 meditations, it is complete with biblical references, theological nuggets, applications, questions, and prayers. This book will be valuable for scholars and beginners. This profound dogma of the Church continues to bear fruit, and this book is like plucking the ripe fruit from the tree.

— **Stephen K. Ray**
CatholicConvert.com,
and author of *Crossing the Tiber: Evangelical Protestants Discover the Historical Church*

Shining in Spotless Splendor is a beautiful and timely book, full of wisdom mirroring its radiant subject, the Immaculata! Throughout this book, Fr. Lancton draws profound insights from the richness of Sacred Scripture and the reflections of saints, showing how each one of us are called to imitate Mary: "to be holy and without blemish" (Eph 1:4). Lest we feel incapable of this degree of wholeness and holiness, the saints make it clear that this is a work of God's grace, accomplished through the merciful love of Christ, reaching the depths of our sin, brokenness, and shame. We, like the Immaculata, must only give our "Fiat." These are a few of the gems that inspired me personally: "Mary remained sinless throughout her life because she always remained in His love" (Jn 15:9); and, "She lived constantly from that place of always having been loved. Sin is behavior flowing from the need to be loved, as if we were not already fully loved. Sin arises from a heart that believes it is unloved and so desperately screams to be loved. Unaware that the living water — the Spirit of love — gushes forth from within, the sinner searches for love outside"; and, "We are purified by His love when we allow Him to love *us in every aspect of our being, even in aspects that are dirty or shameful.*"

— **Bob Schuchts**
Founder, John Paul II Healing Center,
and author of *Be Transformed:*
The Healing Power of the Sacraments

Shining IN SPOTLESS SPLENDOR

Consecration to the IMMACULATE CONCEPTION

Fr. Thaddaeus Lancton, MIC

Available from:
Marian Helpers Center
Stockbridge, MA 01263

Prayerline: 1-800-804-3823
Orderline: 1-800-462-7426

Websites:
Marian.org
TheDivineMercy.org
ShopMercy.org

Cover artwork by José Castrillo.

Library of Congress Control Number: 2023941616
ISBN: 978-1-59614-599-3

Imprimi Potest:
Very Rev. Chris Alar, MIC
Provincial Superior
The Blessed Virgin Mary, Mother of Mercy Province
Feast of the Immaculate Heart of the Blessed Virgin Mary
June 17, 2023

Nihil Obstat:
Robert A. Stackpole, STD
Censor Deputatus
June 17, 2023

Note: The *Nihil Obstat* and corresponding *Imprimi Potest* are not a certification that those granting it agree with the contents, opinions, or statements expressed in the work. Instead, they merely confirm that the work contains nothing contrary to faith and morals.

ACKNOWLEDGMENTS

I dedicate this book to the Immaculata, whose faithful heart reveals to me the mystery of God's love. Through and with her, I have been privileged to know the Father's tender care, the Son's humble obedience, and the Spirit's powerful love.

I want to thank our Founder, St. Stanislaus, for his fidelity to the Lord and his own suffering, that enabled the Holy Spirit to inscribe this mystery of the Immaculate Conception on his heart. Through him, I receive the grace to be a Marian and bear Mary's name and witness to her Immaculate Conception.

Lastly, I want to thank those who accompanied me during the time that I wrote this book. They encouraged me to never lose hope that His mercy and grace are always more powerful than darkness, and that I, a sinner, can hope to become a saint.

In Jesus and Mary Immaculate,
Fr. Thaddaeus Lancton, MIC

Table of Contents

INTRODUCTION

Immaculata Virginis Mariae Conceptio
Sit Nobis Salus et Protectio

May the Virgin Mary's Immaculate Conception
Be Our Health and Our Protection.

— Saint Stanislaus Papczyński

The invocation above is a prayer of St. Stanislaus Papczyński (1631-1701), the Founder of the Congregation of Marian Fathers of the Immaculate Conception. He frequently recited the prayer, since he "always placed his great hope of attaining heavenly goods in this special privilege of the Blessed Mother" — her Immaculate Conception.[1] His spiritual sons, the Marians, still conclude their communal prayers with this invocation. We share his hope of receiving heavenly graces and blessings — health, salvation, protection, and more — through her Immaculate Conception. I invite you to join us in praying this invocation to receive all the "heavenly goods" that the Immaculata desires to grant you.

The Immaculate Conception describes the sinless conception of the Blessed Virgin in St. Anne's womb. But if there were nothing more hidden in this mystery, it would be only her unique privilege. It would not affect our lives nor touch our hearts. Saint Stanislaus Papczyński, however, experienced this mystery as the "sign, strength, and joy" of his vocation, giving purpose, meaning, and direction to his life. This mystery — together with the founding of the Marians — was engraved on his heart.[2]

The Holy Spirit continues to imprint this mystery on our hearts by purifying us of all sin and healing its effects, so that we too may be immaculate like the Virgin. By our entrusting of ourselves to the Immaculata, the Holy Spirit brings this mystery to life in the Church today. "That which the Father brought to pass in the life of Mary through the Holy Spirit, he wishes to realize in us as well, although in a different fashion."[3] Through the 39 days outlined in this book, we tap into the living reality of this mystery, so that the Holy Spirit may accomplish in us what He first wrought in the Immaculata. By the unpacking of her mystery, the heavenly blessings contained within it can be received, experienced, and shared in the Church and in your life.

The Church in the Liturgy of the Hours asks the Lord, "Bridegroom of the Church, cleanse her from every stain."[4] If we listen, we will hear the Holy Spirit within who *groans* for us to be entirely healed and saved *like the Immaculata* (see Rom 8:23-27). Our Blessed Mother wants to share with us all the graces of her Immaculate Heart. The Immaculata explained the symbolism of the Miraculous Medal (originally called the "Medal of the Immaculate Conception") to St. Catherine Labouré (1806-1876): "These rays symbolize the graces I shed upon those who ask for them. The gems from which rays do not fall are the graces for which souls forget to ask."[5] There are abundant riches concealed within this mystery, but we must ask, lest these gems fall to the ground. With filial trust, let us dare to ask the Father for the grace to be immaculate like her.

The Immaculate Conception is a mystery still being fulfilled in the Church and in the heart of each baptized Christian. The historical fact that the Marians in 1910 were reduced by persecution to one member and then revived by Blessed George Matulaitis (1871-1927) testifies that Divine Providence sees this mystery as important both to the life of the Church and to your life. Relating his own experience of this mystery, Blessed George wrote in his journal, "I thank You, Lord, for having given me such extraordinary feelings of love for the Immaculate Conception of the Blessed Virgin Mary … how sweet it is to fall at her feet and to immerse myself in prayer! Overwhelmed by these feelings of incomparable sweetness, my soul swoons and my body is filled with wondrous, incomprehensible, and inexpressible tremors."[6] My hope is that the Holy Spirit will grant you also such "extraordinary feelings of love" and "incomparable sweetness" for the Immaculata.

For the first 100 years of our existence, the Marians were placed under the patronage of the Franciscans — known for their promotion of this mystery. Saint Maximilian Kolbe, a Conventual Franciscan (1894-1941), was convinced that the proclamation of the dogma in 1854 was only the "first page" of the history of the Immaculate Conception. He wrote, "Now that the dogma has been approved, is the matter finished? Are we to cross our arms and consider it done with? … Oh, never! It is right now that we need to get busy, to disseminate devotion to the Immaculate Conception throughout the whole world and instill this devotion in every soul."[7] He believed this mystery to be a "fire, not only revealing itself to the human heart and guiding it, but all the while enkindling and transforming that heart into the likeness of the

Immaculate Heart."[8] These daily meditations provide tinder to inflame your heart — like the Immaculate Heart — with the Holy Spirit.

In Eastern iconography, Mary is depicted as the *burning bush*: the one all-enveloped in the flame of love, and yet not consumed, not burned. The Immaculata invites us to be *aflame* with the same Spirit: to be unafraid of entering this fire! Out of fear, we may attempt to tame, control, extinguish, or even manipulate that blaze of love, which burns and purifies but also provides warmth and life. The Immaculata invites us not only to ponder the mystery from the outside but to enter into it as into a fire, like the three youths in the fiery furnace (Dan 3:23ff). When we allow the fire of the Holy Spirit to touch our hearts, as He filled the Immaculate Heart, then everything in us is transformed into divine life and love. "As fire transforms into itself everything it touches, so the Holy Spirit transforms into the divine life whatever is subjected to his power" (*Catechism of the Catholic Church*, 1127).

Within the furnace of fire, the three youths encountered one looking "like a son of God," that is, Jesus (Dan 3:92). By learning more about the Immaculata and falling in love with her, we come to know Christ and love Him as she does, for she is the gateway to knowing and loving Christ, who surpasses knowledge (Eph 3:19). As Our Lady of Fatima told Lúcia, "My Immaculate Heart will be your refuge and the *way that will lead you to God*."[9]

In the Liturgical Year, during the 39 days from October 31 to December 8, we can prepare ourselves to live this mystery. If you so choose to make this consecration on the Solemnity itself, the preparation in this book ends with Mass on December 8. This book can, nevertheless, be utilized at any time of year, for this mystery extends to everyday life through our living fully the baptismal call to holiness and seeking to be daily transformed by the Holy Spirit. Infused with the fullness of grace, the Immaculata responded to the Father with ever-greater love each day, and she invites and inspires us to do the same throughout the year. If you do use this consecration book at another time of year, keep in mind that some meditations — at the beginning and at the end — make some references that show its connection with the liturgical calendar.

The Second Vatican Council teaches that "devotions should be so drawn up that they harmonize with the liturgical seasons, accord with the sacred liturgy … and lead the people to it."[10] While the meditations are not connected to the daily Mass readings, they nonetheless reflect the primary themes of the liturgical season. As such, this book is intended not primarily as an extra devotion but as an accompaniment of this liturgical season, so that the readers may be more fully aware of the meaning of this mystery, participate more actively in the Liturgy, and "cooperate with divine grace."[11] For the Church invites us to participate in this mystery ever more deeply each year through the Eucharist. In doing so, we are enriched by the effects of this mystery, as were St. Stanislaus Papczyński, Blessed George Matulaitis, and St. Maximilian Kolbe.

Jesus invites us, like St. John, to take the Immaculata "into our own home" (Jn 19:27). In Greek, this translates as accepting Mary not only physically into our house, but into all that we are: our thoughts, emotions, decisions, relationships, work, prayer, and more. Jesus Himself invites us to a personal relationship with His mother, from whom we receive an "inexhaustible outpouring of the Spirit."[12] Only under the presence, protection, and guidance of the Immaculata can we be fully freed from sin, just as Jesus' humanity was preserved from sin under her guidance in Nazareth (Lk 2:51-52).

Saint Stanislaus Papczyński encourages us to "fly to her and to 'learn also to take refuge in her in case of doubts, anxieties, and difficulties, and to give continuous thanks to the Lord, because he chose and made her his own Mother and our advocate.'"[13] The Immaculata takes care of us in the same way she cared for her own Son: "I know that she is concerned for us in no other way than she was concerned for Christ the Lord, her only and most beloved Son, since she recognizes that we are His members."[14] As we say in St. Stanislaus' brief invocation, she, the Immaculate Conception, is our protection from all that is harmful or tarnishes the spotless splendor of holiness. Let us call upon her in every difficulty, for it is Jesus' personal decision to entrust us to His immaculate Mother and her to us.

This book thus aims not at providing more facts about the Blessed Mother. Rather, the goal is to lead you to a deeper relationship with the Immaculata and, through her, with the Holy Spirit. Saint Maximilian Kolbe wrote:

> When you start to read something on the Immaculata, do not forget that at that moment you are coming into contact with a living being, who loves you, who is pure, without any stain. Also, remember that the words you see are unable to express who she is, because they are human words, drawn from earthly concepts, words that present all things in a

human manner, while the Immaculate is a being totally of God. Thus, she is in some way infinitely more sublime than all that surrounds you. She will reveal herself to you through the phrases that you read and will convey to you thoughts, convictions, [and] feelings that the author himself could not possibly even imagine.

Consider carefully, also, that the purer your conscience is and the more you wash it with penance, the closer to the truth your knowledge about her will be. Recognize also with sincerity that without her help, you are utterly unable to do anything in the work of knowledge and, consequently, of love of her. Acknowledge that she alone must enlighten you more and more. She alone must draw your heart toward herself with love. Remember, therefore, that all the fruit of your reading depends on prayer to her.

Do not start reading, then, before appealing with some prayer for her help. Do not worry about reading much, but rather interweave your reading with elevation of your heart to her, especially when feelings of another nature awaken in your heart. Then, when you finish your reading, entrust to her the yield of an ever more beautiful fruit.[15]

Icon of the Pneumatophore:
The Mother of God Carrying the Holy Spirit

DAY 1

WHAT DOES "IMMACULATE" MEAN?

Immaculata Virginis Mariae Conceptio Sit Nobis Salus et Protectio

What does *immaculate* mean? Immaculate derives from the Latin *im*, "not," and *maculare*, "to stain." To be *im-maculate* is, according to the Merriam-Webster Dictionary, to be "spotlessly clean, having or containing no flaw or error, having no stain or blemish, having no colored spots or marks." Synonyms for immaculate include *clean, spotless, pristine, unsoiled, unsullied, speckless, gleaming, unblemished, pure, undefiled, impeccable, untarnished, stainless, incorrupt, sinless.*

Catholics frequently associate *immaculate* with the sinless conception of the Virgin Mary. The Immaculate Conception is her unique privilege. But the Father destines *everyone* to be immaculate. The Father has chosen us in Christ "before the foundation of the world, to be holy and without blemish before him" (Eph 1:4).

Most modern translations of the Bible do not employ the word *immaculate,* so you must seek its synonyms. Thus, the Greek *amomos,* "without blemish," could be translated as *immaculate.* Saint Paul wrote a staggering truth: the Father has predestined us and taken the initiative in Christ to make us holy and immaculate, like Mary, through His Spirit. The Father desires to make you clean, spotless, and pristine, as well as all the other synonyms of *immaculate*!

On October 31, All Hallows Eve, we contemplate the numerous canonized and countless uncanonized saints, in whom this verse of St. Paul has been fulfilled by the Holy Spirit. On November 1, All Saints' Day, we read about this "great multitude which no one could count" that "stood before the throne and before the Lamb ... wearing white robes." An elder asks, "Who are these wearing white robes, and where did they come from?" He then responds to his own question: "These are the ones who have survived the time of great distress; they have washed their robes and made them white in the Blood of the Lamb" (Rev 7:9-14). That great multitude prefigures all the saints, both canonized and uncanonized, "from every nation, race, people, and tongue." Like the Immaculata, these saints have been made immaculate by the Blood of the Lamb, as is symbolized by their white robes.

Through His Blood, we too are washed of all stain of sin. We are called to join their ranks, for we have also been given such white robes in Baptism. These white robes symbolize our Christian dignity, as sons and daughters of the Father. At Baptism, we were enjoined to "bring that dignity unstained [*immaculate*] into the everlasting life of heaven."[16] We must, like white-robed saints, survive the "time of great distress," the time when we suffer many temptations and can easily stain these robes by our sins. In the Mass of Christian Burial, this white garment reappears as the cloth that covers the casket of the deceased, symbolizing the hope that the deceased will be clothed in that stainless robe amid the multitude of heavenly saints.

The Second Vatican Council teaches the *universal call to holiness*: Each baptized Christian is called to the perfection of holiness.[17] For Jesus teaches *all* His disciples: "Be perfect, just as your heavenly Father is perfect" (Mt 5:48). Jesus is anything but a minimalist: If we are to enter Heaven, our holiness must go beyond that of the "scribes and Pharisees" (Mt 5:20) who punctiliously followed the Law. The Father is a maximalist: He created the Immaculata "full of grace" and holiness. He created us for the same goal of beauty and perfection.

But how is that possible for us sinners? My second-grade religion teacher asked our class, "Who wants to become a saint?" Few raised their hands. "Who wants to go to Heaven?" All raised their hands. Paradoxically, we admit we want to enter Heaven, but we feel incapable of being saints, much less immaculate! Such perfect holiness is out of the question. We know far too well how sinful we are, and so prefer to remain on "humbler," safer ground.

Yes, we are sinners, staining that white garment. But the merciful Father provides the Sacrament of Confession as a sort of washing machine to cleanse our once-white robes of all the stains caused by our daily sins. Like bleach, the Precious Blood of Jesus — applied to our contrite hearts in confession — makes us immaculate anew. Our Lady, revealing herself as the Immaculate Conception at Lourdes to St. Bernadette, repeated: "Penance, penance, penance!" For sinners, penance and contrition are our path to share in her immaculacy of heart and be robed anew in white. The Church, in her members, is stained, yet the Immaculata calls us forth along the path of penance to seek renewed immaculacy and innocence of heart.

Authentic humility recognizes that the last word is His abundant mercy. Only pride stubbornly believes that our sinfulness is stronger than His love. The Immaculata is a *living icon* of the Father's merciful love, proof that sin is entirely defeated.[18] She is visible evidence that the precious Blood is able to not only forgive sin but heal us from all stain — every effect — of sin. In the Immaculata, we glimpse who we are to become: shining in spotless splendor. What the Holy Spirit has accomplished already in the Immaculate Conception, He yearns to fulfill in the entire Church and in each of her members, including you. This is our *Christian hope*: that Christ's definitive victory over sin and death be extended to our hearts and lives, and through us, to the entire world.

As happened in Mary's life, the Holy Spirit has been at work since your conception to fulfill the Father's plan for your life: that you be holy and immaculate before Him (Eph 1:4, 5:25; 1 Thess 4:3). The Good News is that the Father has taken the initiative — and continues to do so each day — in making you holy. Imitating Our Lady's *fiat* — "May it be done *to* me" (Lk 1:38) — your part is to allow this Spirit to realize this mystery in your heart. The Immaculata teaches us to be docile and surrender to the Holy Spirit's gentle work of making us immaculate.

For many, this *fiat* was first expressed by your parents in Baptism, when the Holy Spirit began to dwell in you through sanctifying grace. The role of parents is fundamental in this task of teaching cooperation with the Holy Spirit's work. Mary was able to preserve her immaculacy of heart because she grew up in the context of sanctity in the home. We cannot imagine the Immaculate Virgin without remembering her parents, St. Joachim and St. Anne.

Most of us, however, did not grow up with saints for parents. Although my parents' lives were marked by serious sin, I believe they are among the multitude of uncanonized saints. They allowed the grace of God to have the final word in their lives. They became an example to me that the Holy Spirit can transform me — a sinner — into a saint. Like my (uncanonized) parents, the saints were sinners, subject to temptation and the weakness of the flesh: "Though the just fall seven times, they rise again" (Prov 24:16). How comforting authentic biblical holiness is!

We often have an idea of holiness predicated on "never falling." But saints are forgiven sinners who persevere in rising anew each day. Saints felt overwhelmed with sadness. They were weakened, sometimes paralyzed, by discouragement. They made use of the Sacrament of Penance to repent, place their trust ever more in God, and work with greater determination. They were humble, repentant, and confident in His Mercy. Jesus told St. Faustina, **"You see, My child, what you are of yourself. The cause of your falls is that you rely too much upon yourself and too little on Me. But let this not sadden you so much. You are dealing with the God of mercy, which your misery cannot exhaust. Remember, I did not allot only a certain number of pardons"** (*Diary of Saint Maria Faustina Kowalska*, 1488).

But would the Immaculata not be the exception to this — since she never failed? In a paradox, the Immaculata received not less — but more — mercy than any sinner. Like St. Thérèse, who was preserved from all mortal sin, Our Lady was "forgiven" *more,* not *less,* than Mary Magdalene and the "great sinners" who converted.[19] For the Immaculata was spared sin, "forgiven" before it should happen. Thus Our Lady never places herself above any sinner, for she knows in her humility that she has needed more mercy than even the worst of sinners.

In consecrating ourselves to the Immaculate Conception, we are taking the Immaculata as our "ideal" or goal. But we must remember that she is not an idea but a living person who embodies and shares the fullness of holiness God desires for us.

Saint Maximilian wrote:

> Sometimes one might ask himself: how do you have the courage to strive to become a saint, being weak as you are. Precisely the weaker one is, the better. The Immaculate is the embodiment of God's mercy. If She has raised up wretches or souls for which there was no hope that anything would ever come of them to such a sanctity as they had not even dreamed of, if She has raised up the most prodigal and weakest ones — then let us too strive for sanctity.[20]

The only limit to our holiness is the limit of our trust in what God can accomplish in us. For God "is able to accomplish far more than all we ask or imagine, by the power at work within us" (Eph 3:20-21). You have only to trust in Him and His work, echoing Our Lady's *fiat* so as to grant Him freedom to accomplish the Father's plan in you, starting today.

QUESTIONS

- How do you understand the universal call to holiness as applying to you?
- What image do you have of the saints and of holiness?
- How do you experience your weaknesses, and how can you, in effect, "rise again" each day?

PRAYER

Pray the "Prayer to the Immaculate Conception" (p. 204) and the Litany of the Blessed Virgin Mary, Immaculately Conceived (#1 - p. 212).

DAY 2

FOR ALL THE SAINTS

Immaculata Virginis Mariae Conceptio Sit Nobis Salus et Protectio

What does it mean to be a saint? *Saint* translates the Latin *sanctus* as "holy." A saint is a holy person. But what is holiness? The essence of holiness is *charity*, self-sacrificial love, for the thrice-holy God is "love" (1 Jn 4:16). To define love, we need to kneel before Jesus Crucified and contemplate His pierced Heart, overflowing with charity.[21] Saint Paul beautifully describes *agape — love —* in 1 Corinthians 13:4-7, for which Pope Francis provided a moving commentary in *Amoris Laetita.*[22] Although sanctity sometimes is manifest in extraordinary graces (such as visions, levitation, and miracles), the essence of authentic holiness is fulfilling the will of God in daily life. The summary of His will is Jesus' new commandment to love one another as He has loved us.[23]

Now, if being holy means living in love and radiating love toward others, then a saint is one who is filled with the Holy Spirit, for He is love in Person.[24] "The love of God has been poured out into our hearts through the holy Spirit that has been given to us" (Rom 5:5). To be a saint means to be *entirely, completely known and loved by the Holy Spirit, leaving no place of our minds, hearts, or lives untouched by His love.* All the saints — including the Immaculata — are holy because they received the merciful love of the Father and so were transformed by the Holy Spirit. Chosen in love by the Father, Mary was completely permeated with His love, was imbued by it, was rooted in it, was created by it, and remained in it. The Immaculata is the radiant image of the goal toward which we are heading: a human person, fully radiating the light and glory of the Holy Spirit. She is the *Panhagia,* the "All Holy," because she believed in His love, and so was touched by His Spirit of love, in every aspect of her body, mind, spirit, and life.

Saint Francis of Assisi called Our Lady the "spouse of the Holy Spirit." Saint Bonaventure called her the "perfect similitude" of the

Holy Spirit, and St. Maximilian Kolbe described her as the "transparent icon" of the Holy Spirit.[25] Because of her Immaculate Conception, there was never a moment when she was not was filled with the Holy Spirit. She never experienced life without the Father's love. Through her uninterrupted fidelity to the inspirations of the Holy Spirit, she became indissolubly united to Him.

Saint Maximilian Kolbe states that because the union of the Immaculata with the Holy Spirit is so permanent and deep, the Father "infuses no supernatural life into the soul except through the Mediatrix of all graces, the Immaculata, with her consent, with her collaboration. She receives all the treasures of grace in property and distributes them unto whom and to the extent that she herself wants."[26] Pope Benedict XVI similarly affirmed of the Immaculata: "She, the *Tota Pulchra*, the Virgin Most Pure, who conceived in her womb the Redeemer of humankind and was preserved from all stain of original sin, wishes to be the definitive seal of our encounter with God our Savior. There is no fruit of grace in the history of salvation that does not have as its necessary instrument the mediation of Our Lady."[27]

There is a modern icon that vividly portrays this intimate communion between the Immaculata and the Holy Spirit. It is called the "Icon of the Pneumatophore (*new-mát-o-for*) Mother of God Carrying the Holy Spirit" (see p. 14).[28] *Pneumatophore* comes from two Greek words: *pneuma*, meaning "Spirit," and *phoros*, "bear, carry" (compare *Christopher*, "Christ bearer"). We more often depict Mary carrying Jesus in her arms as the *Theotokos*, "God bearer." But before Mary could bear Jesus in her womb, she first carried the Holy Spirit within her heart. The Holy Spirit is the Divine Person closest to us, and it is only through Him that we have contact with Jesus.[29] For it is by the Holy Spirit that the Word became incarnate in Mary, and by Him Jesus is present in the Eucharist. Because she was first a *pneumatophore* (carrier of the Spirit) she became the *Christophore* (carrier of Christ).

The icon reveals our own destiny in light of the Immaculata. We, too, are all called to be *pneumatophores*, carriers of the Holy Spirit. Whereas Mary received the Holy Spirit at her conception, we are given the Holy Spirit first at Baptism. The icon visibly depicts the reality of sanctifying grace: holding close to our hearts this gift of the Spirit. To be a saint means being a *pneumatophore*, a bearer of the Holy Spirit. We are to be intimate partners with Him, moved, vivified, and loved by Him constantly.

This requires living beyond the minimal fulfilling of duties. For those who not only profess faith in Christ but also are led by the Spirit of Christ belong to Christ (Rom 8:14). Although we could point to many human crises in the Church, there is always one root cause: when Christians in the Church fail to press and hold the Holy Spirit to their heart and fail to guard the Spirit there. Thus, St. John Paul II stated that the crisis of the modern world is a crisis of saints: we need more saints, more *pneumatophores.* Too often, we try to hold other creatures to our heart *together with the Spirit,* forgetting that to attain this pearl of great price we must sell everything else (Mt 13:45-46). The entirety of our Christian life is for the sake, not only of possessing, but of *enjoying* the Holy Spirit.[30] We have the privilege of delighting in His presence and love within our hearts, similar to the joy we experience when we spend quality time with close friends or family. He is our only *true possession,* a source of inexhaustible joy and peace, that no one else can take from us (Jn 16:22).

As is visible in the Immaculata, the Holy Spirit wants to fill us with the fullness of holiness, to make us full of grace like her. If we do not realize this as His primary will regarding us, then we will be confused as to why God permits so many things in our lives and in the world. For Divine Providence can be understood only from the point of view of the *fullness of holiness* for which we are destined in Christ. We are often "reluctant saints," desiring God in our hearts, but encountering difficulty in the sacrifices entailed in seeking such holiness. But only by living the fullness of Christian life in the Spirit can we dare to hope to enter Heaven, where the Spirit is our life!

The saints were not superheroes who had some innate capacity that we do not have. Saints — including the Immaculata — were filled with the same Holy Spirit given to us in Baptism. Their motivation was grounded in their faith in God and His love. This faith enables them to persevere amid the adversities they face, leading them to victory through the Cross (1 Jn 5:4-5; Rom 8:37). Now, the essence of the Cross is not suffering, but obedience and self-sacrificial love that reveal the presence of the Spirit of love.

The Immaculata teaches us how to live in such a dynamic union with the Holy Spirit. It is far from being difficult or complicated: the Immaculate Virgin reveals the utter simplicity of such a life. Although the most exalted of all creatures, she is also the humblest and most down-to-earth. My favorite contemporary painting of the Virgin Mary shows her hanging clothes to dry with the Infant Jesus playing at her feet. Her immaculate holiness was hidden amid her daily tasks — cleaning, cooking, prayer, fellowship — but fulfilled in deep love of God and neighbor. She responded fully to the gift of God's love for her: She immersed herself in it through prayer, reciprocated it through the fulfillment of His will, and shared it through daily love of neighbor. For His gift of love evokes the response of our love.

The holiness of the Immaculata grew on the foundation of everyday life. Saint Faustina wrote many times about her monotonous life, which contained hidden treasures of grace (*Diary*, 62, 245, 296, 385, 592). Neuroscientists have discovered that part of the human brain is "programmed" to look for and notice what is novel or new.[31] We have an innate desire for such newness. But, like Qoheleth, we discover sooner or later that "nothing is new under the sun" (Eccl 1:9). While there may not be exciting, "new" things, persons, or events each day, the grace of God — the inspirations of the Holy Spirit — offered to us at each moment is new and unique. Holiness consists in fidelity to His subtle inspirations: "Faithfulness to the inspirations of the Holy Spirit — that is the shortest route [to holiness]" (*Diary*, 291).

The Immaculata's life was similar to our own: She experienced everyday difficulties and the trials of human life. It would be erroneous to imagine her in a sort of life where she never touched the dirty soil of this earth. She lived in the "darkness" of faith, of not knowing all the answers or how everything will play out ahead of time. Like Jesus, she experienced the temptations and suffering of interior battles, particularly during His Passion. Her holiness was not an unchanging ingredient given to her at the beginning of her life.[32] Rather, it entailed the unending process of living in communion with the Holy Spirit — a living Person — at each moment, being embraced and permeated by Him, and sharing Him by loving others. Her Immaculate Conception reveals the path begun at our Baptism: living in newness of life given to us in the Holy Spirit, entering into ever deeper intimacy with Him, until we, too, become His "transparent icons."

QUESTIONS

- How can you live in union with the Holy Spirit in daily, human life, in imitation of the Immaculata?
- Where do you experience most the monotony of daily life, and how can you learn to be sensitive to His inspirations?
- Where do you need to be permeated by His love?

PRAYER

Pray the "Prayer to the Immaculate Conception" (p. 204) and the Litany of the Holy Spirit (#1 — p. 205).

DAY 3

FOR ALL THE SOULS

Immaculata Virginis Mariae Conceptio Sit Nobis Salus et Protectio

Mary is the assurance of our hope of holiness; she embodies the holiness for which we strive. In her person, the Church has already been made immaculate. For, "while in the most holy Virgin the Church has already reached that perfection whereby she is without spot or wrinkle, the followers of Christ still strive to increase in holiness by conquering sin."[33] The Book of Revelation focuses on the unveiling of the bride of the Lamb in the "bright, clean linen garment," like the saints in Revelation 7. Saint John explains, "The linen represents the righteous deeds of the holy ones" (Rev 19:8).

Between Revelation 7 and 19, we read about plagues, trials, wars, and persecutions. All these purifications are part of the Father's plan to prepare the bride for His Son's Second Coming, so she will be immaculate. Our deeds are not always righteous, and our wedding attire — the bright, clean linen garment — is often stained. Being invited to the wedding feast is insufficient; we must be properly clothed, too (Mt 22:12). We need the abundance of Divine Mercy to purify us completely and so make us immaculate like the Immaculata.

The Immaculate Conception unlocks the *secret* of understanding Divine Mercy. Through the prism of this mystery, we glimpse the purpose of Divine Mercy Sunday, the Sunday after Easter: for the Church, in all of her sinful members, to become like the Immaculata. Jesus promises that, by reception of Holy Communion, we will be freed from all sin and punishment due to sin (*Diary,* 300, 699, 1109). In other words, He will make us immaculate, as if we received a second Baptism. Even more, because Divine Mercy Sunday is on the eighth day of the Easter Octave, it symbolizes eternity, the Day when human history ends and the Lord returns to bring His bride to dwell with Him forever in the heavenly Jerusalem. As the Immaculate Conception prepared Mary to receive the Word in the Incarnation, Divine

Mercy readies us to receive Jesus — in the Eucharist, at death, or at the Second Coming.

Both Jesus and Mary explicitly tell St. Faustina that the message of the Divine Mercy is to prepare the world and the Church for the Second Coming (*Diary*, n. 635, 848, 1146, 1588). This message proclaims the overflowing abundance of Divine Mercy on us, to create and provide a place — the Church — for Jesus to enter this world anew. Just as the Father provided an Immaculate Mother for Jesus to enter the world, so He now prepares an immaculate bride for His Son. This requires the Church to be purified and clothed in her white linen for the "wedding feast of the Lamb." The victory song in Revelation (19:6-8) reads, "For the wedding day of the Lamb has come, his bride has made herself ready. She was allowed to wear a bright, clean linen garment." In Song of Songs, the bridegroom uses a Hebrew word related to *immaculate* to describes the perfection — the physical beauty and moral integrity — of his beloved bride (Song 5:2, 6:9).[34] Jesus, the Bridegroom, desires the same for His bride, the Church, for whom He died to clothe her in stainless white, so we shine with spotless splendor like the Immaculata.

But what or who is Divine Mercy? Saint John Paul II wrote that Divine Mercy is "personified and actualized" in the Holy Spirit.[35] By pressing the Holy Spirit to our hearts, like the *Pneumatophore,* we hold tight the Divine Mercy that flows forth from the pierced Heart of Jesus. The dove represents the purity and innocence of the Holy Spirit.

Now, if that were the only symbol of the Holy Spirit, we might conclude that He is always gentle and rather innocuous. But we ought not confuse the title "Comforter" (one way of translating the Greek *Paraclete*) with "comfortable."[36] To impart His purity and innocence to us, the Holy Spirit must purify and challenge us. In my own journey, He often has made me quite *uncomfortable* and seems to specialize in leading me out of my comfort zone along the path of conversion. The Holy Spirit is both a gentle whisper (1 Kings 19:12) and a driving wind (Ex 14:21, Acts 2:2). He is a "living flame of love," as well as a "consuming fire" (Dt 4:24; Heb 12:29) who burns away all dross from our hearts (Is 1:25).

Saint John of the Cross states that the same Holy Spirit Who produces tender touches of sweetness in purified souls first cauterizes our wounds of sin.[37] The Divine Mercy is like a doctor who applies stringent medicine that sterilizes an infected wound to enable healing. Intense suffering is part of His "severe" mercy: The Holy Spirit purifies us with His burning love to bring salvation. God's mercy consists not in lowering the bar of His goal that we be immaculate, but rather in always offering His forgiveness so that we continue to strive to be immaculate in His sight. Gazing on the Immaculata is our comfort, for she reveals what the Holy Spirit is accomplishing within us. Like her, we are privileged to receive the gift of the Father's mercy: the Holy Spirit Who forms Jesus Christ in us.

Our participation in this mystery of the Immaculate Conception starts with *purgation of sin*. Saint Ignatius of Loyola begins his rule for discernment of spirits with the statement that the Holy Spirit brings pain and affliction to a soul in sin, to induce it to contrition and repentance.[38] The Spirit Who brings glory to the saints in Heaven (All Saints) is the same Spirit who purges by fire those not yet immaculate (All Souls). We cannot share in the positive aspect of immaculacy (glory, grace, beauty, peace, harmony, splendor) without its negative aspect (purification).

In November (in the northern hemisphere), autumn has arrived. Trees once alive lose all their leaves. The seasons — including the lengthening of the hours of darkness — direct our attention to death. The Liturgy as well selects readings that lead us to ponder the end — either of our life (death) or of the world (the Second Coming). The Immaculate Conception, celebrated on December 8, directs our gaze to our own end, beckoning us to ask ourselves whether we are taking the appropriate paths that lead us to our destination: Heaven. While we may admit the need to repent of all mortal sin (to avoid hell), we may yet have difficulty in repenting of all venial sin (to avoid Purgatory). We might imagine we would be lucky to make it even to Purgatory. But there is no luck involved: we determine where we go after death by our daily choices for or against God and His will.

If we aim for Heaven, then on account of venial sins we may spend time in Purgatory. If we aim for Purgatory (i.e., if we become complacent in venial sin), then we may end up in hell. Jesus warns about spewing out those who are "lukewarm" (Rev 3:16). Now becoming immaculate — free of all sin — is impossible by our own efforts alone. But the Holy Spirit accomplishes what we cannot do. Our part is to be willing and cooperative: to allow the Spirit to purify us of all sin, even the smallest and most insignificant. The highest holiness is attained by the smallest steps — repenting of seemingly negligible, minor sins.

Sooner or later, if we want to enter the heavenly Jerusalem, we must be purified of all sin. "But nothing unclean will enter it [the heavenly Jerusalem], nor any[one] who does abominable things or tells lies" (Rev 21:27). If we are docile as regards His purifying work on earth to make us immaculate, then we will enter Heaven directly at death. But those who, even though they are in sanctifying grace and so in friendship with God, retain sin and its stain must first pass through Purgatory to "achieve the holiness necessary to enter the joy of heaven" (*Catechism*, 1030). Both this life and Purgatory are like hospitals, where sinners convalesce and wounds are healed.[39] But *we must be made immaculate*, whether by docilely suffering in this life or by Purgatory.

Saint Stanislaus Papczyński, who had such notable devotion to the Immaculata, was also gifted with powerful experiences of the souls suffering in Purgatory. He wrote that one of the greatest works of mercy is to pray for the deceased, because they suffer so much and yet are invisible to our human eyes.[40] One manner of alleviating their suffering is by obtaining for them indulgences, which are a "remission before God of the temporal punishment due to sins whose guilt has already been forgiven" (*Catechism*, 1471). An indulgence shortens the figurative "length" of Purgatory that a person undergoes, and can be either plenary (removing all the time in Purgatory) or partial (removing part of it). Although indulgences can be gained for oneself, they can also be obtained for the deceased, as a spiritual work of mercy.

November 2, All Souls' Day, reminds us to intercede for those souls who are now suffering in Purgatory (*Catechism*, 1032). There, they endure the purifying fire of the Holy Spirit, to be prepared to enter the Kingdom. We share with them the hope of being made immaculate, and so are united with them in our own sufferings and trials, gazing on our Immaculate Mother.

QUESTIONS

- How often do you remember and pray for the souls in Purgatory?
- When have you experienced the Holy Spirit as a purifying fire of mercy?
- How do you compromise with sin rather than allowing God to grant you the "holiness necessary to enter the joy of heaven"?

PRAYER

Pray the "Prayer to the Immaculate Conception" (p. 204) and the Litany of the Holy Spirit (#2 — p. 207).

DAY 4
ON PURIFICATION

Immaculata Virginis Mariae Conceptio Sit Nobis Salus et Protectio

Whereas the Holy Spirit *preserved* the Immaculata from sin, He *purifies* us of all our sin, even the smallest; the manner is different, but the goal (immaculacy) is the same. The mystical experiences of St. Stanislaus Papczyński manifest the connection between these two uniquely Catholic doctrines, Immaculate Conception and Purgatory. Both are necessary to let us better understand the Person and purifying work of the Holy Spirit.

Purgatory — and our intercession for those suffering there — flows organically from the Immaculate Conception. Those who are not made immaculate in this life must endure the necessary purgation after death so as to be prepared for entering Heaven, where no sin may enter.[41] We cannot enter Heaven unhealed (with mortal sin) or partially healed (with venial sin, even the smallest). Since Heaven is the place of perfect bliss, how could we be fully happy if we were still plagued by sin or its effects (pain, suffering, death, broken relationships)? How could we leap for joy if we still limp?

Now, *purification* carries a negative connotation, since it usually involves pain. Yet the word *pure* derives from a root word meaning "fresh, new, clear."[42] We tend to focus on the negative aspect because pain grabs our attention. But the goal of such purification is to renew, refresh, and rejuvenate us for eternal life. For we believe that when our bodies are resurrected, they will be perfect, *immaculate*, free from the wrinkles of age and decay, with wounds radiating glory, similar to the wounds of Jesus Himself (Jn 20:20-21).[43]

It is in our own best interest to patiently endure the purgation of this life, for the goal is our own glorious resurrection in body and soul. Then, we will not need to undergo further purification in Purgatory. Because we are directly in the presence of the Lord Who purifies us of sin, the pain experienced in Purgatory is more intense than purification in this life (though some saints also add that the joy of those souls in Purgatory is also greater than earthly joy, for they are assured of salvation).

Do not put off the needed purification of sin — do not extinguish the consuming, purging fire of the Holy Spirit. In this life, we have the Church — including friends and family — to support and comfort us. We can yet grow in merit (holiness) in this life (*Catechism*, 2006-2011). In Purgatory we no longer grow in merit; we depend entirely on the prayers of others.

Sooner or later, we must face our unhealed wounds. Living at a frenzied pace, we desperately try to avoid seeing ourselves as we truly are. We are often ashamed of our brokenness and wounds, attempting to cover them over in myriads of ways. We become more like Martha than like Mary (Lk 10:38-42): occupying ourselves with noble tasks in service to Jesus but we become frustrated, complain, and lack joy in our service. We even begin to question Jesus — asking whether He sees us in our busyness, placing the blame for our pain on Him. But we are unwilling to be Mary, for we are afraid to face Jesus and encounter Him in genuine intimacy.

In our frenzied world, we can easily become too busy with good things, afraid to make a full stop and be present to our hearts. For we know that if we were to stop for more than a few minutes, we would be likely to feel just how burdened and exhausted we are. We distract ourselves and so try to numb the pain or least no longer pay any attention to it. We seek a solution to extinguish the Holy Spirit's work of purification. To numb that necessary but healing pain, we turn to any number of distractions: TV, radio, alcohol, etc. For although we profess faith that we are "redeemed," we have a silent despair: we believe our hearts and lives cannot be fully healed. Certain problems repeat themselves, and we find ourselves in Confession for the same sins. Certain painful wounds continue to ache. We quietly begin to lose hope that the promise of radical salvation in Jesus applies to us. It may somehow work for others, particularly the saints, but we feel incapable of truly being healed and saved.

Now, we would never state this aloud, for we know it is contrary to our faith. But the heart is slow to believe (Mk 16:14, Lk 24:25).

This does not mean that every illness will be healed in this life. Saint Joan of Arc was assured of her deliverance — a promise made to her by St. Michael the Archangel. She understood that to mean she would be freed from captivity, but Divine Providence intended that to mean her deliverance through dying at the stake and her entry into Heaven.[44] Similarly, St. Mark Ji Tianxiang could not overcome his addiction to opium — perhaps due to a lack of understanding as to the nature of addictions — and so asked for martyrdom so as to be assured of salvation. But the truth remains that our Father does want to heal, and our hearts need to be open to that salvation, in whatever way He wills to grant it to us, and to whatever extent we are able to receive it through an active desire of hope.[45]

So we deal with our hidden despair of finding healing for pain by cloaking it with disguises, such as diligent, even excessive work. We attempt to press through the pain in a numbingly busy lifestyle, filled with accomplishments and appointments. Does not *pain make you stronger*? While there is human wisdom in learning to press forward even when we are in pain, we must be careful about the cost of such pushing. Athletes train hard, to go farther and faster than ever before. However, they also must rest and recuperate, to allow time for their body to heal and so be ready for more exertion. Otherwise, the muscles — including the heart — begin to suffer damage.

When we push ourselves too much, without rest, then our hearts easily become hardened. The English *endure* comes from the Latin for "to harden." We prefer to harden our hearts somewhat to protect ourselves from further pain. But such hardness of heart and toughness in the face of pain are a mark, not of Christians, but of pagans. Compassion and mercy begin with sensitivity to our own pain and the awareness of our own need for help and healing.

Pressing forward in pain, avoiding moments of prayer that would inquire about the deeper questions of the heart, reveals our despair — we believe that there is no comfort, no adequate response, for our pain. Some may have cried out in their pain, only to find themselves alone. But the Immaculata, who stood by her crucified Son, reveals that the Father never permits pain without also extending His comforting love in the Spirit. Jesus, who prayed the opening line of Psalm 22 — "My God, My God, why have you abandoned me?" — likely remembered verse 10: "For you drew me forth from the womb, made me safe at my mother's breasts." The last vestige of the Father's love for Jesus amid His human suffering and experience of abandonment was Mary. As the "transparent icon" of the Holy Spirit, she reveals that at every cross, the Father's love in the person of the Holy Spirit is present to comfort and save us.

The Immaculata reveals that, for every pain, there is comfort; for every misery, mercy; for every problem, a solution; and for all sin, forgiveness. Even while the Father permits us to feel the effects of our sins, He gives us Jesus and Mary to be present to us amid such suffering, so that we may have hope. We are never alone, never abandoned, never forgotten. Our Lady's pierced Heart shows us the mystery both of pain and of healing: By keeping our hearts open, even amid pain, to the Holy Spirit, we receive comfort, peace and healing through Jesus Christ.

In every pain, He is silently present, deeper than the natural rebellion of our hearts against suffering. Mary teaches us how to be docile to the curative work of the Holy Spirit. When I do not silence my interior pain, I hear the Holy Spirit interceding "with inexpressible groanings" (Rom 8:26). Mary instructs us how to listen to His "sighs too deep for words" within our pain. For all suffering in the Spirit is part of the process of new birth in Christ.

Jesus taught St. Faustina, "**My daughter, suffering will be a sign to you that I am with you**" (*Diary*, 669). How paradoxical that is, since we quickly interpret suffering as a sign that God is displeased with us and has abandoned us. But if only we remembered this truth: In suffering, He is already with us! And where Jesus is, there is peace of heart.

When the Romans offered Jesus a drug to numb His pain during the torment of His Passion, He refused. Rather than eliminating His pain, He deliberately chose to endure it to the full for *our sake* and *our salvation*. He allowed the Holy Spirit to bring about our redemption in and through the pain of His broken body. Resisting the natural tendency to eliminate all pain requires prayerful surrender to the Holy Spirit in faith, trusting that He is at work within our suffering. That does not mean we cannot alleviate any pain (for instance, by taking Tylenol for a headache or providing palliative medicine for the dying). But this does mean remembering that suffering is not the worst evil. In fact, suffering can be the efficacious means for growing in love and union with Jesus and Mary.

Saint Stanislaus Papczyński teaches us about the necessity of our obedient surrender to see the miracles of divine grace in our hearts and lives:

> Just as the disciples' dedication and obedience (which were roused in them by the encouragement of the Blessed Mother who understood the will of her omnipotent Son) were necessary for the performance of the miracle at Cana, so also

> all of the works to be accomplished in you and through you by divine grace, as well as all of the favors that the good Lord will grant you, require the consent of your will, your concurrence, and your cooperation.[46]

Just as the Immaculata aroused that obedience in the disciples, so she opens our heart to surrender to the healing purification of the Spirit.

For this reason, understanding this mystery is vital to the spiritual life: for only by understanding do we grasp the purpose of such intense purifications. When we keep our eye on the Immaculata, then we are no longer enclosed within the present moment of pain or confused by the lies of Satan. We see before us both the promise and the fulfillment of our hope: By patiently enduring the Holy Spirit's purifying touch, we too will become like her and radiate His glory. The Immaculata reveals to us our glorious destiny in Christ.

QUESTIONS

- What wounds still need healing?
- How do you maintain the status quo?
- How do you numb your pain — what human comforts do you seek?
- How can you turn to the Immaculata in your pain, so as to hear better the "inexpressible groanings" of the Spirit?

PRAYER

Pray the "Prayer to the Immaculate Conception" (p. 204) and the Litany of the Immaculate Conception (#2 — p. 214).

DAY 5
"ALL HOLY"

Immaculata Virginis Mariae Conceptio Sit Nobis Salus et Protectio

The Eastern Church calls the Immaculata the *Panagia,* the "All Holy." In the Roman Catholic Church, we often frame the Immaculate Conception in negative terms: the absence of original sin and of its effects. But positively, this mystery reveals that the gift of the Holy Spirit provides us with new freshness, vigor, and life which sin and Satan cannot destroy. Precisely because she is perfected and filled with His grace, she remains sinless, intact in her virginity, and pure.[47] She beautifully radiates the *healing power* of the Holy Spirit. The Immaculata guides us to encounter that same Spirit as the fountain of life-giving water.

In 1858, Our Lady appeared to St. Bernadette in Lourdes. Before she revealed her name — "I am the Immaculate Conception" — she requested that St. Bernadette dig into the ground in the cave at Massabielle. The Immaculata linked her triple call to penance with the healing spring of water, which continues to heal the sick and bring hope to the despairing. Four years after the official proclamation of this dogma by Blessed Pope Pius IX in 1854, Our Lady opened the treasures of her privileged grace for the healing and salvation of all her children.

The prayer of St. Stanislaus — "*May the Virgin Mary's Immaculate Conception be our health and our protection*" — uses the Latin *salus* for "health." *Salus* denotes both health and salvation (and other synonyms, such as welfare, life, and safety).[48] The Immaculate Conception is a spring of living water for the Church, bringing us healing and salvation from all physical, moral, and spiritual evil. Once we are healed, the Immaculata protects us from further harm, so that we remain intact and immaculate like her — and unlike Adam and Eve, who were created immaculate yet fell into sin. She is our *protectio* — protection from all that would endanger *salus.*

By opening this fountain of grace, the Immaculata makes the total healing of our person accessible to us. Our Lady willingly shares with those who draw near to her the healing graces flowing from her conception. Her Immaculate Conception is the promise of complete restoration, such that sin leaves no stain, no trace on our bodies or souls. The Immaculata is the sign, the promise, and the guarantee of our hope that the redemption wrought by her Son is capable of radically redeeming all sin and healing all wounds, starting in this life and finding its completion in the next. Her Immaculate Conception reveals that there is unlimited grace available to you to thoroughly transform you from a sinner into a saint.

Blessed Duns Scotus (1265–1308) was a Franciscan who wrote a theological explanation of the Immaculate Conception. Without any merit or cooperation of her own, Mary was *perfectly redeemed*.[49] Since the work of redemption was perfectly accomplished by Christ, then there must be a perfect effect: the total healing of sin, such that it never even occurs. That is the Immaculata.

For Christ has made the Church *immaculate* through the "washing of water by the word" so that she may be "holy and without blemish" (Eph 5:25-27). But if Jesus has washed the Church in the *past tense*, then the Church is already immaculate in Mary. For Christ, in making the Church immaculate, deals not with an abstract idea, but rather with a person — Mary. She is the image and model of the Church: Christ's perfect cleansing of the Church has taken place already in Mary.[50] Assumed into Heaven, she now stands as a sign of hope, that what Christ accomplished in her will be fulfilled in the entire Church and each one of us who believes.[51]

The Immaculate Conception thus urges us to have "unlimited trust and confidence" in the redemption wrought by Christ.[52] For by His Cross and Resurrection, He "secured ultimate healing," which is the process of "restoration of body, mind or spirit to a state of wholeness and well-being."[53] We need to ask for ever-deepening faith that allows the Holy Spirit to release the fullness of His healing power in our hearts, our lives, the Church, and the world.[54] By sharing the fountain of her immaculate holiness with us, she wants us to begin the process of being fully healed and made whole, starting in this life and finding its completion in the next.

In English, the word *holy* derives from the same root as *heal* and *whole*: *hal*, meaning "whole, uninjured."[55] The "universal call to holiness" means that the Father wants everybody, without exception, to be authentically holy: mature, whole, and healed. The Holy Spirit purifies us of all sin because He is zealous to make us whole, holy, and healed like the Immaculata. The Immaculata enjoys the wholeness of heart that God intended for us in Eden. The Immaculata is a living image of *salus:* what true health, wholeness, and holiness are. She lived human life fully and wholly. By imitating her, and in union with the same Holy Spirit, we too will attain *salus* and grow to be truly healed, healthy, and holy. But that is a long process, which requires patience in our hope that what seems impossible right now is, through faith, possible by grace.

The Holy Spirit is not content to do half His work in us; He wants to bring it to full completion, as He brought it in her! Healing is a restoration of the whole person: *Salus* implies the healing of every aspect of our being (Mt 13:15; 1 Pet 2:24; Titus 2:14; 1 Jn 1:7). While we look to the Father for salvation, He desires to heal all of us, with no wound left hidden, and yet to be healed. This can be unnerving: God is not satisfied with healing the majority of your wounds. Nor is He satisfied with healing your sin. He is satisfied only when you are entirely saved, healed like Mary: in your emotions, in your spirit, in your body, in your relationships with others, in your relationship with Him. Only then will He rest, and only then will you find refreshment.

Now, some of us may have asked for such healing for quite some time, without success (perhaps like the woman with the hemorrhage in Mark 5:24-35). But the fact that we are not content to surrender to the status quo, that we keep asking for healing, is a sign of the Holy Spirit at work, who groans within us for that total healing. His grace is already at work to begin anew this process, though it may take time, many detours, and healing other wounds that we may not even be aware of. But no matter our "current location," the destination for our "divine GPS" — the Holy Spirit — remains the same: total salvation, starting in this life, reaching its fulfillment in the next.

Nor need we wait until Heaven to be healed and made whole — He is already at work to do so now. For holiness has little to do with being completely otherworldly. Sometimes the Immaculata is presented as being so holy that she is distant from us. But Mary's holiness shines through her humanity that she shares with us! Her holiness makes her not less but rather more human, not farther from but closer to us.

Saint Thérèse of Lisieux wrote, "It is true that Our Lady is Queen of Heaven and earth, but at the same time she is more Mother than Queen."[56] A queen, like a king, is more difficult to approach, because of her royal dignity. Yet a mother is easily approached by her own children.

Mary's holiness makes her more our mother — more approachable.

In Mary, we experience the *utter relief* of holiness that brings us healing and wholeness. Mary teaches us the paths of holiness, healing, and wholeness, opening our daily lives to the Holy Spirit. She will share with you the riches of her Immaculate Conception, so that you can live — a bit more day by day — a *whole, holy, and healed life.* Her immaculate holiness reached every aspect of her life, and that holiness *made her entire life whole.* She is the Mother of God, with wholeness and holiness that make her unlike anyone else. She lived, as we do, on this humble, "dirty" earth — but in profound union with the Holy Spirit. A whole or holy person is one capable of living out all human experience, rather than avoiding it, escaping it, or manipulating it to suit one's own desires. Authentic holiness means being capable of living in the real world according to the limitations placed by God. For all sin has its origin in seeking to surpass or rebel against the "insurmountable limits that man, being a creature, must freely recognize and respect with trust. Man is dependent on his Creator and subject to the laws of creation and to the moral norms that govern the use of freedom" (*Catechism,* 396).

The truly healed person is capable of humbly living in this world with both its glory and its sorrow, in its joys and in its pain. The more one avoids or blunts real pain, the more one also eliminates real joy.[57] This is the Christian paradox of human life: Everlasting happiness is encountered only by first embracing the tragedy of the cross.

The Good News, however, is that God brings not only restoration to our original, sinless state, as in Eden. Christ's salvation is not merely a "bringing back to a former position or condition."[58] The radiant splendor of the Immaculata reveals that Jesus' Paschal Mystery brings even *more blessings* than were lost through original sin. As St. Thomas Aquinas wrote: "There is nothing to prevent human nature's being raised up to something greater, even after sin; God permits evil in order to draw forth some greater good. Thus St. Paul says, 'Where sin increased, grace abounded all the more'; and the Exultet sings, 'O happy fault, … which gained for us so great a Redeemer!'" (*Catechism,* 412; Rom 5:20).[59]

The wholeness that the Holy Spirit brings includes and glorifies our wounds — He does not always eliminate all of them. Rather, these wounds become sources of healing for others. As St. John Paul II wrote, "He gives them this Spirit as it were through the wounds of his crucifixion: 'He showed them his hands and his side.'"[60] Too often, healing is an attempt to erase or hide those tragic aspects of the past. Jesus reveals His glorified wounds as proof of redemption and the forgiveness of sins (Jn 20:20-21). The Immaculata, too, reveals that God creates us anew not by erasing the past, but by using sin and failure! For the Immaculata was created, not apart from the sinful history of Israel, but as its most precious fruit, a gift of His abundant grace.

QUESTIONS

- Where have you given up hope of being fully healed?
- What do you imagine you would be like if you were *holy, whole,* and *healed*?
- What image do you have of Our Lady's holiness, and how can you imitate her "lowly" holiness of everyday life?

PRAYER

Pray the "Prayer to the Immaculate Conception" (p. 204) and the Litany of the Immaculate Conception of Mary, Mother of God (#3 – p. 216).

INTERLUDE
TWO KINDS OF HEALING

There are two primary kinds of healing. In the Gospels, we see Jesus literally healing leprosy, raising the dead, and exorcising demons. Those are clear instances where someone was afflicted, Jesus arrived, and He relieved the malady. If that were the only kind of healing, then we might become discouraged. Many pray and beg God to intervene and help, but their situation remains the same or even worsens. Does God simply refuse to heal?

The name Raphael, in Hebrew, means, "God heals." In my experience, God *always* heals. It is not whether God heals; whenever the Holy Spirit touches us, He *always* heals, too. But, as Scripture states, He "wounds us as He heals" (Job 5:18, Hosea 6:1). Sometimes, the healing process requires more pain, and begs the question: *What is God trying to heal?* Sometimes, we point at one problem that we want the Lord to eliminate, while Jesus is pointing at a deeper wound that He is painfully touching to bring healing.

In the Immaculata, we see the first kind of healing in her conception: She was preserved from all sin. There was the elimination of even original sin that is "passed on to" the children of parents. But when I say that she is totally "healed, whole, and holy," does that mean she never suffered? Does total healing and wholeness mean the absence of suffering and pain?

Here is the difference between Adam and Eve and the Immaculata. Adam and Eve had what theologians call "preternatural gifts." Those gifts include infused knowledge, immortality, and immunity to suffering as we know and experience it today. The Immaculata, like Adam and Eve, was sinless at the moment of her creation, but she did not possess immortality in the same way as them, nor was she spared all the sufferings of this present life, marked by sin and its effects.

Being "healed, whole, and holy" in this present life aligns us with the Immaculata and so leads us to *suffer well,* as she did, not to be *free of suffering,* or even *free of wounds.* For she bears the seven swords of sorrow through her Immaculate Heart. In fact, if one follows the logic of St. Thomas Aquinas regarding the sinless humanity of Jesus, then, as my Dominican professor in seminary noted, it means that the Immaculata *suffered more, not less,* than we do. As sinners, we put up sinful defenses to protect ourselves from pain, whereas the Immaculata was more sensitive to pain, for her Heart was never hardened but always tender.

Let me turn to a different example, of St. Paul. He specifically requested the Lord to remove the thorn from his flesh (2 Cor 12:9-12). But, despite his triple request, the Lord did not do so, but rather responded that His power is made perfect in weakness. Does that mean God did not heal? That He heals only sometimes? This is the second kind of healing: when He heals our weakness by empowering it with grace. This leads to a better definition of healing than imagining it to be a simple removal of problems and pain.

Dr. Matthew Breuninger, in a talk on healing, defines healing as a work of divine grace within us that enables us to go wherever God asks us to go, do whatever God asks us to do, while bringing our suffering with us.[61] This is a beautiful definition that widens how we grasp the meaning of healing and of how we experience the graces that the Immaculata pours upon us through her Immaculate Conception. We are called to be "healed, whole, and holy" like her in this definition: capable of living her *fiat* while we bear our suffering, our wounds, allowing the Father to use even those to accomplish His plan and will.

Perhaps the Immaculata will work an actual, positive healing in our lives, as many experience in Lourdes. But perhaps she will also work a different healing, like St. Paul experienced, that enables us to grow in faith, hope, and love even amid suffering. For every person who receives a miraculous healing in Lourdes, there are many more who leave without such healing. Does that mean Our Lady, the Immaculata, does not heal them or respond to their pain? Perhaps she responds similarly to them as her Son did to Paul: God's power, His love, is perfected in our weakness.

We often hate our weakness and our wounds, wanting to be "strong." But, in truth, that is our need to be self-reliant, instead of being trusting sons and daughters of our Heavenly Father, Abba. If we want to see what healing looks like, we must look at Jesus and Mary, who are sinless, and as such, capable of embracing suffering freely as a means of love. For the ultimate wounding that the Father *always heals* is our incapacity to love. He sends the Holy Spirit to those places of our heart (Rom 5:5) where the truth of His love is not yet present, so that we in turn are able to love, even upon the Cross.

The more we are healed, the more capable we are of suffering *as an act of love,* in union with Jesus. The Immaculata shows forth this kind of *ultimate healing*: She participated in a unique manner in the self-offering of her Son, His holocaust of love. Our healing also leads us to the Cross: not only because it is the source of our healing, as it is the source of the Immaculate Conception, but also because we become capable of loving as does Jesus. To be "healed, whole, and holy" means that we are capable of loving one another as Jesus has loved us (cf. Jn 13:1, 34-35). Hence, this book commences with our own purification and healing but leads us to uniting ourselves, like the Immaculata, with Jesus in His total self-giving holocaust of love.

The more we are healed, the more we rejoice in our weakness, the more we embrace suffering, the more we love in all circumstances, placing love where there is no love; the less we employ "self-protection strategies" aimed at avoiding the Cross, the less we are governed by fears and lies. Jesus, risen from the dead, still retains His wounds, through which He pours forth the Spirit. The Immaculata bears the seven swords of sorrow. These wounds opened her Heart to an even greater love, to loving all of us as a mother loves her very own children.

The Holy Spirit *always* heals. *What* does He want to heal? *How* does He heal? Do not be discouraged if you do not find the first kind of miraculous healing. Remember St. Paul and countless others who found the second kind of healing: of encountering God's grace and power in their weakness, which enabled them to fulfill His will always, like Our Lady.

DAY 6
MARCHING TOWARDS PERFECTION

Immaculata Virginis Mariae Conceptio Sit Nobis Salus et Protectio

Whereas the Immaculata was preserved in her purity at her conception, we must undergo purification to be made pure. But why is such purity important in the first place? Purity is the first step — after which follows maturation in grace — toward perfection.[62] This Old Testament concept of *purity* relates to our ability to enter God's presence and enter into communion with Him. The customs of ritual purity enabled man to recognize his need for purification from sin to enter the presence of the thrice-holy God. Thus, the Law provided a system of purification for things, animals, and people to be ritually and morally clean and pure.[63]

Jesus identifies the source of impurity as the heart (Mk 7:14-23). But how specifically are we purified? "You are already pruned by the word I have spoken to you" (Jn 15:3). His word received in faith is the source of purification. His Word — when received with living faith — has the power to transform the entirety of who we are — intellect, will, and heart.[64] Faith is the door open to the Spirit's touch, which both comforts our pain and cauterizes our wounds. Pope Benedict XVI wrote, "Faith cleanses the heart. It is the result of God's initiative toward man. It is not simply a choice that men make for themselves. Faith comes about because men are touched deep within by God's Spirit, who opens and purifies their hearts."[65] We are purified by encountering the God of love in Jesus Christ.

The Holy Spirit imbues our hearts with *faith* that is total surrender to the Father's Word, faith modeled after Our Lady's *fiat*. She received the Word so deeply into her being that the Spirit gave the Word flesh. Now, Jesus' Word is more than doctrinal information, for it "breathes forth love."[66] His word breathes forth the Spirit. By listening attentively in faith, we let His word penetrate our hearts, opening them up to His love. By washing the disciples' feet, Jesus indicates that His love "to the end" (Jn 13:1) purifies them from all stain of sin.

Authentic purification entails not merely enduring suffering, but also, being broken open to receive the fullness of divine love. This requires allowing our hearts to be pierced by the sword of His Word, as was the Immaculate Heart (Lk 2:35, Heb 4:12).

We are purified by His love when we allow Him to love *us in every aspect of our being, even in aspects that are dirty or shameful.* "We have come to know and to believe in the love God has for us" (1 Jn 4:16). The ritual purity of the Old Testament is thus not replaced by moral purity in the New Testament. If this were so, we would be loved only if we maintained moral standards. Rather, we are purified because the Father reveals His love in Christ, Who died for us while we were still sinners (Rom 5:8).

When we gaze on Jesus Crucified and Risen, our shame and sin are burned away by His love. But we must learn to remain still in such moments, rather than flee from them. When we do persevere, we learn that His love alone remains. "Faith in Christ brings salvation because in him our lives become radically open to a love that precedes us, a love that transforms us from within, acting in us and through us."[67]

What does this mystery of the Immaculate Conception reveal about our faith? The mystery reveals that we are always, already loved by the Father, Who breathes forth His Spirit — the Lord and giver of life — upon us from the first moment of our existence. We need not search for others to love us. In this fallen world, we live in a meritocracy: if we are good enough, if we perform enough, if we are "holy" enough, then we will be loved. But that obscures the fundamental truth: we have been loved into being. All other knowledge is secondary. Saint Faustina wrote, "My soul is being inflamed by His love. I only know that I love and am loved. That is enough for me" (*Diary*, 1828). Before we do or do not do anything, we are already, always loved.

"Each of us is the result of a thought of God," Pope Benedict said. "Each of us is willed, each of us is loved, each of us is necessary."[68] The Immaculate Conception is the clearest affirmation of unconditional love, or in biblical language, being "saved by grace" (Eph 2:8). We are saved by the Father's *pure gift of grace*, which is the Spirit of love, poured forth in Christ. This gift of grace then enables us, as St. Paul states, to fulfill those good works prepared for us from eternity (Eph 1:10).

Mary remained sinless throughout her life because she always remained in His love (Jn 15:9). She lived constantly from that place of *always having been loved*. Sin is behavior flowing from the need to be loved, as if we were not already fully loved. Sin arises from a heart that believes it is unloved and so desperately screams to be loved. Unaware that the living water — the Spirit of love — gushes forth from within, the sinner searches for love outside. Jesus lamented to St. Faustina that some **"have no desire to experience that sweet intimacy in their own hearts, but go in search of Me, off in the distance, and do not find Me"** (*Diary*, 580).

Saint Augustine beautifully describes this tragic odyssey:

> Late have I loved you, Beauty so ancient and so new, late have I loved you! Lo, you were within, but I outside, seeking there for you, and upon the shapely things you have made I rushed headlong – I, misshapen. You were with me, but I was not with you. They held me back far from you, those things which would have no being, were they not in you. You called, shouted, broke through my deafness; you flared, blazed, banished my blindness; you lavished your fragrance, I gasped; and now I pant for you; I tasted you, and now I hunger and thirst; you touched me, and I burned for your peace.[69]

God purified St. Augustine through faith, but that required God's calling, shouting, breaking, flaring, blazing, banishing, so that Augustine sought God's love within his own heart rather than in the world.

The saying goes, "Every man who knocks on the door of a brothel is looking for God."[70] When we disbelieve the unconditional love that flows from the pierced side of Jesus — the Holy Spirit — then we often look for substitute loves in all the wrong places. Faith allows us to tap into the mysterious reality that — despite all the painful contradictions provoked by sin — we are already, always loved. But we come to treasure this love only when we surrender our coping mechanisms to assure us that we are loved — by others or by ourselves. For our hearts are made for God by God: we are made by love for love, and nothing else will satisfy us.

The light of faith purifies our hearts by scattering the darkness of sin, which has its roots in the lies of the enemy. Satan, in a myriad of ways, whispers: "You are unloved and unlovable." He uses our sins as his leverage to prove our incapacity and unworthiness to be loved. But God never ceases to love us, and His Spirit arouses faith in our hearts, faith that — despite every seeming contradiction — we are always, forever loved. A *purified heart* is one that believes in His Word of love and so is rendered capable of loving God and neighbor in return.

To be made immaculate means to allow faith to open our hearts to the brilliance of His love, leaving no place remaining in the darkness of doubt. *Doubt* comes from the Old English *tweon* and the Latin *duo,* "two."[71] Doubt indicates being of two minds, faced with two choices. Our worst problem, as Jesus indicated to St. Peter, is our doubt: "O you of little faith, why did you doubt?" (Mt 14:31) We might imagine the real problem to be the storms (trials, tragedies, suffering, etc.) that overcome us in life. But the real issue is the doubt in our heart that perhaps He doesn't love us after all. Satan uses the storms to "prove" that He is punishing, not loving, us. The heart begins to waver, and like St. Peter, we begin to drown. Yet the Immaculata — who stood steadily at Calvary — radiated her faith in His love, even amid that darkness, and the truth of His love. She wants to convince your heart of His love, so that you do not waver between believing and doubting. Take her hand and entrust yourself to His love, the Holy Spirit Who is working to purify your heart of sin and doubt.

QUESTIONS

- Do you believe that you are always, already, unconditionally loved?
- Where do you falter in such faith?
- How do you interpret purification and suffering in light of His love?

PRAYER

Pray the "Prayer to the Immaculate Conception" (p. 204) and the Litany of the Immaculate Conception (#4 — p. 219).

DAY 7
THE EFFECTS OF SIN

Immaculata Virginis Mariae Conceptio Sit Nobis Salus et Protectio

The cornerstone of our faith is that, despite all the evidence to the contrary, we are fully loved. Nothing we do can change that. To discover this truth, though, we must face Jesus, whom we have wounded and pierced by our sins (Jn 19:37; Zech 12:10). By the Holy Spirit, flowing forth from His glorious wounds, we are healed (Is 53:5). For by His Cross, He revealed that His love has conquered our sin and is stronger than death (Song 8:6; *Catechism,* 1040). Mary was not exempt from this: she, too, looked on her Son, and even though she was sinless, she understood that He was crucified for her, too, to save her. For the grace of her Immaculate Conception depends on His death on the Cross.

We know how painful a moment it is to face the one that we wounded, similar to the pain Peter experienced when he faced Jesus after denying Him three times (Mt 26:75). The purifying pain of Purgatory flows from our encounter with Christ, Whose gaze burns us, transforms us, and frees us from our sin. Purgatory's "cleansing fire" is the fire of His love that blazes with the tinder of our sins. If earthly fire can burn us, how much more will the spiritual fire of His love?

Pope Benedict XVI wrote in *Spe Salvi*:

> All that we build during our lives can prove to be mere straw, pure bluster, and it collapses. Yet in the pain of this encounter, when the impurity and sickness of our lives become evident to us, there lies salvation. His gaze, the touch of his heart heals us through an undeniably painful transformation "as through fire." But it is a blessed pain, in which the holy power of his love sears through us like a flame, enabling us to become totally ourselves and thus totally of God.[72]

By facing Jesus crucified by our sins, we receive the healing we need from His glorified wounds: to become "totally ourselves."

The fire of Purgatory is the blazing love of God that is the Holy Spirit. He is already at work in us *today* to make us immaculate. If you are afraid of facing His blazing love, if you feel alone, take the hand of the Immaculata. She gently tempers that flame to our weak hearts, so that we can gradually bear His pure love. She tenderly opens your wounds to Him, particularly those you think would never be healed. The Immaculata invites you today to entrust yourself fully to the Holy Spirit, granting Him the freedom of your heart. She encourages you to be unafraid, even amid the burning of His love, and to trust Him without limit.

Encountering Jesus requires facing the effects of our sin (His wounds) as well as our own interior shame and fear. While shame can be *toxic* — hijacked by the enemy to discourage us and tempt us to despair — it can also be *healing*, guided by the Holy Spirit for reconciling with Jesus. Such healing shame is a necessary experience, part of authentic repentance and heartbreaking contrition.[73] That shame is the reason Peter, upon encountering Jesus for the first time, states: "Depart from me, Lord, for I am a sinful man" (Lk 5:8). We avoid this excruciating experience because of its profound pain. But *contrition* comes from the Latin for "to grind thoroughly."[74] The Holy Spirit can use shame to heal our hearts by grinding their hardness, breaking them open, and offering to God the acceptable sacrifice of a "contrite spirit" (Ps 51:19).[75]

Confession is a sacramental encounter with Jesus that anticipates our judgment. By confessing sins now while it is still the time for mercy, we receive not condemnation but forgiveness. While the Father does reprove us as sons, He does so only on behalf of loving discipline (Heb 12:4-12). Some avoid Confession because of their shame regarding their sins; however, shame is the proper emotion to feel regarding sin! To feel otherwise would reveal that our hearts are not yet fully contrite, as evidenced by sometimes frequent returns to Confession for the same sins. The Holy Spirit works in and through our emotions, including shame, which He evaporates before the love that flows from the pierced side of Jesus. The Immaculata reveals that God's judgment on sin results not in our destruction but in our total redemption and healing, in our becoming "beautiful in every way" (Song 4:7).

Through Confession, we anticipate the purifying experience of Purgatory: facing the one Who loves us so much, wounded by our sins.

Like St. Peter, we gaze on the One whom we have denied, Who yet tenderly gazes on us. Now, Confession begins but does not complete the process of purification. For every sin has a double consequence, and both of these consequences need healing. Sin both ruptures a relationship and brings objective disorder into the world. Every venial sin "entails an unhealthy attachment to creatures, which must be purified either here on earth, or after death in the state called Purgatory. This purification frees one from what is called the 'temporal punishment' of sin" (*Catechism*, 1472). Venial sin cracks the window, making it easier to break the entire window through grave sin. Grave sin "deprives us of communion with God and therefore makes us incapable of eternal life." Hell — the total rupture of intimacy with the Holy Spirit — is the "eternal punishment" for sin.

But such punishment is "a kind of vengeance inflicted by God from without," but rather follows "from the very nature of sin" (*Catechism*, 1472). This punishment is itself the reality of sin (separation from God) and the effects of sin: the negative consequences in our earthly life. "Temporal punishment" describes these damaging effects of sin. Although the Father promptly forgives our sin to restore our relationship with Him, the process of healing the effects of our sin requires time, patience, and penance. The process of Purgatory is similar to that of caring for a wound: Once inflicted, it requires proper care and treatment over time. As revealed in the Immaculata, the Holy Spirit is zealous to mend all our wounds, assuage all our pain, and repair all the damage caused by sin.

Confession removes the eternal punishment due to sin: Our relationship with God as Father is restored. But temporal punishment remains: the cracked window — our hearts — must be fully restored. Even after Confession, there are many wounds that still need healing. *Penance* entails laborious, painful steps needed to repair the objective damage — in ourselves, in others, in the world — caused by sin. By completion of the necessary reparation through penance with "fervent charity," provoking a deep conversion and purification of heart, "no punishment would remain" (*Catechism*, 1472).

"While patiently bearing sufferings and trials of all kinds and, when the day comes, serenely facing death, the Christian must strive to accept this temporal punishment of sin as a grace" (*Catechism*, 1473). Temporal punishment is a grace because it is a sign of the Father's zeal to restore all your life, back to the moment of your conception. This may require prayerfully revisiting tragic moments of life: things that have happened to you as well as things you have chosen to do (or not do). This process is similar to Peter's experience of Jesus' three questions, "Do you love me?" (Jn 21:15-17). Through this repeated question, next to the same charcoal fire as on the night of His Passion (Jn 18:18), Peter revisits his triple denial and so opens his wounds and sins to Jesus and His mercy. Wherever there is any lack of love, wherever the presence of God was "lacking" (at least, not perceived), then temporal punishment is a challenge to return to these unredeemed areas of life, one by one, and allow the Spirit to bring all that become scarred and died to spring forth to life.

The trio of prayerful reading of Scripture, keeping a journal, and sharing with a confidant (like a spiritual director or a trustworthy therapist) can help identify and heal these areas.[76] We need the healing of our memory, inasmuch as we remember the pain of our lives from our perspective. But through Scripture and contemplation, we come to see our lives from the Lord's perspective and notice His consoling presence in ways and at moments we hadn't seen. By reentering such memories in detail, allowing our hearts time to grieve over our pain and loss, we open up the wounds of our hearts to the Holy Spirit, Who comforts us in all our afflictions (Mt 5:4; 2 Cor 1:3-7).

Moreover, just as Our Lady stood by her Son at Calvary, so she stands by us at each of our own "Calvaries" — to embody the presence and healing love of the Holy Spirit amid our pain. We have only to invite her into that pain and allow her to comfort us.

QUESTIONS

- How do you handle or cope with shame?
- How do you accept (or reject) the grace of temporal punishment (the necessary purification of sin's effects)?
- What memories or painful experiences do you need to open to the Holy Spirit and His love?

PRAYER

Pray the "Prayer to the Immaculate Conception" (p. 204) and the Litany of the Holy Spirit (#3 — p. 209).

DAY 8
HEART TIME

Immaculata Virginis Mariae Conceptio Sit Nobis Salus et Protectio

The Immaculata was always embraced by the love of God the Father, in the Spirit, through Jesus. She never knew a history without God. For the healing of our past, up to our conception, we need to allow the Holy Spirit — today — to imbue our past without God with God, through surrendering those aspects of our lives to Him. This process requires patience, for this is "heart time," rather than clock time, just as the length of Purgatory cannot be strictly measured by clock time but has to do with time of the heart.

As Blaise Pascal (1623–1662) stated, the heart has reasons that the mind does not know.[77] For some people, entering into certain wounds may need to be done with the accompaniment and guidance of a therapist so to work through such memories gently. But the key is not to pretend that one can continue with life as if "time heals all wounds," because only Christ heals all wounds. In surrendering the fallow years — consumed by pain and suffering — to Him, we allow Him to fulfill His promise to repay double for all that evil in this life has destroyed (Joel 2:25-27).

By diligently cooperating with the Holy Spirit's work of purification and healing, we are enabled to enter Heaven directly at death, like the Immaculata, who entered Heaven on her Assumption. For the Immaculate Conception is the Father's promise that every sin can be forgiven, every wrong corrected, all wounds healed, and punishment fully remitted. Seen in this light, Purgatory, far from being a place of punishment, becomes an anchor of hope for authentic justice and redemption.

God the Father does not ignore the pain we have endured nor the havoc sin has wrought. He repairs all that is broken, mends every rupture, and rectifies every injustice. This includes us: He not only desires to rectify how others have harmed us, but also asks that we too make retribution to others we have harmed. Our hope is that His justice will correct all wrongs and redeem this broken world, starting with our hearts. When He does so, the Church, the world, and the entire cosmos will radiate the splendor of the Immaculata.

Through *penance*, we begin this work of repairing and mending what has been broken. At Lourdes, the Immaculata emphasized to St. Bernadette, "Penance, penance, penance!" Her request for penance is not about punishing ourselves for sin but about cooperating with the medicinal work of the Holy Spirit. Penance turns temporal punishment — the damage caused by sin — into an opportunity to grow in grace by lovingly accepting the effects of our sins and seeking to repair them. While holiness is primarily the fruit of the Spirit's activity within us, He nonetheless desires our total cooperation with His work. Immaculacy is both a pure gift of grace and the fruit of our graced effort. Hence, the Immaculata calls us to practice penance. Like St. Bernadette, who dug into the ground to find the spring of living water, so through penance we excavate our hearts to let them be filled with His love.

Saint Augustine provides a useful analogy: "Suppose that God would fill you with honey: if you are full of vinegar, where will you put the honey? That which the vessel bore in it must be poured out: the vessel itself must be cleansed … albeit with labor, albeit with hard rubbing, that it may become fit for that thing, whatever it be."[78] Just as we follow doctor's orders to avoid certain foods or activities for the sake of healing an injury or a sickness, so we practice penance to cooperate with the Holy Spirit to cure sin and wounds. Penance breaks open our hardened hearts and removes all hindrances that block the Immaculata from touching our hearts. Authentic penance opens all that we are to the Holy Spirit, to love in Person.

As St. Maximilian Kolbe wrote, "Let her preach to us such penance. Let us open our hearts, let her come in, and let us generously give up our hearts, our souls, our bodies and all to her without any restriction or limitation."[79] Penance removes these restrictions, so that we can truly take her into all that pertains to us (Jn 19:27), allowing the Spirit who permeates her to imbue us with His love. For the Holy Spirit desires to make us "full of grace," transformed and permeated by His love, like the Immaculata.

That interior transformation — an intimate, total change and renewal of the entire person, including one's opinions, judgments, emotions, and decisions — is what the Greek *metanoia*, "conversion" entails. The Father is never content with the status quo of our lives: His Spirit converts us ever more each day, if we let Him. As sinners, we resist change, attempting in that way to find stability in a changing world. The Father offers security in His unchanging love: Heaven. He needs our cooperation with His Spirit to accomplish His plan to purify and heal us. In a world of immediate gratification, making the choice to deliberately delay assuaging our pain is difficult. But we will never come to know the divine comfort of the Holy Spirit if we always settle for human comforts.

As St. Faustina wrote, "I have come to know that every soul would like to have divine comforts, but is by no means willing to forsake human comforts, whereas these two things cannot be reconciled" (*Diary*, 1443). Human comforts are like acetaminophen or ibuprofen: They reduce the symptom without providing the cure. Only the Holy Spirit provides the cure we most need for our broken hearts. For He is our true Comforter, Who forgives and heals our sins. Penance forgoes the human comforts that numb but do not heal the pain: It allows the Holy Spirit space to touch, cure, and transform our hearts. But this work of the Holy Spirit requires both our passive acceptance of trials and our active participation through penance.

Now, God does not "need" our penance, but we do. While we must avoid external penances unaccompanied by interior conversion, we also must be careful not to believe interior penance alone is sufficient. Since we are our bodies, we need corporal mortification to love God with all we are, for the First Commandment requires our total love for Him, without reserve or hesitation (Mk 12:29-30).

Pope St. Paul VI identifies three tiers of penance. The first consists "in persevering faithfulness to the duties of one's state in life, in the acceptance of the difficulties arising from one's work and from human coexistence, in a patient bearing of the trials of earthly life and of the utter insecurity which pervades it." The second concerns those members of the Church who "are stricken by infirmities, illnesses, poverty or misfortunes, or who are persecuted for the love of justice." They are "invited to unite their sorrows to the suffering of Christ" to obtain for others grace from God and for themselves the blessedness promised to those who suffer. The third tier comprises "some voluntary act, apart from the renunciation imposed by the burdens of everyday life."[80] Such voluntary asceticism is more binding "where economic well-being is greater," both to avoid being led by the spirit of the world and to give witness of charity toward those who suffer poverty.[81]

The daily Examen — as proposed by St. Ignatius of Loyola — is extremely helpful in the practice of penance. For what may be a necessary penance for one person (with a particular weakness) may not be necessary for another. An alcoholic, for instance, will need to avoid alcohol and the company of those who drink. By reviewing each day, one learns where the Holy Spirit is moving so as to cooperate more faithfully with His inspirations, and knows where one still needs to surrender certain human comforts or desires that are not conducive to our salvation or to God's glory.

Saint Ignatius also recommends using the "particular examen," which is a similar practice, but with the focus on growth in a particular virtue. The way to know what penances to practice is through identifying the primary vice one needs to uproot, and such uprooting is achieved by cultivating the opposite virtue. For instance, one can choose from the Ten Evangelical Virtues of the Immaculata (see page 223). For penance ought to foster virtue, and virtue bolsters penance so that it leads to authentic holiness. Without such connection, penance can not only be unhelpful but also harmful.

By faithfully practicing penance — both by accepting trials and by the voluntary practice of mortification — one can endure Purgatory on earth. The Holy Spirit, amid the busyness or dreariness of daily life, works in countless ways to purify us of all sin and mold us according to the model of the Immaculata. For the question is not whether becoming immaculate is necessary, but when and how. By fidelity to the delicate work of the Spirit, one can be freed from all sin and confirmed in grace.[82] While that is a lofty goal, which not many attain in this life, it remains the Father's plan for each person. Purgatory ensures that His plan is fulfilled after this life, and penance enables us to work in this life to accomplish His plan now.

QUESTIONS

- Where do you find yourself impatient with the time your heart needs for healing?
- When do you seek human comfort rather than divine?
- What penances — from each tier — do you need to apply to cooperate with the healing work of the Holy Spirit?

PRAYER

Pray the "Prayer to the Immaculate Conception" (p. 204) and the Chaplet of the Ten Evangelical Virtues (p. 223).

DAY 9
INTERIOR PEACE

Immaculata Virginis Mariae Conceptio Sit Nobis Salus et Protectio

Because the Immaculata shared in the victory of her Son over Satan and death through participating in His Passion, she shares in His Kingship. She is Queen of Heaven and Earth, the Queen of All Hearts, the Queen of All Creation. But first, she is *queen of herself*: she is entirely the master of herself, her Heart, her entire being. As a result of her Immaculate Conception, she did not experience the inner tension of concupiscence nor the antagonism between her flesh and spirit, as we do. There was no discord within her, no point where her mind, will, and emotions went in different directions. Think of how often we are distracted — our minds in one place but our emotions and will in another! Her heart knew only peace and harmony among all aspects of her interior, because her will was one with God's.

But she maintained this mastery or queenship over herself through daily collaboration with grace. The Immaculata had to face challenges daily and so grow in virtue. She is, for us, an example of how to live in peace, above all, with ourselves. For if we lack interior peace with ourselves, we will be incapable of peace with others. This requires patience with our weakness, patience that opens our hearts to the gentle mercy of the Father toward our sinfulness.[83] As Blessed George Matulaitis wrote, "Perfection also means knowing how to bear your own imperfections patiently: in other words, knowing how to combat them patiently and steadfastly."[84]

Through Baptism, we are made partakers in Christ's three-fold-mission of being priest, prophet, and king. In Him, we are all kings, which means that we must rule first and foremost over ourselves, our hearts, and our decisions. This is no easy task, as our hearts often elude the guidance of our minds. Because of sin, we experience an inner brokenness, and our hearts — even though they are our own — are a sort of unconquered territory.

Since we are in a spiritual combat, we need to be prepared for battle. In the Old Testament, the Lord left the "nations" in the Promised Land to test His Chosen People so that they might learn "warfare" and be faithful to God's law (Judges 3:1-4). We must extend the Kingdom of God into every area of our hearts and lives, and this requires effort, time, and penance to eradicate all sin (*Catechism*, 405).[85] For "Baptism, by imparting the life of Christ's grace, erases original sin and turns a man back toward God, but the consequences for nature, weakened and inclined to evil, persist in man and summon him to spiritual battle" (*Catechism*, 405).

This requires *asceticism* — from the Greek word for "exercise, train" — and it is not optional but is a requirement of divine law for all the members of the Church.[86] As St. John of the Cross comments, "The world is the enemy least difficult to conquer; the devil is the hardest to understand; but the flesh is the most tenacious, and its attacks continue as long as the old self lasts."[87] The battle to bring the flesh under the dominion of the Holy Spirit is arduous and requires equal tenacity.

Saint Paul describes this inner tension well in Romans 7:13-25: we experience a war within ourselves. Through asceticism, we conquer our hearts anew for Christ. This means allowing His Kingdom — His Spirit — to enter our hearts entirely, leaving nothing untouched by His love.

Now, we believe that the soul is the spiritual element that is united to the flesh of our body (*Catechism*, 363-367). While the flesh is limited and physical, the soul is spiritual and capable of the infinite. There is a dynamic tension between the soul's aspiration to what is infinite and spiritual and the flesh's desires for what is finite and material. Yet the Father *creatively willed* the *complementarity* of body and soul for man to live in harmony, and our redemption is completed only by the resurrection of the body.[88]

There was no opposition before original sin; but afterward, concupiscence has brought a destructive antagonism of the flesh toward the Spirit (Gal 5:17). But *flesh* there refers to the totality of *unhealed, unredeemed human nature, both body and soul.* The Spirit is not opposed to the human body, which is His temple. We need not punish our body, as if it were the culprit of sin. Sin has its origins in the human heart and flows from the will (*Catechism*, 1849).

Those zealous after a recent conversion sometimes practice harsh penances for past sins. Even some saints, like Ignatius of Loyola, later admitted that their lives were shortened by excessive penance. Various saints write against such harsh treatment of the body, drawing on their own experiences from which they learned: St. Francis of Assisi, St. Catherine of Siena, and St. John of the Cross, to name a few. But excessive corporal penance misdirects vast amounts of energy and time, perpetuating rather than healing the wound of interior division.

Sometimes called "mortification of the flesh," penance tempers desires of the flesh that war against the spirit (Gal 5:17). This has nothing to do with condemning the body or seeking "spiritual" liberation from the body. Rather, mortification liberates us from being enslaved by concupiscence, which is inflamed through our five senses. Indeed, in the words of *Gaudium et Spes*, the "whole of man's history has been the story of dour combat with the powers of evil, stretching, so our Lord tells us, from the very dawn of history until the last day. Finding himself in the midst of the battlefield man has to struggle to do what is right, and it is at great cost to himself, and aided by God's grace, that he succeeds in achieving his own inner integrity" (37.2).

We are to *tame*, not kill, the body: for just as the Spirit tamed the chaos without violence, so He calms our flesh *by His gentleness*. The flesh can be imagined like a horse. The horse contains *much more power* than the person riding it, yet, when the rider intelligently *guides* the horse, all that horsepower is at the rider's disposal. Without a rider (or a fence), the horse *goes where it desires, just as the flesh wanders aimlessly* without our intellect to guide its desires.

Yet, even when a horse rebels, we need to be *firm*, not violent. Once, I rode a horse that had been stung in its rear by a hornet. Unlike the other horses, it was not very responsive to my commands to stop or turn. I became rather afraid as we raced toward a barbed wire fence. From my trainer, I learned that I need not *force* the horse to stop, but rather, *amid my fear, maintain composure and keep pulling on the reins.* In the same way, one deals with the "unruly" flesh: *not* by forcibly punishing it, but by being firm in directing it constantly. Similarly, our flesh needs the gentle but firm direction of the Spirit.

Christian holiness is *not* the dominance of the spiritual over the material but the harmonious union of the soul and body in one whole.[89] The Immaculata reveals this in her Assumption: her holiness is manifest in the integrity of her body and soul sharing in the glory of her Son. The Father is not pleased by our cruelty to ourselves, nor is He appeased if we crush ourselves in affliction. Authentic *mortification* or *penance* puts not the body but sin to death. As the Father revealed to St. Catherine of Siena: "They have placed all their labour and desire in the mortification of the body, rather than in the destruction of their own will."[90]

What doctor would castigate a patient who comes in, severely ill and at the door of death? The doctor would immediately take care of the patient to heal him. Then, once he is stabilized, the doctor will recommend medicine for the patient to take, activities to do, and activities to stop. *Penance* entails *full cooperation with the Divine Doctor*, taking the medicine we need, performing the activities that strengthen us, and leaving behind activities that bring harm. That *change of lifestyle* is conversion, and the concrete *steps* involve penance.

Mortification applies to those bad habits that *impede health* and *prevent healing*. Both penance and mortification — as a "no" to sin — ought to serve as a deeper "yes" to *freedom*: the capacity to live in accord with the Spirit, Who dwells *precisely in our flesh*. When we possess what we most *deeply desire*, then we no longer are concerned about superficial desires that lead not to freedom, but to death. A great help in this is a spiritual director, who can instruct us in how to persist in gently submitting our flesh to the Holy Spirit, so that, like Our Lady, even our body radiates the glory of God.

What is it like living in union with the Immaculata, a life governed solely by the Holy Spirit? When the flesh has been calmed by the Spirit — just as the formless land and the waters were under the power of the Spirit — then all those forces that oppose God's kingdom in our lives are silenced. We experience peace. The internal cacophony of opposing desires, thoughts, and impulses is transformed into a harmonious but silent symphony.

Saint Paul lists the characteristics of living in the Spirit as His one, multiform fruit (Gal 5:22-23). Similarly, the qualities of love in 1 Corinthians 13:4-7 describe this kind of life, which the Immaculata enjoys and which she wants to share with us. In short, we begin to taste Heaven in our hearts — and share the peace of her Immaculate Heart.

The mystery of the Immaculate Conception reveals the utter priority of God's grace. But His grace in turn undergirds our efforts and makes them possible, so that — strengthened by His grace — we might collaborate with Him in the spiritual combat to extend His Kingdom.

QUESTIONS

- Where do you most experience the tension between the flesh and the Spirit, between cravings of the body and yearnings of the soul?
- In your daily life, how can you deny your own will and submit to the Spirit?

PRAYER

Pray the "Prayer to the Immaculate Conception" (p. 204) and the Litany of the Blessed Virgin Mary, Immaculately Conceived (#1 — p. 212).

DAY 10
THE CALL FOR PENANCE

Immaculata Virginis Mariae Conceptio Sit Nobis Salus et Protectio

In heeding the Immaculata's call for *penance,* one might think of *fasting* or *abstinence,* such as we practice in Lent. However, another helpful penance is imitation of Our Lady's *prudent silence.* "Silence is so powerful a language that it reaches the throne of the living God. Silence is His language, though secret, yet living and powerful" (*Diary,* 888).

Now, such silence is not a somber absence of life; rather, it is the prerequisite for allowing space for communion with the Immaculata, to speak to her freely from the depths of our heart about what concerns us. When we transition from one activity to another, those silent moments open us up to her presence and love. Moreover, the mystery of her Immaculate Conception occurred in such silence and hiddenness. To witness the great things the Almighty accomplishes, we need profound silence — a fruit of interior peace — to see "in secret" (Mt 6:4, 6, 18).

Silence also fosters communion with Jesus through the Holy Spirit. Our Lady instructs St. Faustina, "*My daughter, strive after silence and humility, so that Jesus, who dwells in your heart continuously, may be able to rest. Adore Him in your heart; do not go out from your inmost being*" (*Diary,* 785). To live in such union with the Holy Spirit, we need exterior silence and profound interior silence. "I am trying my best to be faithful throughout the day to the Holy Spirit and to fulfill His demands. I am trying my best for interior silence in order to be able to hear His voice ..." (*Diary,* 1828). Notably, these are the last words of the *Diary.*

Saint John of the Cross stated, "The Father spoke one Word, which was His Son, and this Word He always speaks in eternal silence, and in silence must It be heard by the soul."[91] That "eternal silence" is the Holy Spirit, and when this is lacking, it is impossible to hear clearly the Father's one Word. Cardinal Robert Sarah, in *The Power of Silence*, comments that the dictatorship of noise in the world is a subtle blasphemy against the Holy Spirit.[92] For while the Word is spoken, the Spirit remains silent, and in silence alone do we enter into profound union with the Spirit. Saint Faustina warns:

> God does not give Himself to a chattering soul which, like a drone in a beehive, buzzes around but gathers no honey. A talkative soul is empty inside. It lacks both the essential virtues and intimacy with God. A deeper interior life, one of gentle peace and of that silence where the Lord dwells, is quite out of the question. A soul that has never tasted the sweetness of inner silence is a restless spirit which disturbs the silence of others (*Diary*, 118).

To know the Holy Spirit — and to be known by Him — we need to practice profound silence, not only with our lips, but with our hearts. This requires not only bridling our tongue but directing our thoughts and affections to God: "We … take every thought captive in obedience to Christ" (2 Cor 10:5). Saint John of the Cross advises: "Cast off concern about things, and bear peace and recollection in your heart. Keep spiritually tranquil in a loving attentiveness to God, and when it is necessary to speak, let it be with the same calm and peace."[93] Now, if only we could turn off all our thoughts! But it is important to remember that we cannot shut off our thoughts; we can only choose to direct our attention to God amid a barrage of distractions and worries. The goal is to never lose touch with the Holy Spirit, so that one always remains in His love. An aid to redirecting our attention to Jesus and remaining in His love is the use of brief ejaculatory prayers. For this reason, the Eastern churches highly value the repetition of the Jesus prayer — "Jesus Christ, Son of the living God, have mercy on me, a sinner" — throughout the day.

This entails being focused on and engaged in the will of God at each moment. While that sounds penitential, it is actually quite freeing. How often we are distracted, worried, and concerned about many things at once, so that our heart loses its interior peace and we accomplish little that we need (Lk 10:41; Gal 5:17)? How liberating to be present in the present moment, without having to carry the weight of everything else! By avoiding or checking our dissipation or distraction, we are able to do what we are doing, to live in the present, with filial trust that the rest is in the hands of the Immaculata. By letting go of anything other than her will — which is always guided by the Holy Spirit — we live our consecration to her moment by moment (as we shall see later in this book). The goal is communion with the Spirit, to always and everywhere be guided by Him. In remaining docile to her, we are ready to receive the graces the Spirit pours forth — even at the most unexpected moments. Those who are faithful in little things — even the subtlest inspirations of the Spirit — will be entrusted with greater ones (Mt 25:23). Silence is the readiness to recognize and respond to the Spirit, Who moves where He wills (Jn 3:8).

This silence requires a letting go of oneself — one's own ideas, thoughts, etc. The word idiot comes from the Greek *idios*, "one's own." An idiot is one who clings to or solely identifies with "one's own" — opinions, thoughts, ideas, will. One consecrated to the Immaculate Conception clings to the Immaculata's thoughts, ideas, will, and emotions. John took Mary into *ta idia* — the plural of *idios* — "into all that was his own" (Jn 19:27). Saint Maximilian Kolbe wrote that, "... we have to dwell in Her soul, think Her thoughts, etc., so that there might be no difference between what She thinks about something and what we think about it, just as there are no differences between Her desires and the will of God."[94]

By silence, we make room for the Immaculata, allowing her to enter into all that is our own. We dwell in the same Spirit that dwells in the Immaculata, and we radiate her love, grace, and virtue in our daily activities and words. We surrender what is "our own" by silencing the ways that we express ourselves. Now, not all such self-expression is wrong or harmful. However, much of our self-expression flows from inordinate self-love, and silence provides space for divine love to be present and permeate us. When we do this, then — to use the wording of St. Maximilian Kolbe — we are "transubstantiated into the Immaculata."[95] By surrendering what is "our own," we share and live her virtues, thoughts, emotions, and will.

This communion with the Immaculata through the Holy Spirit entails not allowing anything to absorb our attention or distract us from this union. The goal is to be interiorly united with the Holy Spirit through interior silence and peace even amid external work and activities. "The silent soul is capable of attaining the closest union with God. It lives almost always under the inspiration of the Holy Spirit. God works in a silent soul without hindrance" (*Diary*, 477).

Now, in this life, we cannot be truly thinking explicitly of the Immaculata; but we can give our attention, minds, wills, to those things which pertain to her will, her mind, and her heart. The purpose of penance — including silence — is adjusting our will to the will of God, which the Holy Spirit reveals to our heart in silence. Our Lady taught St. Faustina, "I strongly recommend that you faithfully fulfill all God's wishes, for that is most pleasing in His holy eyes. I very much desire that you distinguish yourself in this faithfulness in accomplishing God's will. Put the will of God before all sacrifices and holocausts" (*Diary*, 1244).

One can break silence by being silent when one ought to speak as well as by speaking when one ought to be silent. The point is to remember that our words are always to be spoken in the breath of love. "Idle" words are those spoken out of self-love or, worse, out of hatred — words spoken without the breath of the Spirit. These include gossip, slander, detraction, lies and rumors. Jesus warned: "I tell you, on the day of judgment people will render an account for every careless word they speak" (Mt 12:36). James (1:26, 3:1-12) also warns about the tongue, noting that the one who can control the tongue is "perfect." "We are sensitive to words and quickly want to answer back, without taking any regard as to whether it is God's will that we should speak" (*Diary*, 477). Taking a calm breath before speaking can be a subtle but helpful practice to invoke the Holy Spirit to inspire what we say.

Moreover, we infringe silence by allowing anything or anyone to "absorb our attention and distract that attention from that to which God desires us to attend."[96] How often do we — like Martha (Lk 10:41) — become worriedly occupied with many things making ourselves overly busy with tasks that are more than what He asks of us! Even more subtly, we may be applying ourselves to His will but, with excessive anxiety and concern, making it more about us (and our will) than about Him. Every daily activity — even the most important — is means to loving God, Who alone is our goal and reward. So we apply ourselves to our activities in the way and the measure that the Holy Spirit intends.

Saint Maximilian Kolbe wrote:

> Fulfilling a duty cannot absorb us; we ought to apply ourselves to work, but without any disordered impetus. In calmness you will achieve more, because you will commit fewer mistakes. Hence we are to avoid that which does not belong to our duties in a given moment. This gets in the way of work and of inspirations. We are to fulfill that which is the will of God. Then we will find time for ejaculatory prayers, which are so important in the spiritual life and for

> conversation with Our Lady. Slowly we will be able to get used to this. Then the soul will remain in interior peace.[97]

Saint Maximilian refers here to ejaculatory prayers, which are short prayers that we can repeat either interiorly or aloud in a free moment, to refocus our mind and attention to Jesus or Mary. The prayer at the opening of each day — *Immaculata Virginis Mariae Conceptio Sit Nobis Salus et Protectio* — is such a prayer, as is *Jesus, I trust in You*. By nature, such prayers are brief and quick, enabling us to pray amid our activities. Brother Lawrence has written a classic on how to maintain the presence of God throughout the day, which can be helpful in putting this into daily practice.[98]

By letting go of any excess of worries and distractions, we make room for an interior dialogue with the Immaculata. Not only that, but we perform our duties with greater care and attention, for we focus on what is before us rather than dwelling on the barrage of thoughts within. Thus, St. Faustina — who prayed silently as she gardened — worked more diligently (even while sick) than the other sisters and grew larger tomatoes than the others.[99]

Through silence, we enter into the "atmosphere" of the Spirit, where the Father can speak His Word. We also enter into the atmosphere of Our Lady, who always dwells in the Spirit. By silence, we enter into communion with her, and we will witness how the Spirit works to accomplish this mystery within our own hearts.

QUESTIONS

- Where do you need most to practice silence and adjust your will to His will?
- In moments of transition, how can you allow the Immaculata's presence into your daily life?
- What "idle words" do you speak?

PRAYER

Pray the "Prayer to the Immaculate Conception" (p. 204) and the Litany of the Holy Spirit (#1 — p. 205).

DAY 11
THE CHOICE

Immaculata Virginis Mariae Conceptio Sit Nobis Salus et Protectio

The mystery of the Immaculate Conception reveals the Father's triumph in Christ over the full power of sin and of Satan. Her conception is like the morning star that foretells the coming sun: the light of victory. The Father desires to extend this victory of her Immaculate Conception to every heart, including yours. The triumph of her Immaculate Heart, promised at Fatima, begins with this interior victory over Satan, his lies, and his temptations. As was discussed yesterday, silence is necessary for conquering the power of Satan and persevering amid suffering: "Silence is a sword in the spiritual struggle. A talkative soul will never attain sanctity. The sword of silence will cut off everything that would like to cling to the soul. A silent soul is strong; no adversities will harm it if it perseveres in silence" (*Diary*, 477).

We participate in this triumph through choosing — in union with the Immaculata — faith over doubt, hope over despair, and love over hatred. Just as this mystery reveals the Father's love for the Immaculata, it also manifests Satan's hatred of her. The Immaculate Conception sheds light on the total opposition between the Holy Spirit and Satan. Through original sin, Satan has been able to inject his venom of distrust into every heart, except that of Jesus and Mary.[100] As God pronounced after the fall of Adam and Eve: "I will put enmity between you and the woman, and between your offspring and hers" (Gen 3:15). By entrusting ourselves to the Immaculata, we become her spiritual offspring. We can expect — and ought to prepare for — the enmity of Satan (Sirach 2:1-6; 1 Pet 4:12, 5:8-9). Jesus Himself bluntly warns us: "If the world hates you, realize that it hated me first. If you belonged to the world, the world would love its own; but because you do not belong to the world, and I have chosen you out of the world, the world hates you" (Jn 15:18-19). We ought not be caught off guard by Satan's hatred.

If we desire to draw near to the Immaculata, we must be ready as well for the attacks of Satan, who opposes this mystery — the presence and work of the Holy Spirit in her Immaculate Heart. The Immaculata, like her Son, endured Satan's fierce hatred. Firm in her faith and remaining steadfast in love, she never consented to his temptations and so remained always free of his venom. Saint Maximilian Kolbe also urges us, "Let us prepare to fight against Satan, the world and ... ourselves — to save and sanctify our souls and as many other souls as possible — let us prepare to suffer and to work."[101]

The victory of the Immaculate Conception did not occur without real combat unto death. Her Son died on the Cross so as to defeat Satan. But as Jesus conquered Satan with Our Lady's cooperation and suffering, so He renews this victory in the Church and us through associating us with this spiritual combat. To share the fruit of this mystery — total freedom from sin and from Satan — we also must share in the battle.

In other words, we enter the scene of Revelation 12 as active participants. The woman of Revelation 12 symbolizes Israel, the Church, and the Immaculata.[102] In the pangs of birth, she faces the threat of the dragon who seeks to consume her offspring. But she and her son are protected by divine intervention, and then a battle ensues between St. Michael and the holy angels and Satan and his fallen angels.[103] Unsuccessful in regard to Mary and her Son, Satan pursues her spiritual children to bring them to ruin (Rev 12:17). "Although the church is protected by God's special providence (Rev 12:16), the individual Christian is to expect persecution and suffering."[104] We know that Christ has conquered Satan, and the Immaculata is proof of that total victory. The Church, too, will share in that triumph. However, we also know that God's providence permits persecution and suffering as part of the necessary purification of the Church, for growth in virtue and holiness (*Catechism*, 675).

Saint Michael the Archangel warned St. Faustina, "The Lord has ordered me to take special care of you. Know that you are hated by evil; but do not fear — 'Who is like God!'" (*Diary*, 706). The closer we draw to God, the more we will be hated by evil and face its fury against us in spiritual combat. The saints of the latter days — which may indeed be our own day — will be pitted against the power of Satan, unleashed anew on the world (Rev 20:7-8). But they will be preserved and strengthened through their devotion to the Immaculata.

The Immaculata — as at Lourdes and Fatima — calls us to penance so as to bear the appropriate arms for this spiritual battle against Satan and demons. For just as Christ conquered through the Cross, so we, too, can defeat Satan only through sacrificial love offered on the altar of the Cross. We are called, with Our Lady, to unite ourselves to Jesus Crucified, offering ourselves as victims in union with Him. We thus live our royal (baptismal) priesthood, offering ourselves as living sacrifices to God (1 Pet 2:5; Rom 12:1-2).

It is necessary to study our opponent, to understand his tactics, and so not fall prey to his persecution. The name *Satan* derives from the Hebrew for "accuser." "For the accuser of our brothers is cast out, who accuses them before our God day and night" (Rev 12:10). Satan accuses us of our sin before God, attempting to prove that we are unworthy of being counted among God's elect. But we know that the Father has irrevocably chosen us in Christ and forgives our sins. So, Satan's attacks are primarily directed toward us, as he attempts to convince us that we are worthy, not of merciful love and forgiveness, but of condemnation.

Satan provokes a response of fear — as if we had to brace for punishment from an angry God — rather than a response of trust. Satan places our sins before us to insinuate, "You are unlovable, because you are so miserable and sinful." But the Holy Spirit convinces our hearts, "You are a sinner, but you are still loved, and this love will heal your sins." Satan's accusations are a hidden temptation toward despair, while the Holy Spirit's conviction of our sin leads to hope in the Divine Mercy. Like a doctor who indicates the illness so as to provide the necessary treatment, the Holy Spirit identifies our sins as He brings us to the pierced side of Jesus, the font of mercy.

Since we are still sinners, sometimes there is truth in Satan's accusations. Hence, his tactics are quite tricky and sly, for he would induce us to flee from the Father because of our sins rather than plead for forgiveness. Satan portrays God the Father as a "just judge," who is entirely impartial to us and devoid of merciful love. Satan clouds our vision of God as a good Father, making Him appear as a tyrant whom we need to escape to find freedom, life, and joy. But apart from the Father's house, we encounter only emptiness and pain, like the Prodigal Son who endured famine and misery in a foreign land (Lk 15:14). God is not intent on accusing and condemning us for our sins.

The mystery of the Immaculate Conception heals how we envision God. By drawing near to the Immaculata, the "fully healed" one, we come to know better how to recognize Satan, who is quite subtle in his attacks against us. Her tender love reveals his coy malice. Through her, the Holy Spirit heals our image of God, so that we, like Jesus, dare to call Him "Abba" (Gal 4:6). "We need not fear our own brokenness, for the Immaculata has chosen us because we are weak."[105]

The Immaculata is a transparent icon, a quasi-incarnation of the Holy Spirit. Her femininity reveals the personality and personal qualities of the Holy Spirit. As we more clearly experience the unconditional love of God through the faithful love of a mother, so through the Immaculata we grasp the Holy Spirit Who is love in Person. The Immaculata, through her maternal yet virginal femininity, reveals a particular characteristic of God's compassionate mercy so that we trust in Him.

In Hebrew, *rahamim,* "tender, compassionate mercy," is the plural of *rehem,* "womb, uterus." The idea is that God *feels* the *tender love* that a mother experiences toward her own child. "Can a mother forget her infant, be without tenderness for the child of her womb? Even should she forget, I will never forget you" (Is 49:15). The Immaculata stands beside her Son in judgment to remind us that we are before the God of merciful, tender love.

Do we not pray for this with every Hail Mary? "Pray for us sinners, now and at the hour of our death." Yet the Immaculata — filled with spiritual beauty and merciful love — is terrifying to Satan. The Church has applied this line to her: "Beautiful as Tirzah are you, my friend; fair as Jerusalem, fearsome as celestial visions" (Song 6:4).

The oldest known prayer to Our Lady — from the third to fourth century — invokes her "tender compassion." The Greek word used is a translation of *rahamim*: literally, her "good innards" where she feels compassion for us. "Beneath your compassion, We take refuge, O *Theotokos* [God-bearer]: do not despise our petitions in time of trouble: but rescue us from dangers, only pure, only blessed one." With her, we will gain victory over Satan and will be protected by her tender, compassionate mercy.

QUESTIONS

- How do you envision the moment of judgment, and where is Our Lady in that moment?
- Where do you stand "accused" by Satan, and when are you convinced by the Spirit?
- How can you have more frequent recourse to Our Lady's "tender mercies" in your daily trials?
- How do you differentiate between the subtle hatred of Satan and the love of the Spirit?

PRAYER

Pray the "Prayer to the Queen of Heaven and Earth" (p. 204) and the Chaplet of St. Michael (p. 224).

DAY 12
TEMPTATION

Immaculata Virginis Mariae Conceptio Sit Nobis Salus et Protectio

The Immaculata, who radiates the merciful love of the Father, enables us to discern ever more easily the difference between the good spirit and the evil spirit. Her beauty — the splendor of divine grace — unmasks the machinations of Satan, who wants to pose as an "angel of light" (2 Cor 11:14). Saint Ignatius of Loyola developed two sets of rules, based on his prayerful experience, to enable us to differentiate between the two spirits. "Good spirit" refers both to the Holy Spirit at work within our hearts and to the holy angels who assist us. "Evil spirit" refers to Satan and other demons who tempt us as well as to our fallen nature (concupiscence). As stated previously, the good spirit and the evil spirit are entirely opposed to each other, and the Immaculata — totally aligned with the Holy Spirit — is at enmity with the serpent, Satan, and with all evil spirits.

The Holy Spirit, in all that He does, heals us so as to elevate us to share in the divine life of self-giving love. The Cross is a symbol of the Holy Spirit, for it expresses the *agape — love —* that is God: total, self-giving love. This same love burns in the human, Sacred Heart of Jesus Christ. The Immaculate Heart, too, shares in that same fire of love, for she sacrificed her own private good — having her Son alive — for the common good of our salvation. Satan, on the other hand, actively works to harm us through temptation to sin — through inordinate self-love.

Because we are social creatures, our personal good depends on the good of others. Inordinate self-love means choosing one's own private good in opposition to the common good. For instance, someone who accumulates excessive wealth for himself is amassing a private good, which may be detrimental to the common good, that is, the just distribution of wealth, particularly as it affects the poor (*Catechism,* 1938). At its root, this self-love is actually self-hatred, by which we harm ourselves because we choose not what is authentically good for us but only what is apparently good.

Satan's tactics include separating and isolating us as individuals, apart from the Church and from the Communion of Saints. The name *devil* comes from the Greek "to divide." In nature, wolves encircle sheep so as to lure one of them — typically, the weakest — away from the others. Once the sheep is isolated — divided from the flock — the wolves are able to attack. Satan always destroys communion, separating one person from another and from God.

Today, however, individualism is touted as the path to freedom and happiness. The Holy Spirit, on the other hand, creates and fosters communion. The only path to defeating Satan is through the Communion of Saints, which requires us to beseech the heavenly intercession of the Immaculata and the saints, but also the human help of others in the Church on earth. When we seek our own private good, we separate ourselves from the flock and so are easily hounded by Satan. United with the Immaculata in prayer just as the disciples at Pentecost, we are not only protected from Satan but filled with the Spirit. It is worth noting that the Spirit is given only to those united with others in prayer (Acts 1:14-15).

Jesus calls Satan "a murderer from the beginning" (Jn 8:44) because he seduces us through temptation to kill the gift of divine grace in our hearts. Satan accomplishes this through lies, namely, that we are unloved and unlovable, that even God does not love us, because He hates sin. The Holy Spirit, on the other hand, leads us into "all truth" (Jn 16:13), so that our hearts taste and know the unfathomable reality of God's love. The truth, then, is not merely doctrinal or intellectual but, above all, life itself — and apart from that, there is only death.

When we lack truth, we lack life and mercy; when we remain in the truth, we are filled with life. For authentic mercy is only encountered in the fullness of the truth: "Love and truth will meet" (Ps 85:10). Our deepest wound is not that of any suffering or pain inflicted by others, but rather, the wound of sin — disbelief in His love. For the sin of which the Spirit convicts us is that of not believing in Jesus, in His Person and His love that He sends in the Spirit (Jn 16:8-9).

By accusing us and tempting us to despair over our sin, Satan obstructs any attempt to find healing. When Satan maintains a stronghold over certain unhealed wounds, then we live in bondage to sin. "Amen, amen, I say to you, everyone who commits sin is a slave of sin"

(Jn 8:34). Adam and Eve were given dominion over all visible creation, but by original sin they ceded part of this freedom to Satan and to their own instincts, reducing themselves to slaves. Such slavery is visible in addiction, whereby addicts lose the freedom they once had to choose what is actually good. They instead "choose" — repeatedly and despite any attempt to the contrary — what is harmful. This moral and spiritual bondage is maintained through sins that are not confessed and wounds that are not healed.

As described in previous days, the Sacrament of Confession makes available to us the mercy we need to be free from bondage to sin and Satan. Why do we need to confess our sins to a priest, rather than directly to God? First, by every sin, we harm not only ourselves and our relationship with God, but also the Communion of Saints — the Church. By Confession, we draw near anew to the Lord's flock. As Jesus is not only the Shepherd but also the "gate" (Jn 10:9), so the priest stands as the "gate" to let the flock enter anew.

Penance thus entails not only spiritual practices (fasting, prayers), but also repairing any harm we have done to others. This may entail asking for forgiveness, repaying debts, or restoring relationships to restore communion. As Jesus Himself warns: "If you are to go with your opponent before a magistrate, make an effort to settle the matter on the way; otherwise your opponent will turn you over to the judge, and the judge hand you over to the constable, and the constable throw you into prison. I say to you, you will not be released until you have paid the last penny" (Lk 12:58-59). We ought to forgive and work toward reconciliation with others in this life, lest we be thrown into prison — Purgatory (see *Catechism,* 2838-2845). For Heaven is the fullness of communion between the Trinity and the saints. All relationships need to be healed for that to come about. Although reconciliation requires participation of both sides, the willingness to reconcile and be in relationship with the other (forgiveness) is necessary to enter Heaven.

Second, while it is true that God can directly forgive our sins, He ordinarily grants absolution to us through the Church. *Absolution* comes from the Latin *absolvere,* "set free, loosen, acquit." The root, *solvere,* means "to loosen, dissolve; untie, release; dismiss."[106] In granting absolution, the priest uses his sacramental authority to untie or loosen us from the bondage of Satan. This loosening is more powerful than exorcism, for it has the power of a Sacrament, whereas exorcism is an extensive blessing.

Picture Lazarus at the moment that Jesus resuscitated him from the dead. He was alive, but he was still bound by the burial cloths. "The dead man came out, tied hand and foot with burial bands, and his face was wrapped in a cloth. So Jesus said to them, 'Untie him and let him go'" (Jn 11:44). Jesus alone has the power to raise Lazarus from death, but He chooses to instruct others: "Untie him and let him go." That is a vivid depiction of absolution, which is more visible in the Latin translation: "untie" is *solvite,* the imperative of *solvere.* What good is it to be alive, but still bound by the effects of our sins? Jesus desires to loosen the bonds of sins, to free us from their bondage and from Satan's grasp.

God desires that we participate in loosening this bondage. In his *Spiritual Exercises,* St. Ignatius of Loyola recommends a general Confession. This entails examining our whole life, to confess those things that we may not have recognized as sins or that we did not remember. Whereas we easily remember those sins that are more obvious to us, to be fully unbound we need to confess at a minimum all our mortal sins. Confessing all venial sins is also extremely helpful. What good would it be to be freed from the majority of our sins, if we still are held bound by others? As St. John of the Cross wisely observed: a bird is prevented from taking flight whether by a heavy chain or a thin thread.[107]

Similarly, we cannot fly until every disordered attachment of our hearts to creatures is purified. Imagine a patient in the hospital who tells the doctor all his life-threatening symptoms but ignores other, less painful symptoms. One might be free of cancer, but if one has flu, one doesn't feel healthy. Similarly, we bring all our sins to the Divine Doctor in Confession, so that He can heal all our wounds and untie all our bonds.

The Holy Spirit gives us *parrhesia*: Fully convinced of being loved, He enables us to speak forth our sins, so as to find healing forgiveness (*Catechism*, 2778). Satan, on the other hand, mutes our voices, filling us with fear and making us avoid Confession. Remember that Satan depicts God as a fearsome judge, while the Holy Spirit — through the Immaculata — reveals His tender compassion and forgiveness. Through confessing all our sins, small and great, we will be clothed, like Our Lady, with His tender mercies and so become ever more immaculate. The point here is not to be scrupulous, but rather to be complete and make an *integral* Confession, whereby we confess every sin, even the most insignificant. By exposing our misery to His mercy, we receive the torrent of His grace and love — the same torrent that washed the Immaculata when the side of Jesus was pierced at Calvary. When we are washed clean, then we will be able to see and distinguish properly between the good and the evil spirit. As Jesus taught St. Faustina:

> **Daughter, when you go to confession, to this fountain of My mercy, the Blood and Water which came forth from My Heart always flows down upon your soul and ennobles it. Every time you go to confession, immerse yourself entirely in My mercy, with great trust, so that I may pour the bounty of My grace upon your soul. When you approach the confessional, know this, that I Myself am waiting there for you. I am only hidden by the priest, but I Myself act in your soul. Here the misery of the soul meets the God of mercy. Tell souls that from this fount of mercy souls draw graces solely with the vessel of trust. If their trust is great, there is no limit to My generosity. The torrents of grace inundate humble souls. The proud remain always in poverty and misery, because My grace turns away from them to humble souls** (*Diary*, 1602).

QUESTIONS

- How do you discern when making decisions?
- How do you experience the attacks or strongholds of Satan in your life?
- What sins do you still need to confess, to find healing and freedom from bondage?

PRAYER

Pray the "Prayer to the Queen of Heaven and Earth" (p. 204) and the Litany of the Holy Spirit (#2 — p. 207).

DAY 13
SPIRITUAL COMBAT

Immaculata Virginis Mariae Conceptio Sit Nobis Salus et Protectio

The Immaculata, although entirely separated from sin, is not separated from sinners. She is the "Refuge of Sinners," embracing us, with all our wounds, close to her Immaculate Heart. When we draw near to her to seek her unconditional love in our sinfulness, she in turn leads us to the Church to experience that love in the Sacrament of Confession. When we confess aloud our worst sins, we are embraced by the love of God and led into the fullness of His truth. At the moment when we would have every reason to imagine we deserve to be punished and unloved, the Father renews His gift of love to us through the Holy Spirit.

The Holy Spirit not only forgives our sins. He Himself is the forgiveness of our sins. For sin is wherever there is a lack of the Holy Spirit in our hearts, and sin is removed when that void is filled anew with His presence and love. Mary was conceived immaculate and remained immaculate precisely because there was no aspect of her being that was empty or devoid of the Holy Spirit. On the other hand, wherever there is a void of the Holy Spirit, then Satan comes to fill that emptiness with his lies.

This is one of the most pernicious tactics of Satan. Jesus warns:

> When an unclean spirit goes out of someone, it roams through arid regions searching for rest but, finding none, it says, "I shall return to my home from which I came." But upon returning, it finds it swept clean and put in order. Then it goes and brings back seven other spirits more wicked than itself who move in and dwell there, and the last condition of that person is worse than the first (Lk 11:24-26).

The house may be "swept clean and put in order," but as long as it is not filled with the Holy Spirit, then the demons can return with a vengeance.

We all have areas of our lives where we are bound by sin, even though we outwardly may be presentable. Satan firmly keeps his stronghold over any unhealed wound, lest he lose his foothold in our lives. Moreover, he even prefers that the outside look "put in order," lest anybody suspect his pernicious influence. This entails that our participation in our healing does not end with Confession. We need to attend to the interior house, closing every open door, lest Satan return. Only through penance do we prevent the demons from returning, for penance includes taking the necessary measures not only to remove Satan from our lives but to keep him out permanently. Like a soldier guarding a fortress, so we must vigilantly protect our hearts and lives from Satan, who is the thief who comes to destroy (Jn 10:10).

The paradox of mortification, however, is that if it is merely self-protection, then it does not open us to the Holy Spirit. All penance is to lead us toward charity, toward self-giving love, for only then is our heart filled with the Spirit. As Jesus taught, "Whoever finds his life will lose it, and whoever loses his life for my sake will find it" (Mt 10:39, also 16:25; Mk 8:35; Lk 9:24, 17:33; Jn 12:25). To be fully alive, we must embrace the death of Christ — a death that is an expression of self-giving love. By practicing such penance — impelled by God's grace — we grow in grace. The Holy Spirit inspires us to do penance, and in turn, our practice of penance leads to deeper union with Him and enables us to merit more grace and deeper holiness.

Whenever a wound is not healed, sin easily returns. When wounds are untended, they will fester and become re-infected. When we confess our sins, we pluck the bad fruit off a tree. But as long as the roots are alive, more fruit will appear — whether sooner or later. We need to do more than cut off a branch, or even the trunk itself. We need to remove the taproot. That entails digging deeply, as taproots extend very deep depending on the size of the tree! Only by excavating the root will we stop the sin from returning.

Human wounds are like fertile soil for the seeds of sin to continue to sprout, grow, and flourish. Sin does not appear out of nowhere. Satan shrewdly places his temptations in soil where they can grow: He proposes false solutions in those areas where we desperately want to leave behind or numb our pain. The Seven Deadly Wounds that give rise to the Seven Deadly Sins are: abandonment, shame, fear, powerlessness, rejection, hopelessness, and confusion. We identify such wounds through the false beliefs that they generate and the promises we make to ourselves to avoid feeling the pain of the wounds.[108]

History has shown that when people are desperate, they more easily accept a radical solution, as in Germany under the Nazi regime after the humiliation of the Treaty of Versailles. All temptations lead us away from the Cross, which is the source of all healing, for it is the place where the Holy Spirit is poured forth on us. The healing of the Immaculate Conception flows from the pierced side of Jesus. But we must stay by the Cross, as did Mary and John, to be washed in that torrent of mercy.

Satan, as St. Ignatius of Loyola calls him, is the "enemy of human nature."[109] Satan studies our human nature for the sake of using it against us and he knows it quite well. Satan seeks to harm and destroy us, and for that reason hell is filled with torture. Those who, through the free choice of their sin, have placed themselves under Satan's dominion, experience his constant harm and ruin. On the other hand, those who place themselves, with their wounds, under the Holy Spirit find healing and salvation.

The first weapon necessary in the spiritual combat is authentic self-knowledge, lest our undiscovered weaknesses be used against us. We are only as strong as our weakest point, and St. Ignatius of Loyola recommends paying attention to these weaknesses to strengthen them against attack. Moreover, to address human wounds, we may need to make use of human means, including sound, Christian psychotherapy. For God may bring our healing through means other than prayer. Indeed, many wounds — such as trauma provoked by death, tragic accidents, or disasters — are healed only through healthy relationships that convey God's love. Just as the paralytic was brought to Jesus by others, so we often need others to assist us in being brought to Jesus for healing (Mk 2:1-12).

Now, many such wounds may not be our own fault. For instance, how we were treated or mistreated by our parents, friends, or others is not our fault. However, we are responsible for how we deal with such wounds, for the worst response would be to ignore them or imagine they do not exist. The mystery of the Immaculate Conception is the healing of the *entire* human person — with every wound, caused by whatever event — through the touch of the Holy Spirit. As this healing takes place, then Satan is gradually conquered. He no longer has an entry point nor any stronghold within which to hide.

The Holy Spirit purifies, heals, and transforms our broken humanity by the work of His grace. When we pay insufficient attention to our humanity — emotions, pains, joys — then we remain immature, undeveloped, and untransformed. At times, we may cover such immaturity, even with devotions and pious disciplines. But the Immaculate Conception conquers Satan by filling our humanity with the holiness — the Spirit — of God. Authentic growth in holiness is manifested through every deepening maturity, security and purity.[110]

The Immaculata was not exempt from wounds; in fact, as "Our Lady of Sorrows," she is depicted with seven swords that pierce her Immaculate Heart. She told St. Faustina: "Know, my daughter, that although I was raised to the dignity of Mother of God, seven swords of pain pierced my heart" (*Diary*, 786). Because her heart was never hardened by sin, she was even more sensitive to pain and suffering than we are. Yet her wounds were never infected by sin or resentment, as often happens when we suffer; in fact, her pierced heart became a source of grace that flows forth to others. For Christians, healed wounds are not those that disappear or cease to cause pain, but rather those which are sources of love for God and others.

The wounds of her Immaculate Heart never became doors for Satan to enter in because there was always love gushing forth. Amid her suffering, the Immaculata never ceased loving God and neighbor, even at the cost of the pain of losing her own Son before her eyes. Similarly, when suffering comes, we must beware that Satan will knock on the doors of our wounds: and unless a wound is filled with the Holy Spirit (amid the pain), Satan will force his way into the emptiness and infect the wound.

Remember that Satan does not need outright commission of sin to gain a stronghold: he needs only sins of omission, areas where the Spirit is lacking, to gain entry. Now, we could point to many problems that Satan creates in the Church — heresy, persecution — but the most difficult one is our own mediocrity and hypocrisy. We profess a faith that — unlike the Immaculata — we do not live with complete generosity and steadfastness. But the Immaculata can help us overcome ourselves, for she will strengthen our trembling hearts with her grace and tender love.[111]

QUESTIONS

- Where do you have a swept and clean house, but are still not filled with the Holy Spirit?
- How would you classify your wounds according to the Seven Deadly Wounds?
- What false beliefs or lies do you have about yourself, God, or others?

PRAYER

Pray the "Prayer to the Queen of Heaven and Earth" (p. 204) and the Litany of the Holy Spirit (#3 — p. 209).

DAY 14
THREE WEAPONS

Immaculata Virginis Mariae Conceptio Sit Nobis Salus et Protectio

The Father, in His wise plan, permits Satan to besiege us (*Catechism*, 395). He permitted Satan to test Adam and Eve, who fell, and to test Jesus and Mary, who remained firm. Through this testing, we are forced to make a choice: either to grow in virtue like Jesus and Mary, or to fall into sin like Adam and Eve. But we cannot remain neutral, for possessing freedom means that we must, in some fashion, make a *definitive* choice: either for or against God Himself. As with Job (2:4-6), Satan presumes that we love God because of His blessings. Satan's bet is that, if he makes us suffer enough, then we will stop loving God for His own sake. Will we continue to bless God, even when we feel cursed? By persevering in his fidelity, Job received abundant blessings for the suffering he endured (Job 42:10-17). Jesus, through His obedience unto the Cross, was raised from the dead and transformed the Cross into the source of grace for us.

Amid her sorrow and pain, the Immaculata conquered Satan, since she never ceased loving the Father and obeying His will, even when this required the sacrifice of her Son. By her fidelity amid the attacks of Satan, she with her Son gained for us our salvation. Since she knows from her own experience the pain of such trials, she accompanies us, as she accompanied her Son, when we are hounded and pressed by Satan. For she knows that we are in a struggle unto death, and there is no ground for neutrality: there are only victors and losers, saints and sinners. This battle is the most important one of our life, and even should all else fail, this is the one we must win — even at the cost of our lives — to gain the crown of glory (Rev 2:10).

Perhaps the most beguiling of temptations in the modern world is indifference. Many claim to be agnostic as regards God: They remain supposedly neutral, without stating yes or no as to whether He exists. They remain indifferent to Him and make no conscious choice as regards Him: but their negligence is itself a choice against Him, for it shows that they choose to love other things or persons over God, Who is worthy of all our love. Saint Faustina thus warns, "I noticed one thing: that most of the souls there are those who disbelieved that there is a hell" (*Diary*, 741).

Since you are reading this book, however, you probably are attempting to make a definitive choice for God. But Jesus does warn us: "I know your works; I know that you are neither cold nor hot. I wish you were either cold or hot. So, because you are lukewarm, neither hot nor cold, I will spit you out of my mouth. … Those whom I love, I reprove and chastise. Be earnest, therefore, and repent" (Rev 3:14-19).

The Father permits Satan's attacks to cure us of our selfishness, so that we serve and love Him for Who He is, not only for what He gives us. An indispensable aspect of holiness is healing our impure — mixed — motives. That mixture must be purged either now or in Purgatory. For loving God with all our being, as in the First Commandment, is our true healing toward which everything else is geared. When we learn to love as He has loved us first, then we are truly healed and made immaculate. For love alone covers and heals a multitude of sins (1 Pet 4:8).

But as the Father explained to St. Catherine of Siena, we love as God has loved us only when we selflessly and generously love our neighbor:

> I ask you to love me with same love with which I love you. But for me you cannot do this, for I love you without being loved. Whatever love you have for me you owe me, so you love me not gratuitously but out of duty, while I love you not out of duty but gratuitously. So you cannot give me the kind of love I ask of you. This is why I have put you among your neighbors: so that you can do for them what you cannot do for me — that is, love them without any concern for thanks and without looking for any profit for yourself. And whatever you do for them I will consider done for me.[112]

We defeat Satan by remaining firm in God's love and loving our neighbor in return.

In the spiritual combat, our weapons are prayer, fasting (penance), and almsgiving (charity). Through prayer, we open our hearts to the Holy Spirit so as to receive the imprint of His grace. Since our destiny

— immaculacy of heart — is beyond our natural, human strength, we need supernatural help. Grace empowers us to attain what is beyond our human capacities. This presumes an attitude of humility, namely, the recognition of our incapacity and our utter need for the help of the Holy Spirit. Prayer opens us to receive grace: but without prayer, we receive nothing.

The Immaculata, the paragon of humility, is a woman of deep prayer. By placing ourselves in her "school" of prayer, we learn to pray as she does — in deep communion with the Holy Spirit.[113] She not only prays *with us,* to teach us to pray: she is our advocate, who lifts our prayers to her Son: and our Mediatrix, who pours forth the graces we need.

In Ephesians 6:1-17, St. Paul writes clearly on the reality of spiritual warfare against the principalities and powers of darkness. *Spiritual combat,* however, is not the same as military battles. The goal of our warfare is not primarily to defeat Satan but rather to glorify God and aim for Heaven. Otherwise, we can become caught up in the metaphor of spiritual battle because it corresponds to our broken experience upon earth. But after the Second Coming, there will be no war, no fighting, no battle. If we are accustomed to war, we may find it difficult to be in a place with "no action"! If we live only in a defensive, combative position, we will become exhausted, and Satan will always return to fight when we are least prepared.

The example of St. Joan of Arc is instructive here. Well-known for her exploits in battle, she is often depicted in shining armor. The city of Philadelphia, for instance, has a golden statue of her in full amor mounted on her horse. But her greatest battle took place when she had no armor: when she was imprisoned, placed under trial, and burned at the stake. Her most stunning victory — of total surrender to Jesus and Mary — occurred in apparent defeat.

While we might gladly follow St. Joan of Arc into battle, we may hesitate to follow her example of being consumed by fire. Because we are aware of our vulnerability, we prefer having armor to protect us. But we forget that, in the spiritual battle, the greatest weapon is the Cross, where Christ was naked, vulnerable, and wounded. The self-giving love of Christ and the Immaculata at Calvary defeated Satan, and he is defeated anew by our self-giving love in union with them. In other words, we win the spiritual battle by making thousands of choices to love — always, everywhere, amid all suffering — and so preparing ourselves for that final, definitive choice to love forever in Heaven.

That we defeat Satan by loving, even while vulnerable on the Cross, does not mean, however, that we are without any heavenly protection. Surely the Immaculata, the Queen of the Angels, was assisted by them in her own earthly life. When Jesus struggled to say, "Your will be done," during His Agony, He was strengthened by an angel, which Tradition holds to be St. Gabriel (Lk 22:43). This is in accord with Gabriel's name, which means "strength of God." When we find ourselves in weakness, we need to invoke his presence and assistance: He strengthens us through obedience and faith in God's Word. Notably, St. Gabriel is the same archangel who received Mary's similar response at the Annunciation: "May it be done to me according to your word" (Lk 1:38).

Saint Michael the Archangel is often invoked for protection and defense in the spiritual battle. He is a powerful intercessor and leader! "At that time there shall arise Michael, the great prince, guardian of your people; It shall be a time unsurpassed in distress since the nation began until that time. At that time your people shall escape, everyone who is found written in the book" (Dan 12:1). Revelation 12:7-9 depicts this battle, wherein St. Michael defeats Satan and so protects the Virgin and her Son, as well as those who follow her Son.

We also need St. Raphael the Archangel, whose name means "God heals." Saint Raphael is an angelic exorcist in the Bible, as he cast out Asmodeus (demon of destruction and impurity) from Sarah (see the Book of Tobit). How necessary St. Raphael is today, amid the contemporary plague of impurity! Saint Stanislaus Papczyński had an altar to St. Raphael in Góra Kalwaria, Poland. On that very altar, he performed a miracle, raising a child from the dead. Saint Stanislaus, so devoted to the Immaculata, was devoted to St. Raphael.[114] Satan would like to infect our wounds with sin, but St. Raphael brings healing to our wounds with divine love.

From the Immaculata, we learn that we defeat Satan not primarily by intelligence or willpower, but rather by humble trust in God's merciful love. As Immaculata, the fully healed one, she heals by her very presence. In exorcisms, Our Lady does not come to attack Satan. *Her very presence* scatters Satan. She does not fight him; she simply prays, and her very holiness brings unbearable pain to Satan. But her mere presence, her beauty, brings healing to us. Is that not what the world needs today — a healing beauty, harmony and peace? The Immaculata is our assurance that the lost paradise has already been found again. She teaches us that we recover such a paradise not by revolutions, not by violence, not by wars, but by trust, humility, and love. Just as light scatters darkness by its very presence, so Satan is defeated by the presence of God dwelling within our hearts. The *true path* to healing after the example of Our Lady is not through constant battle. Rather, it is through obedient surrender to the will of God, whereby the Holy Spirit dwells in every aspect of our hearts and lives. Then, we are enabled to make our definitive choice: to love God above all and to love others with that very same love.

QUESTIONS

- Where do you struggle to repeat or confirm your choice to love God and neighbor?
- Where do you find yourself lukewarm or indifferent, particularly toward the poor?
- Where might you ask for the protection and assistance of holy angels?

PRAYER

Pray the "Prayer to the Queen of Heaven and Earth" (p. 204) and the Chaplet of St. Michael (p. 224).

DAY 15
HELL

Immaculata Virginis Mariae Conceptio Sit Nobis Salus et Protectio

Our salvation depends on silent surrender of our will to the Holy Spirit in imitation of the Immaculata. For sin is an impairment in our relationship with God, namely, our partial or total opposition to surrendering to His love. William of Saint Thierry — a Benedictine abbot, theologian, and mystic (1085-1148) — wrote that the Holy Spirit is the will of God "in Person."[115] Since God is love, His will is love. The Holy Spirit is also the *impulse* or *breath* of the divine will of both Father and Son united in love.

When we bear this in mind, the realities of Heaven, hell, and Purgatory describe our manner of relating to the Holy Spirit as a living person within our hearts *in the present moment.* Because we are embodied spirits, we are bound by space and time. So we imagine hell, Purgatory, and Heaven to be different places. That is true, inasmuch as we will have our bodies anew at the Second Coming, and Jesus assures us that some arise to resurrection of life, others to resurrection of damnation (Jn 5:29). Our hearts, broken by sin, already struggle to live in communion with the Holy Spirit. But the Immaculata — as the *Pneumatophore* — teaches us how to live now in interior communion with the Holy Spirit, preparing our hearts to be a worthy temple of His glory.[116]

As a warning to those who procrastinate their repentance, Our Lady of Fatima showed hell to the three children. Hell is the result of those who refuse to surrender to the Holy Spirit, who persist in their sin to the end. This persistence is blasphemy against the Holy Spirit (Mk 3:28-29): a refusal to open up to Divine Mercy, unstinting resistance to the purifying work of the Spirit.[117] That sin is unforgivable not because God will not forgive it, but because the sinner refuses to receive His mercy, choosing sin over His love. Jesus warns us of this sin because we all, as sinners, tend to choose what is pleasant over what is painful. We delay our total conversion because we are unwilling to submit ourselves to the purifying fire of the Holy Spirit through penance.

Our Lady, shortly after revealing hell to the children, stated that sinners were falling like snowflakes into hell, since there was no one to make sacrifices for them. The Immaculata — the All Holy — is most concerned about those who, through unrepentant mortal sin, are not holy at all. Our Lady warned the children that sins of the flesh are the most common reason for damnation to hell. The Immaculate Conception behooves us to choose the Spirit over the flesh, and one way to do so is the practice of penance. Another reason for damnation is lack of silence: "I have seen many souls in the depths of hell for not having kept their silence; they told me so themselves when I asked them what was the cause of their undoing" (*Diary*, 118).

Mary our mother implores us, who turn to her with love, to help her intercede for them through offering our sacrifices and penances on their behalf. If they will not perform the necessary penance for their salvation, then we ought to do so, as Christ and the Virgin have done for us. As we practice penance to open our hearts more fully to the Holy Spirit, so we sacrifice on behalf of others to implore the gift of the Spirit for their hearts, too.

Hell as our own self-will — based in the desires of the flesh — is isolated from and disobedient to the Holy Spirit.[118] Hell is the interior experience of one at enmity with the Holy Spirit, namely, a state of constant disharmony between one's heart and the Holy Spirit, the will of God in Person. Hell is a cacophony like two musical instruments — in this case our will and God's will — in disharmony. This stubborn, persevering opposition to Him by insistence upon our own will is the "unforgivable sin."[119] Our opposition flows from the attempt to create a self different from the self the Holy Spirit is creating — in the likeness of Jesus. Western, individualistic culture believes we mold our own identities according to our own likes and dislikes, placing our ego at the forefront of this process, regardless of moral norms or other persons, including the Holy Spirit. Enshrining the individual will leads to isolating our deepest self from everyone else, a veritable foretaste of hell. For the only point of contact between our deepest selves and the rest of reality (God, other persons, creation) is the Holy Spirit. Without Him, we have no genuine contact with others. Would this not explain the gnawing anxiety and burdensome depression of so many, even of many who are surrounded by fame, riches, and all the world can offer?

Since you are reading this book, you are not entirely closed to the Holy Spirit, so you need not worry about the "unforgivable sin." But, as sinners, we may succeed in cooperating with Him in some areas while we fail in others. We are learning — through trials and pain — to harmonize our own wills with the Holy Spirit. Still, our cooperation with Him is often unstable or fragile. In the Old Testament, the Judges were anointed by the Holy Spirit for specific tasks. However, in the rest of their lives they remained sinful — as described in detail in Judges. As Christians, we are called to be led permanently, dependably by the Holy Spirit. For those are sons of God, after the example of Jesus, who are stably led by Him (Rom 8:14).

Extraordinary moments force us to seek His guidance and grace. The challenge is perpetually to surrender to Him, as the Immaculata did, so that He can utilize us whenever and however He wishes. Granting such freedom to the Holy Spirit can, however, generate fear and uncertainty. We like to be in control, to examine things beforehand. But that is not the case with the Holy Spirit. What we know is Him, His Person, His love; where He leads us, we do not always know ahead of time. He asks for trust in His Person, trust that allows Him to lead us wherever He desires, like the wind blowing leaves wherever it goes (Jn 3:8).

Our Lady of Fatima told the children that the Father, to avoid the perdition of souls in hell, desires to institute devotion to her Immaculate Heart. The heart, in biblical language, is the center of the human person. Here reason, will, temperament (personality), and emotions converge and form a unity. According to Jesus' words in Matthew 5:8 ("Blessed are the clean of heart, for they will see God"), an immaculate heart is one that has been purified by God's grace; that is, touched, healed, and transformed by the Holy Spirit. Since Heaven is described as the beatific vision, where we shall see God face to face (Rev 22:4), we must beseech Our Lady for an immaculate heart to enter Heaven.

Our salvation thus depends on allowing the Holy Spirit to make our hearts immaculate, like that of the Immaculata. The Immaculate Conception is the victory of the Holy Spirit over Satan in the heart of a human person, and the triumph of the Immaculate Heart is the extension of this victory to the hearts of her children. Her heart is for us a refuge in trial and tribulation, because profound peace always reigns in her heart. Her heart never wavers from the will of God: as Dante wrote in *The Divine Comedy*, "In His will is our peace." That heavenly peace results from the harmony of our will with His will, with the Holy Spirit.

As Pope Benedict XVI put it, Heaven is precisely the place where God's will is perfectly accomplished.[120] Hence the petition in the Our Father that His will be done on earth as it is in Heaven. When we live in His will, we already have a foretaste of Heaven and its unending peace, which is the fruit of the harmony between our wills and His. Devotion to the Immaculate Heart embraces the fundamental attitude of her Heart, namely, her *fiat* ("May it be done to me according to your word," Lk 1:38) as the defining center of one's whole life.[121] *Fiat* expresses not only the permission but the desire that God accomplish His will. We may imagine God's will to be something that we must do, a sort of task list for the day. While it does include our fulfillment of good deeds (Eph 2:10), His will is first to make our hearts pure and immaculate, capable of seeing Jesus. The Holy Spirit forms us, so we can give our *fiat* with Mary, allowing Him to make our hearts immaculate and capable of gazing on the Lord in Heaven.

QUESTIONS

- How do you imagine Heaven, hell, and Purgatory?
- How do you experience those realities already within your heart?
- How can you grow in living Mary's *fiat*?
- How do you live the petition in the Our Father that His will be done on earth and in your life?

PRAYER

Pray the "Prayer to the Immaculate Conception" (p. 204) and the Litany of the Immaculate Conception (#2 — p. 214).

DAY 16
THE SIMPLEST PRAYER, CONTEMPLATION

Immaculata Virginis Mariae Conceptio Sit Nobis Salus et Protectio

By our sharing in Mary's immaculacy of heart, the words of St. Paul come to life in our prayer: "All of us, gazing with unveiled face on the glory of the Lord, are being transformed into the same image from glory to glory, as from the Lord who is the Spirit" (2 Cor 3:18). *Contemplation* is this gazing with unveiled faces on the glory of the Lord. But it is not merely viewing Jesus, as a spectator; rather, this contemplation transforms us to share His same glory — which is nothing other than the Holy Spirit.[122]

Is it any wonder, then, that the Immaculata — so filled with grace and glory — was known to be dedicated to prayer? Twice St. Luke makes the point that Mary kept and pondered these things in her heart (Lk 2:19, 51). Jesus implicitly calls her *blessed*, for she — above all — has heard His word and treasured it in her heart (Lk 11:28). Jesus promised that all who keep His word will receive His indwelling presence: "Whoever loves me will keep my word, and my Father will love him, and we will come to him and make our dwelling with him" (Jn 14:23).

The Immaculate Heart — pondering that Word — is thus a tabernacle of the Holy Spirit. Our hearts are similarly destined to be His temple. Immaculacy of heart is a requirement for the Holy Spirit to fully dwell within us. Scripture, personifying the Holy Spirit as Wisdom, states that "into a soul that plots evil wisdom does not enter, nor does she dwell in a body under debt of sin" (Wis 1:4). The more the Holy Spirit purifies us of sin, the more our hearts become temples of His presence.

Contemplation — the simple prayer of being present to the Holy Spirit — derives from the Latin *templum*, "temple." Saint Augustine, describing how intimately God the Spirit dwells within us, states:

Interior intimo meo et superior summo meo, "Higher than my highest and more inward than my innermost self."[123] While the Holy Spirit is always present to us in the depths of our being, we are not always present to Him because of the busyness of our days.

Christian contemplation — as indicated by the name — is an activity that exclusively takes place *within the temple of the Spirit in our hearts.* By contemplation, we leave the superficial realities of daily life and return to an "interior castle" — the tabernacle of the Spirit. We return to this interior simplicity, where we recognize that all our desires converge on this one longing: "One thing I ask of the LORD; this I seek: To dwell in the LORD's house all the days of my life, To gaze on the LORD's beauty, to visit his temple" (Ps 27:4). Saint John Paul II invites us — through the Rosary — to enter into the "school of Mary," there to learn how to ponder and meditate on His Word, learning to contemplate with her, and to grow in that one desire of dwelling within His temple and gaze upon his beauty. Through contemplation, our hearts are touched by the Holy Spirit, making them subject to Him. The deeper our prayer, the more continuous our union with Him will be, for our will becomes one with His.

Through prayer, we discern what is His will so as to fulfill it in daily life. But He Himself will accomplish His will within us, if only we surrender. Fulfilling God's will is thus not reducible to executing a divine task list. Fulfilling the will of God first means allowing the Holy Spirit to accomplish the Father's plan in Christ to make us immaculate. This entails remaining always in His love (Jn 15:9). His love is the Holy Spirit, and we are called to always remain in that Spirit. Apart from His love, we can "do nothing" (Jn 15:8) that is truly God's will, even if we are busy with many things. Moreover, we are called to remain in His will inasmuch as we are always to love God — whether we lie down to rest or get up in the morning, whether at home or away (Dt 6:7).

Prayer enables us to remain in His love always. Now, Jesus makes clear that love for Him consists in keeping His commandments, that is, His will (Jn 14:15, 1 Jn 5:3). The essence of the love of God is found — not in our emotions, thoughts, or desires — but in fulfilling His will. Fulfilling His will is not always easy. As St. Maximilian Kolbe wrote, "The more difficult this fulfillment will be, the more disgust and repugnance [we have to overcome], the greater will the manifestation of love be."[124] This does not mean that without such difficulties, we cannot love; but the penance of denying our will — every time it differs from His will — often does encounter difficulties.

Jesus instructed St. Faustina: **"Do not be afflicted if your heart often experiences repugnance and dislike for sacrifice. All its power rests in the will, and so these contrary feelings, far from lowering the value of the sacrifice in My eyes, will enhance it"** (*Diary*, 1767). Through prayer, we allow the Holy Spirit space and time to touch our hearts, strengthen them for self-denial, and bring them into accord with His will. Over time, such prayer enables us to rejoice in God's will, even when we at first dislike it. Jesus Himself needed this space of prayer in Gethsemane, for He spent three hours praying in agony as He repeated: "Take this cup away from me; still, not my will, but yours be done" (Lk 22:42). If Jesus needed such time for prayer to accept that cup, how much more do we need it!

Contemplation gives precedence to the work of the Holy Spirit within our hearts. Humility acknowledges His constant but hidden presence. Just as the Holy Spirit was at work in Mary's conception, before she was conscious or able to cooperate with Him, so in our own lives, the Holy Spirit is at work within us before we are aware. Prayer attunes us to His presence and His work, enabling us to cooperate with Him. But He is always the primary Actor — we always follow His lead and initiative.[125] By our incorporating prayer into daily life, our attention — which often becomes clouded by worries or stress — returns to His presence amid our activities.

When we lose sight of the Holy Spirit — when we leave the atmosphere of faith nourished by prayer — we work alone, as we were orphaned, without help. Then, our awareness narrows to the tasks on our list, and impatient anxiety prevails as we try to accomplish everything in time. We can easily become disorderly, attached to our work, proud of our accomplishments (as if they were our own), and angry with those who interfere with our plans. Then we focus so much on a task that we no longer remain in His love and His will, which always bring peace of heart.

Resolving to avoid this trap, St. Faustina wrote: "I will not allow myself to be so absorbed in the whirlwind of work as to forget about God" (*Diary*, 82). I remember hearing that St. Mother Teresa implored others to pray that she not "get in the way" of the Lord, since what she did was the Lord's work, nor hers. How easily we appropriate the Lord's work as our own, taking it into our own hands, doing it our own way, and leaving our mark on it. Promoting a culture of life requires adopting an attitude of heart whereby we value persons over tasks, starting by valuing our own human person (particularly life in the Spirit) above all the myriad of tasks and worldly demands that are placed on us and that prevent deeper prayer.

The Immaculate Conception teaches us to do less and allow the Holy Spirit to do more. The frenzied pace of modern life keeps us too busy to remain in His love. The need to "keep up" with others is a trap set by Satan, whereby we forget that the focus is on the lead actor, Who is the Holy Spirit, rather than on ourselves or others. By learning contemplation with the Immaculata, we shift from seeking respect or esteem to learning to receive as a gift the abundance of His love. As Jesus instructs us, we must receive the Kingdom like a child — as a pure gift of love, not based on our merits (Mk 10:15).

We recognize that it would do no good to ask a fruit to mature more quickly than it can, or a child to somehow grow more rapidly than possible. Both need time, though today we often live under the lie that we never have enough time. Perhaps we do not have enough time, but then we ought to remember: The Lord allots us enough time to fulfill His will. If we add more to that will, then we exhaust ourselves and become discouraged.

The Blessed Mother, through prayerful contemplation, remained in the Holy Spirit, in God's will. Her heart knew only peace, without having to be frenzied by her activity. Through her Immaculate Conception, she reminds and teaches us to slow down and allow the Holy Spirit freedom to work in our hearts and lives, starting with deep prayer.

QUESTIONS

- When do you find yourself caught up in a whirlwind of exterior work or emotions?
- How can you intersperse prayer with work (*ora et labora* — prayer and work)?
- How can you turn to the Immaculata more often to learn from her intimacy with the Spirit?

PRAYER

Pray the "Prayer to the Immaculate Conception" (p. 204) and the Litany of the Immaculate Conception (#3 — p. 216).

DAY 17
TIME TO REST

Immaculata Virginis Mariae Conceptio Sit Nobis Salus et Protectio

The Spirit draws us into communion with Jesus through deep prayer. The Immaculata is depicted in paintings in a pose of prayer. She is always caught up in deep, interior contemplation: From her union with the Holy Spirit, she pours forth His graces on us, her children. How do we imitate the Immaculata's depth of prayer? First, prayer itself is a gift, a work of the Holy Spirit within our hearts. We do not achieve contemplation but receive it, for it is pure grace. But we can, nonetheless, dispose ourselves to be capable of praying, in such a manner that we are ready to receive this grace. In spiritual theology, this is called "remote preparation," that is, the kind of practices in daily life that help us be prepared for such contemplation.

The most natural way of learning to surrender is sleep. Here I leave this world for a moment and entrust myself, as if in a little death, into the hands of the Father. Surrendering to God in prayerful contemplation begins on the natural level of letting go of our daily worries and occupations through giving ourselves sufficient time to rest. Pope St. John XXIII, after a day of work in the Vatican, told the Lord, "Well, Lord, it's your Church. You take care of it; I'm going to sleep."[126] We tend to become worried about our problems, so much so that we become strangled by them.[127] Yet Jesus was capable of sleeping even amid a violent storm (Mk 4:38-40).

Through rest, we let go of our own activity and give place to His work, which continues beyond what we do or do not do. Sleep is an apt image for this. "This is how it is with the kingdom of God; it is as if a man were to scatter seed on the land and would sleep and rise night and day and the seed would sprout and grow, he knows not how" (Mk 4:26-27). "All this God gives to his beloved in sleep" (Ps 127:2).

We might think that in sleep we are doing nothing, but in reality scientists have discovered that much is going on while we sleep.[128] In fact, without sleep, we run the risk of many health-related and psychological problems. For there are certain processes that happen in the body and brain only during sleep. Similarly, while certainly there is time for us to be active each day, there is also time for us to be receptive. But Satan tends to eliminate more and more time for leisure and prayer, so that we are always on edge, keeping up with others in activity, with little receptivity.

Contemplation is essentially entering and remaining within that interior temple where the Holy Spirit is present. There, we surrender to Him, to His presence, activity, and love. Remember: He is the Divine Person closest to us. Through contemplation, we enter into contact with God Himself. Rather than being another activity that we must master, contemplation is what the Holy Spirit does within us.

The more direct effect, beyond medical problems, of a lack of sleep is incapacity to be present to the Holy Spirit through contemplation. Many of us probably know this experience quite well: We sit down for prayer, and after a few minutes we are fighting drowsiness and sleep. Part of remote preparation for a deeper prayer life is sufficient sleep (and not merely more coffee!). While the Lord does understand the tiredness we bring to prayer (Mt 11:28), He also wants us to make a conscious shift away from living according to the world's incessant demands, which so drain our energy that we are unable to be present to Him in prayer. "Do not conform yourselves to this age but be transformed by the renewal of your mind, that you may discern what is the will of God, what is good and pleasing and perfect" (Rom 12:2). Satan, by ever increasing the demands of daily activities on our energy and time, leads us to be negligent of our primary duty, namely, union with God.

In a beautiful poem, Charles Peguy comments on sleep:

> Just sleep. Why don't people make use of it? I've given this secret to everyone, says God. I haven't sold it. He who sleeps well, lives well. He who sleeps, prays. He who works, prays too. But there's time for everything. Both for sleep and for work. Work and sleep are like two brothers. And they get on very well together. And sleep leads to work just like work leads to sleep. He who works well sleeps well, he who sleeps well works well.[129]

His words echo the biblical admonition of Qoheleth: "There is an appointed time for everything, and a time for every affair under the heavens" (Eccl 3:1).

It is little wonder that, in a world that sleeps less and less, Sunday has been virtually eliminated as a day of authentic rest. *Authentic rest* refers to those periods of time when we refrain from activity so as to be receptive, above all, to God and His love, as well as to our neighbor. Saint Augustine wrote, "The charity of truth seeks holy leisure; the necessity of charity accepts just work."[130]

In many countries, Sunday does remain a day free of work for many, yet it is filled with various other activities, particularly sports. While there is nothing wrong with sports or other such Sunday activities, it is worth asking whether they help us to commune more with God or simply keep us at the same busy pace of the week. The purpose of the Sabbath — Sunday for Christians — is to leave this world, leave its pace, and enter into God's "world," His Kingdom. If God Himself rested on the Sabbath, we too should do so! Even more, the Sabbath — according to Exodus — is a day of liberation, of jubilee, in which the Lord frees us from the burden of slavery. But in a paradox related to sin, we often prefer to keep ourselves busy than to rest in loving contemplation of His face. We (like the Israelites) prefer Egypt to the task of being freed and living as sons and daughters of God.

The Immaculate Conception reminds us, poignantly, of the primacy of grace over human activity, effort, and merit. In other words, the Immaculate Conception reminds us of the presence of the Holy Spirit at the origin of who we are and what we do. In turn, a practical way to let grace retain its primacy in our lives is to ensure that our lives are conducive to prayer.

One step toward this is keeping Sunday holy. This involves, of course, going to Mass, but it ought to extend to the entire day. In my own childhood, this took the form of not having any radio or television until after noon. In the morning, we prayed the Rosary before the statue of Our Lady of Fatima. At the time I found this incredibly boring and annoying (as I could hardly imagine what to do without the television or video games), but I recognize now how formative the experience was for me. That moment of silence helped me to recognize the Holy Spirit, and later, I was drawn by Him into deeper prayer, into seeking solitude with Him. This recognition of the Holy Spirit occurred concretely through Our Lady: through the family recitation of the Rosary.

It may be worth a period of prayer to imagine how the Holy Family organized their time, particularly their Sabbath. While it is clear from Jesus' teaching that He did not see the Sabbath as a day only about rules and restrictions, He nonetheless retains the importance of the Sabbath as a day when we focus exclusively on love of God and neighbor. So perhaps it would be good to visit our elderly parents, or help the poor, or reach out to family members who are suffering (*Catechism*, 2186).[131]

Saint Teresa of Avila stated that one reason our prayer is not deepened is our lack of love of neighbor.[132] To be truthful, many of us are simply too busy to be fully attentive to our neighbors, to give them the time they need. As a result, while we all agree that we want to be the Good Samaritan, in truth it is not so easy. Like the Levite and the priest, we quickly pass by our neighbors; our minds are focused on the long task list. But we cannot encounter Jesus in prayer when we pass Him by on the street or in our home. Saint Mother Teresa, as she walked through Rome to the Vatican for a meeting with Pope St. John Paul II, encountered a drunk man dying on the street. She instructed her sisters to tell the Pope she had to reschedule. The man died some hours later in her arms. For Mother Teresa, Jesus was hidden under the appearance of that drunk, dying man, just as Jesus is hidden under the appearance of the Eucharist.

Union with God and love of neighbor interrupt our busy lives and can wreak havoc on our plans. As Thomas à Kempis wrote, "Man proposes, God disposes."[133] "The human heart plans the way, but the Lord directs the steps" (Prov 16:9). But that disposition by God shows us just how often we are far from His plan, far from His will. We are caught up in our little world and so are frustrated when our plans are ruined. But the saints — and the Immaculata — did not lose their peace when the Lord disposed differently from what they had planned. For they lived in surrender to His will, always in union with the Holy Spirit, who "blows where He wills" (Jn 3:8).

By living a life of remote preparation, we dispose ourselves to receive the grace of deeper prayer with the Immaculata, and through her with the Holy Spirit. She teaches us how to rest in His peace by surrendering to His will even when His plans are different from our own. Then we will be able to "run and not grow weary," for we depend on the Lord (Is 40:31).

QUESTIONS

- How do you balance rest, prayer, and work?
- How do you react when your plans are frustrated?
- How do you celebrate Sunday as the Day of the Lord?
- How do you imagine the Holy Family celebrated the Sabbath rest?

PRAYER

Pray the "Prayer to the Immaculate Conception" (p. 204) and the Litany of the Immaculate Conception (#4 — p. 219).

DAY 18
THE LIVING FLAME

Immaculata Virginis Mariae Conceptio Sit Nobis Salus et Protectio

Contemplation is a privileged means of participating in this mystery, for by it we receive the purifying and sanctifying work of the Holy Spirit without resistance, in imitation of the Immaculata. With her, we learn to allow the Holy Spirit to bestow all the gifts He desires on us, touching and transforming our hearts by love. Saint John of the Cross, writing about the final stages of union with God in this life, titled his work "The Living Flame of Love." The title refers to the Holy Spirit, Who dwells within our hearts through faith as this living flame. The depictions of the Immaculate Heart of Mary always include the flame, a symbol of the Holy Spirit burning within her. Contemplative prayer fosters this flame, adding the necessary fuel so that it will burn more brightly.

The living flame is painful to those who remain in sin but delightful to those who are purified. We can expect the Holy Spirit — even in prayer — to bring dryness while He purifies us. Only as we persevere in contemplation, when His flame has burned away the dross of sin, do we begin to feel His delightful love, peace, and joy, and all His other fruits. The difference is not in the Holy Spirit, who always remains the same. Rather, it is in us, who shift and vary day by day.

Saint John of the Cross also gives wood and fire as an analogy to explain this process of deepening union with the Holy Spirit through contemplative prayer. When the wood is wet — a symbol of a soul permeated by sin — then the wood crackles and pops amid the heat of the fire. The first action of the Holy Spirit is to dry the wood — that is the process of purgation. Then, slowly, the fire begins to ignite the wood, raising its temperature. That is the process of growing in virtue. After some time, the wood and the flame become one: Both are fire. That is union. The Immaculate Heart endured the full heat of the Holy Spirit at Calvary, and for our hearts to be aflame also, we need to permit the Holy Spirit to burn us from within, to evaporate all sin, heal us, and transform us into love in Him.[134]

In contemplation, we place ourselves directly within this flame of love. We learn to cooperate and surrender more fully to the Holy Spirit, His work, and His love. Since the Immaculate Conception reveals the absolute initiative of God in His work of sanctifying, contemplation provides the natural atmosphere where this priority of grace over human effort is experienced. In contemplation, we learn to be *docile,* to be *molded* and *shaped* like clay without resistance. This gift of deep prayer, in our world of rapid activity, is often not esteemed sufficiently. Saint Stanislaus Papczyński wrote that "there is no better good and gift of God ... than the gift and benefit of contemplation."[135] Whether such contemplation be according to Ignatian or Carmelite spirituality is not as important as the necessity of contemplation.[136]

Because of original sin and its effects, man is born into a world or state of resistance to the Holy Spirit. Contemplation is time designated for learning to cooperate with His Spirit, first by surrender and receptivity. For there is no other time when one can so palpably experience the work of the Spirit, where He is the primary actor. There, you take the back seat, so as to allow Him to lead. We need to allow the Holy Spirit to pray deep within us. If you do not have sufficient time to simply be with Him in silence when there are no external distractions, it will be even more difficult to cooperate with Him amid the legitimate tasks and distractions of daily life. Because we are so constantly busy, we need to learn to pray deeply, so as to learn the receptivity necessary for cooperating with the Holy Spirit.

Because all that is good — in whatever form — comes from God, Who is Goodness itself, whatever good actions or deeds we perform belong more to the Holy Spirit than to us.[137] His will guides and leads our own. Thus, when we live by His grace, He is the principal actor in our lives. Only when we sin or do evil are we the primary actor. Jesus indicated this to St. Faustina: Her only possession is her misery (*Diary,* 1318). While we may not recognize the Holy Spirit as the driving force or energy behind our good actions, He is the author of all inspiration, creativity, fecundity, and beauty. Even if those feel like spontaneous desires from within, discernment glimpses its true source: the Holy Spirit, the Lord and Author of life.

Through contemplation, our interior freedom grows and matures in the Holy Spirit. Christian freedom is not the freedom to do whatever we want without restrictions (license or "freedom of the flesh" in biblical language), nor is it mere spontaneity (freedom from neuroses or inhibitions). Authentic freedom in Christian virtue is more akin to dancing with another person, which requires discipline, training, and repeated practice. On the *tilma* of Our Lady of Guadalupe, her feet are uneven, indicating — according to the Aztecs — that Mary is in a position of dancing, which for them was a posture of prayer.

Dancing often requires two persons. One takes the initiative, the man; and the other follows, the woman. Before the Holy Spirit we are always the "woman," in a place of feminine receptivity. That provides a visible image of the primacy of grace, and the need for prayer before all human activity. If mortal sin is refusing to dance at all, venial sin is dancing but stepping on the toes of the Spirit. Heaven, in turn, is a perfect dance, such as we see in professional dancers: After much practice and many mistakes, they dance freely, with elegance and grace!

In discussing the Trinity, the Greek Church Fathers used the word *perichoresis* to describe how each of the Divine Persons lived in synchronous harmony with the others. The Greek *perichoresis* literally means "dancing around [each other]," giving a visual image of how the three Persons live in harmony, all possessing one will. To live by grace means to enter into this dance, whose rhythm and choreography are initiated by God, rather than by us. But we are not merely passive: Our human freedom means that we do participate and add something of our own, born of the creativity of the Spirit in our hearts.

In the Trinity, none of the Divine Persons acts apart from the other Persons. Everything they do, they do in common, even as they remain distinct Persons. Christian freedom imitates this Trinitarian freedom, whereby we are authentically free only when our will is united with other persons — God and neighbor. Heaven is the complete and perfect harmony of our will with the Father's will, like a symphony with Jesus as the conductor. For Jesus Himself does only what He sees the Father doing (Jn 5:19). The Holy Spirit moves us to obey Him, training our will thereby to be in harmony with the Father's will.

Through such contemplation and the dance of daily life, we enter into ever-deeper personal union with the Holy Spirit. As Our Lady is Spouse of the Holy Spirit, so we are also called to be spouses of the Holy Spirit: inseparably, indissolubly linked to Him. While the Immaculate Conception — and our Baptism — marks the beginning of the path, the goal is spiritual marriage with God, which occurs only in and through union with the Holy Spirit. It is to this intimate union with the Holy Spirit that the Immaculata wants to lead us, so that we might enter into the perfect dance with the saints in Heaven.

QUESTIONS

- How often do you ask and dispose yourself for the gift of contemplation?
- How much time do we consume focusing on what we are doing, without considering the Holy Spirit at work within and through us?

PRAYER

Pray the "Prayer to the Immaculate Conception" (p. 204) and the Litany to the Holy Spirit (#1 — p. 205).

DAY 19
THE GIFT OF HOLINESS

Immaculata Virginis Mariae Conceptio Sit Nobis Salus et Protectio

The Immaculata shines forth brilliantly with the full gift of holiness bestowed on her through the Holy Spirit. Gazing on her, we learn how holiness is first a gift, given by the Holy Spirit, received through the Sacraments, and deepened through prayer. Contemplation serves as the school of ***disposing the human heart*** to receive the gift of God, the Spirit in full. Without contemplation, it is impossible to live out the call to the fullness of holiness, since such holiness is primarily a gift received, cherished, and nurtured rather than a state attained by strenuous effort.[138]

We often associate holiness with a laundry list of things that we must accomplish before we can consider ourselves holy. When we do that, we often compare ourselves and our lives with the saints and find that we always come up short.

To grow into the full maturity of Christ (Eph 4:13), namely the fullness of holiness that the Father has destined for each of us, we need to grow in deepened prayer. While contemplation is itself a gift (and not a method or technique to be mastered), we can nonetheless learn to dispose ourselves properly to receive this gift and enjoy it, as described in the preceding days. Through contemplation, we learn the receptivity that Our Lady had and maintained throughout her life, so that we not only state but live her words: "May it be done unto me."

The Immaculate Conception is a revolution in terms of how we grasp holiness. Just as salvation is first a *pure gift*, not attained by our own works, so holiness is not achieved through our efforts (Eph 2:8-9). While we must cooperate with the Holy Spirit in growing in holiness and in carrying out good works, it is helpful to keep in mind the framework of a *gift* before it becomes a *duty*. When holiness is overlaid with duties, Christian living becomes more of a burden, something that one would rather avoid so as to enjoy life. But holiness is about receiving the renewed gift of grace in the Holy Spirit, treasuring it, and cooperating with it, to be ready for the gifts that are yet to be given.

This reality of the *gift of grace* is essential to St. Paul's conversion (Acts 9:1-22; 22:3-16), which provides an example of how the Holy Spirit continues the mystery of the Immaculate Conception in a sinner. Saint Paul's emphasis on being saved by grace is the *essence* of the mystery of the Immaculate Conception.[139] We are saved by the gift of God, and Christian life is patterned on this free self-giving in love. Whereas St. Paul spent his youth as a zealous Pharisee, expending every effort to fulfill the Law and so ensure his own righteousness, his conversion taught him that all such efforts to justify himself were vain and even rubbish (Phil 3:7-11). Moreover, he was adamant that the two do not mix: that one cannot both seek salvation or holiness based on one's own efforts and seek it through faith in Christ. Rather, faith in Christ radically departs from seeking holiness by effort alone. The Immaculate Conception is the paradigm of St. Paul's theology of being justified and saved by grace.

The Immaculata could not and did not do anything to make herself holy at that first moment of her existence. Rather, the Father poured forth that holiness into her as a pure and free gift. He desires to do the same with us: to infuse holiness into us in His Spirit. Once filled with this grace, we are then able to be perfected in holiness by the Holy Spirit — a process that requires our own cooperation. *Merit* is not primarily about *earning* holiness, but rather about *receiving* and *growing in* holiness. Merit is the *quality* or *depth* of our cooperation with the sanctifying work of the Spirit. As St. Paul wrote of himself, "Just one thing: forgetting what lies behind but straining forward to what lies ahead, I continue my pursuit toward the goal, the prize of God's upward calling, in Christ Jesus" (Phil 3:13-14).

All our human effort in terms of growing in holiness is not so much about striving or jumping high enough but rather about being directed toward receptivity to and cooperation with the gift of holiness. Saints are not athletes: They are not among those who simply ran fast enough for a period of time and so were crowned. While even St. Paul uses athletes to provide an image of running a race (1 Cor 9:24-25), we always need to remember the primacy of grace as gift. Otherwise, we incur the risk of becoming Pelagians.

Pelagius was a heretic of the early Church, who believed that we make the first steps to God by our own moral effort, which is only later aided by grace. While few may know the name of this heresy, many today live as semi-Pelagians, for while they acknowledge the necessity of grace, they still see self-reliance as a good quality or even a virtue. Hence, we have such phrases as "pulling oneself up by the bootstraps," and "God helps those who help themselves." The truth is that we cannot help ourselves. We are, before God, entirely helpless. Pope Francis recently warned about this ancient but common heresy of relying ultimately on ourselves rather than on His grace.[140] In fact, self-reliance is the source of our failures, as Jesus told St. Faustina: **"The cause of your falls is that you rely too much upon yourself and too little on Me"** (*Diary,* 1488).

In contemplation, God accomplishes far more than we could do on our own or even what is possible by our graced efforts. By letting go of "doing" and "striving," we let go of this need to always be busy and active: We become utterly simple and open before the Spirit and what He desires to accomplish in and through us. Contemplation enables us to experience the truth of St. Paul's words: "Now to him who is able to accomplish far more than all we ask or imagine, by the power at work within us, to him be glory in the church and in Christ Jesus to all generations, forever and ever. Amen" (Eph 3:20-21).

Through deep prayer, docility to the Spirit, and adoration, one gives the Holy Spirit space and time, so He can work the miracles of His grace within one's heart. The Father looked on Mary's nothingness at her conception, and He accomplished "great things" in her, pouring forth His Mercy on her (Lk 1:49). Similarly, by the same Holy Spirit, He desires to accomplish great things within us also, precisely where we feel and experience our lowliness and weakness. This mystery highlights all that the Spirit can accomplish in us, even apart from us, when we are incapable of anything, if only we trust in His goodness.

For the Holy Spirit dwells in our weakness, since He manifests His power more fully within such weakness, as St. Paul experienced (2 Cor 12:9). Saint Peter, who once denied Christ and fled from the Cross, later died in imitation of Christ, crucified. As Fr. Wilfred Stinissen explains, the Holy Spirit "comforts by giving a certain taste for poverty. He teaches you to love your littleness… Instead of making you strong, the Spirit teaches you to accept and even love your poverty."[141] The Holy Spirit illumines our weakness, so that from there, we learn to rely not on ourselves, but only on His grace.

The "Little Way" of St. Thérèse is the path of total distrust of self and total trust in the Father. The Immaculata, more than anyone else, recognized her utter nothingness before the Father, and that everything in her comes from Him alone. She reveals what the Holy Spirit can do in the face of our nothingness and willingness to surrender to Him, as she proclaims: "He has looked upon his handmaid's lowliness; behold, from now on will all ages call me blessed. The Mighty One has done great things for me, and holy is his name" (Lk 1:48-49).

She is, as the Second Vatican Council teaches, the first among the *anawim*, the poor who place their trust entirely in God.[142] She teaches us the truth of the beatitude: "Blessed are the poor in spirit, for theirs is the kingdom of heaven" (Mt 5:3). Precisely there — where we are lacking, empty, incapable — we possess the Kingdom. Perhaps, where we feel competent, able, and strong, we may lack the Spirit, for we rely too much on ourselves.

In contemplation, our focus is not so much on what we are doing as on the Holy Spirit and His delicate work. Saint John of the Cross emphasizes that as long as we insist upon the natural use of our faculties — thinking, choosing, remembering — we will never be brought to the height of holiness. Rather, we need to allow the Holy Spirit to calm our normal, human activity, so that He can be at work within us unhindered.[143]

We have only to think of how often our natural, human activity fills our minds with distractions, preventing deep interior silence. Such a focus on what we can accomplish (devotional prayers, penances, etc.) can lead to the danger of losing focus on what God alone can accomplish. Such souls do not attain the height of sanctity, because they interfere with the work of the Holy Spirit rather than giving Him freedom to do as He wishes. They return to meditation or to too much activity, thereby impeding the delicate, intimate, and hidden work of the Holy Spirit.

But no amount of our own activity — on its own — can replace His divine activity. Growth in the spiritual life is measured by simplicity: As we do less on our own, we give space for the Spirit to do more, even when we feel nothing happening at all. Sometimes, when we feel we are not praying at all, then the Holy Spirit is truly praying within us, on a deeper level. That does not mean we abandon our normal practices of prayer and penance, but rather, that we persevere in them, trusting that the Holy Spirit may be at work in ways we cannot immediately sense or recognize.

The Immaculate Conception reminds us of the radical revolution of the Gospel: that His gift of grace precedes and accompanies all of our efforts. Even more, rather than achieving holiness by exhausting effort, we grow in holiness by being open and responsive to His grace, given each moment to take the next step in following Jesus as His disciple.

QUESTIONS

- How do you experience holiness as a gift?
- How do you foster that gift in your life?
- Where do you experience the Holy Spirit at work in your weakness?
- Are there areas where you find yourself semi-Pelagian?

PRAYER

Pray the "Prayer to the Immaculate Conception" (p. 204) and the Litany of the Holy Spirit (#2 — p. 207).

DAY 20
WORK AND VIRTUE

Immaculata Virginis Mariae Conceptio Sit Nobis Salus et Protectio

The Immaculate Conception teaches us to choose the better part, the one thing necessary: love, the Holy Spirit (Lk 10:41-42). As in the icon of the *Pneumatophore*, our privilege as Christians is to hold the Holy Spirit and possess Him within our hearts. Without Him, everything becomes dreary, gray, and boring. Thus, when life becomes a burden, we need to turn to the Holy Spirit in prayerful contemplation. When we no longer rely on grace, life depends on us and our efforts. Without the fuel of renewed grace, we quickly become exhausted.

To tap into such grace we need a slower rhythm of life; when the daily schedule becomes too demanding, the interior life dries up. This does not necessarily mean — for those who have to work exhausting hours to make ends meet — that one can simply quit working and enjoy more free time. We are bound by the duties of our state in life! But even amidst those duties, we can choose our attitude toward them. Blessed George, for instance, was a man of intense work, waking up around 4 in the morning and working all day, but he intentionally prayed throughout the day and offered each hour of his work for a different intention. At the end of such a day, we will likely be tired and even exhausted, fully spent in giving of ourselves.

Now, our tiredness is precious to the Lord, Who invites us to draw near to Him in our weariness. When we heed His call to draw near, He offers us His Spirit to renew and energize our hearts. When we experience the sweetness of the Lord's love — when we are strengthened by the Spirit — His burden becomes light and sweet (Mt 11:30). Then, we undertake great tasks with renewed energy and strength of heart for His name.

For that reason, we must guard against the danger of sacrificing prayer so as to do more work, even work for the Lord or other good causes. Satan utilizes this trick to slowly separate us from the Holy Spirit, thereby cutting us off from the source of grace. Blessed George warns:

> A person often tends to defer attaining spiritual perfection or even neglects it altogether when faced with an opportunity of doing something good for others. Sometimes the person allows himself to become so involved in this whirlwind of good works that he has no time left for himself. Living in this frantic activity, the spirit gradually diminishes and dries up, becomes weak and dissipated. When our spirit has cooled, nothing is left to fire our zeal and then even our good works lose their vitality. That is why our spiritual life should always come first.[144]

Life is more than tasks to be accomplished and problems to be solved (yielding stress and perfectionism). Our life is measured not by success alone but rather by the virtues we are called to embody (like faith, hope, and charity). Capitalist values of productivity and efficiency have, sadly, become supreme values, to which even Christian values are often subordinated. Activity — by itself — does not yield more fruit in the vineyard of the Lord. Good intentions do not replace discernment of God's will, which is often different from what we expect or imagine. We must cooperate with the Spirit not only in *sincerity* but also in *truth* (1 Cor 5:8). When we do not trust in the Holy Spirit, then our plans and intentions — even the best — fail, for they rely on the weakness of human flesh rather than on the strength of the Spirit (Mt 26:41).

Since the world today places a premium on relentless activity, we need to be firmly anchored in prayerful contemplation for that activity to bear fruit. As St. John Paul II wrote, "Ours is a time of continual movement which often leads to restlessness, with the risk of '*doing for the sake of doing*.' We must resist this temptation by trying '*to be*' before trying '*to do*.'"[145] We need to be careful not to become so focused on exterior work we individually lose contact with the Spirit at work within us.

Saint John Paul II also reminds us that we must observe an "essential principle of the Christian view of life: *the primacy of grace*. There is a temptation which perennially besets every spiritual journey and pastoral work: that of thinking that the results depend on our ability to act and to plan. God of course asks us really to cooperate with his grace, and therefore invites us to invest all our resources of intelligence and energy in serving the cause of the Kingdom. But it is fatal to forget that 'without Christ we can do nothing' (Jn 15:5). It is prayer which roots us in this truth. It constantly reminds us of the primacy of Christ and, in union with him, the primacy of the interior life and of holiness. When this principle is not respected, is it any wonder that pastoral plans come to nothing and leave us with a disheartening sense of frustration? We then share the experience of the disciples in the Gospel story of the miraculous catch of fish: 'We have toiled all night and caught nothing' (Lk 5:5). This is the moment of faith, of prayer, of conversation with God, in order to open our hearts to the tide of grace and allow the word of Christ to pass through us in all its power: *Duc in altum!*"[146]

Now, there is a natural vocation, given at creation, for man to work (Gen 2:15). But work must be evaluated from the point of view of the *worker*, not only from the point of view of the *product*.[147] In assessing the goodness or value of our own work, we first need to ask: Are we becoming better persons through our work? Or do we focus primarily on what is accomplished, even if in the process we have not grown but become hardened or cooled in our charity for God and neighbor?[148] This is the unnoticed byproduct of a capitalist culture which judges itself based upon levels of production without taking into account the good of the worker.

Christian work is primarily a question of *quality*, not of *quantity*. Imitating the Lord, Who did all things well (Mk 7:37), we recognize that the primary prerequisite for fruitful work is the quality of love (holiness) and purity of heart rather than talents or strategies. Personal sanctity makes us more useful in building the Church and transforming our world than does keeping ourselves busy. The Immaculata's intercession on our behalf is most efficacious because of her immaculate purity and holiness. Saint Faustina wrote, "Now I can be wholly useful to the Church by my personal sanctity, which throbs with life in the whole Church, for we all make up one organism in Jesus. That is why I endeavor to make the soil of my heart bear good fruit. Although the human eye may perhaps never see it, there will nevertheless come a day when it will become apparent that many souls have been fed and will continue to be fed with this fruit" (*Diary*, 1364).

This holiness on her part — entirely hidden during her lifetime beneath her daily tasks of gardening, and baking, and her suffering — has indeed borne fruit in the conversion of countless hearts. But the almost incredible fruitfulness of her suffering and life depended on the depth of her love. Now, a single act of perfect love accomplishes more than many acts of imperfect love (*Diary*, 576). All our works will be tried by fire (1 Cor 3:13), either in this life or in Purgatory. Only the work accomplished in obedience to God's will, out of love for Him, will stand on the Last Day (Is 2:11) and accompany us in Heaven (Rev 14:13).

Saint Faustina wrote, "And God has given me to understand that there is but one thing that is of infinite value in His eyes, and that is love of God; love, love and once again, love; and nothing can compare with a single act of pure love of God. … I have come to know that only love is of any value; love is greatness; nothing, no works, can compare with a single act of pure love of God. … [Jesus told her,] **A single act of pure love pleases Me more than a thousand imperfect prayers**" (*Diary*, 778, 1092, 1489).

Saint Paul reminds us: we can do many things, even heroically, but if we have not love, then we have done and are "nothing" (1 Cor 13:1-3). Many people are quite busy, convinced that they are doing much good. But to lack prayer is to cut the tree of life at its trunk, while attempting to bear fruit at the branches. Jesus offers the "secret" of bearing "much fruit": "Remain in me, as I remain in you. ... Whoever remains in me and I in him will bear much fruit, because without me you can do nothing" (Jn 15:4-5). In other words, we must always remain within the Holy Spirit, who allows us to remain in Jesus and in His love. For once we go beyond this love, even for the sake of serving others, we can do nothing that bears supernatural fruit, even if we are doing many things to keep ourselves busy.

By our uniting of prayer with work, our lives will bear more abundant fruit. Instead of relying on our own strength, we will be sustained by His grace. Jesus told St. Faustina, **"No action undertaken on your own, even though you put much effort into it, pleases Me"** (*Diary*, 659). Like children, we need to be entirely dependent on the Father and His will; only then will we see our efforts filled with grace and bearing fruit. The Immaculate Conception reminds us of this *primacy of grace*, the *primacy of the interior life*, and the *primacy of obedience to His will.* Echoing the words of her Son, she invites us to set out into the deep of the spiritual life to bear abundant fruit in the Spirit.

QUESTIONS

- How do you maintain the primacy of grace and of the interior life?
- When you become busy, what do you do so as to remain rooted in prayer and in His love?
- How does work help you to become more virtuous, a better person?
- How do you grow toward perfect love?

PRAYER

Pray the "Prayer to the Immaculate Conception" (p. 204) and the Litany of the Blessed Virgin Mary, Immaculately Conceived (#1 — p. 212).

DAY 21
MYSTERY AND SECRECY

Immaculata Virginis Mariae Conceptio Sit Nobis Salus et Protectio

What does it mean to say that the Immaculate Conception is a *mystery*? In common usage, a mystery is comparable to the riddles or enigmas that Sherlock Holmes solves. Or a mystery is something that is incomprehensible to us, inaccessible and inexplicable. *Mystery* in the biblical sense is not either of these. "In biblical terms, a mystery is a 'secret truth' or 'secret plan' that is hidden from the common knowledge of men. Mysteries are known to God, and they must be disclosed through revelation in order to be known by his people."[149]

There is an element of secrecy pertaining to mystery, so that only God can reveal the truth of such mysteries to us. The Immaculate Conception is a revealed truth, not one that we deduce by human reason. It requires the assent of faith to God, Who reveals it. While Mary's biological conception is a historical reality, her Immaculate Conception is a spiritual reality, known to God alone when it occurred and revealed to us by faith.

What if we started, not from a place of knowing more information, but from a place of mystery? A dogma verbally enunciates a mystery in the Church. When a dogma is declared by the Church, this means that an aspect of the mystery of Christ is revealed, which we are to believe by faith. Often, it simply means that more information is added to what we know about our faith. We also know that Neptune is a planet, but this changes nothing in our daily lives. Professing our faith in dogmas leads us to contact the mysteries they reveal. Otherwise, we'd be professing faith in mere knowledge, which, although important, do not save us. For *gnosis* — mere knowledge — does not save; but participation in the mysteries of our faith does save.

A dogma sheds into our minds a ray of divine light, through which we peer into the mystery it illumines. Now, we can never fully understand divine mysteries, just as we cannot gaze directly on the sun. But we can, bit by bit, ponder this mystery and so enter into its deeper reality. We will never understand the Immaculata or this mystery perfectly; only God fully grasps the beauty of the work He has accomplished in her. But the mystery is, for us, quite consoling, for it reveals the beauty of His grace at work within us and the masterpiece He desires us to be.

Thus, the mystery of the Immaculate Conception invites us to an attitude of awe and wonder that is expressed in contemplation. We know the Immaculata not merely through information but through the openness of our hearts to the mystery of her person. Moreover, contemplating this mystery, we witness and glimpse the image of the Triune God, Who has accomplished in Mary the great work of redemption by preserving her from original sin and granting her the fullness of grace.

In her is fulfilled the plan of God for our salvation in Christ: "In the New Testament, the Greek word *mysterion* (mystery) can refer to some aspect of God's plan of salvation in Christ that is being made known in and through the Church's preaching, liturgy, and faith (1 Cor 2:7-8; Eph 3:3-6). A mystery is an act of God in history, and to truly understand this historical action is to understand the divine mystery, which it bears."[150] The mystery of the Immaculate Conception reveals both His plan of salvation and the Triune God. This mystery reveals something not only about the *Immaculata,* but above all about the *Triune God.*

In our contemplating of this mystery, the Immaculata leads us to plumb the "depth of the riches and wisdom and knowledge of God" (Rom 11:33). As the seat of wisdom, the Immaculata possesses Christ, "in whom are hidden all the treasures of wisdom and knowledge" (Col 2:3) and communicates these unfathomable riches to us.[151] The Church applies certain aspects of "Lady Wisdom" in the Bible to Our Lady. "For whoever finds me finds life, and wins favor from the LORD" (Prov 8:35). In finding Our Lady, we find *life — the life that is the Spirit* — and favor: *grace* from the Lord. She pours forth grace and life upon us from the abundance she possesses within her heart; we need only to be properly disposed to receive what she wants to give.

While we are not present in the moment when this mystery occurred, we nonetheless do have access to the mystery through the Holy Spirit. For *mystery* includes the idea of being *initiated into that mystery* through *rituals.* The word *mystic* comes from the same root — someone initiated in a religious ceremony.[152] In the Eastern Church, the Sacraments are referred to as *mysteries.* Through the Sacraments, particularly Baptism and the Eucharist, we are enabled to personally experience and participate in the grace of the Immaculate Conception. Baptism and Confession are for Christians what the Immaculate Conception is for Mary: the gift of the Holy Spirit for the forgiveness of sin. We receive — like the Immaculata — the gift of the Holy Spirit, Who cleanses us of all sin and makes us His temple. By first receiving the Holy Spirit, we are then prepared to receive Jesus in the Eucharist, just as the Immaculata received Jesus in the Incarnation.

In the Eucharist, we are present at Calvary, where Jesus shed His Blood, which had already made Mary immaculate. He continues to pour Himself forth so that we — the Church — may be immaculate. In the Eucharistic Liturgy, not only does the Church remember the mystery of the Immaculate Conception, but the Holy Spirit *makes this mystery present to the faithful,* so that they are enabled to participate in it *in the present.* For instance, the collect (opening prayer) for December 8 ends with the petition "so, through her intercession, we, too, may be cleansed and admitted to your presence."[153] While we adore the Triune God in the Liturgy for what He has worked in the Immaculata, we ask that He work the same within us too.

Blessed Columba Marmion (1858–1923), an Irish Benedictine abbot, wrote, "The Fathers of the Church speak more than once of what they call the *vis mysterii* — the virtue and signification of the mystery which is being celebrated."[154] *Virtue* here refers not to any of the moral virtues (such as courage) but to *power:* the Liturgy makes the *power* of this mystery present for the faithful who participate in the Mass. Participation in this mystery begins in the Sacraments and extends to the entirety of life.

The first reading for December 8 is from Ephesians 1:3-6, 11-12. In Christ, we have been chosen before the foundation of the world to be holy and blameless (immaculate) in the Father's sight (Eph 1:4). Moreover, in Ephesians 1:6 Paul uses *echaritosen*, which shares the same root (*charis*) as the word that the Archangel Gabriel uses in his greeting to Mary in Luke 1:28, *kecharitomene*: "full of grace," or better, "completely transformed by grace." Like Mary, we have been abundantly bestowed with divine favor and grace. For the Father "does not ration his gift of the Spirit" (Jn 3:34). The mystery of the Immaculate Conception is the stupendous sign of the definitive pouring forth of the Spirit on all mankind (Joel 3:1; Acts 2:17). This pouring forth without ration or measure begins with the Immaculata and is fully revealed at Pentecost, with Our Lady at prayer amid the disciples (Acts 1:12-14).

What is said of the Virgin can be ascribed both to the Church and to each individual Christian. "In the inspired Scriptures, what is said in a universal sense of the Virgin Mother, the Church, is understood in an individual sense of the Virgin Mary ... In a way every Christian is also believed to be a bride of God's Word, a mother of Christ, his daughter and sister, at once virginal and fruitful. These words are used in a universal sense of the Church, in a special sense of Mary, in a particular sense of the individual Christian."[155] The mystery of the Immaculate Conception consists *primarily* in the work of the Holy Spirit, first in Mary, then in the Church as composed of individual Christians. This work is the full application, to each person of the redemption of Christ. Although the Holy Spirit has fully accomplished this work in a historically unique and unrepeatable manner in the Immaculata, He nevertheless wants to accomplish the same work, the same redemption, within each Christian through faith, prayer, and the Sacraments. He wants us to be "other Marys," by faith in this mystery.

QUESTIONS

- What relevance does this mystery have for you?
- How does this mystery connect to your experience of the Sacraments (Baptism, Confession, Eucharist)?
- How are you aware of the Spirit's work in your heart to make you "another Mary"?

PRAYER

Pray the "Prayer to the Immaculate Conception" (p. 204) and the Litany of the Immaculate Conception (#2 — p. 214).

DAY 22
THE COMING OF THE KINGDOM

Immaculata Virginis Mariae Conceptio Sit Nobis Salus et Protectio

The Immaculate Conception is a mystery, not only to be believed but to be lived by all the faithful. Saint Maximilian refers to our age as the "era of the Immaculate Conception," beginning with the manifestation of the Miraculous Medal to St. Catherine Labouré in 1830, the dogma of the Immaculate Conception in 1854, and the apparitions at Lourdes in 1858. We are called to live the "second page" of this mystery: to "elicit such love toward the Immaculata by kindling it in one's heart and to communicate such fire to those who live around us; to kindle all souls, and each one individually, with such love: the souls who live now and shall live in the future. To set such flame of love within oneself ablaze ever more forcefully and without restrictions, all over the earth."[156]

Elsewhere, St. Maximilian Kolbe rhetorically asks:

> Could we be content just with drawing the plan of a house without ever trying to carry it out? … Rather, is it not true that the plan is laid out only because it is the prerequisite for building the house itself? … There opens the second page of our history then; namely, to sow that truth into the hearts of all those who live and will live until the end of time, and to ensure that growth and the fruits of sanctification. To introduce the Immaculata into the hearts of men, so that she may erect in them the throne of her Son, lead them to the knowledge of Him, and inflame them with love toward His Most Sacred Heart.[157]

When we accept the Immaculata into our hearts and lives, she erects in them the throne of her Son — His Kingdom. The center of the mystery of the Immaculate Conception shifts from the Immaculata herself to the Kingdom of her Son, by Whom and for Whom she is granted this privilege.[158] To understand the connection between the Immaculate Conception and the Kingdom of God, we need to take a bit of a detour into biblical history.

In the Old Testament, the Aramaic word *raz*, "mystery," appears exclusively in the Book of Daniel. Eight out of nine times, *raz* describes King Nebuchadnezzar's dream regarding the statue and the stone that destroys it (Dan 2:18-47). God Himself will shatter the world empires by hurling a stone that would grow into an everlasting kingdom (Dan 2:44-45). "In other words, the Danielic mystery is a vision of the Kingdom of God in history."[159] *Mystery* in the Bible is intrinsically connected to the Kingdom of God prophesied in the Old Testament and inaugurated by Jesus in the New.

Jesus possibly understood Himself as the stone from the dream (Dn 2:34; Lk 20:17-18), for in His Person, the Kingdom has begun on earth. He also speaks of the mysteries (plural) of the Kingdom, often in parables (Mt 13:11; Mk 4:11; Lk 8:10). In the writings of St. Paul, the mystery of God is the divine plan of salvation for the world that was hidden in former times but now made known through the Gospel (Rom 16:25; Eph 1:9, 3:9; Col 1:26). Although Paul speaks of individual aspects of the mystery (Rom 11:25), its essence is the Person and work of Jesus, which the apostles make known to the nations. In Revelation, the word *mystery* describes the Kingdom of God, which supersedes all earthly kingdoms (Rev 10:7; 11:15): This alludes to the relationship between mystery and Kingdom of God in Daniel.[160]

Now, according to St. Gregory of Nyssa, the Kingdom of God is the Holy Spirit in Person. In Gregory's time, the Our Father in Lk 11:2 had a textual variant. Instead of "Thy kingdom come," the Greek text read, "Thy Holy Spirit come down upon us and purify us." Saint Gregory thus deduced that the Holy Spirit — in His Person — is the Kingdom.[161] The fullness of grace within Mary is the effect of the indwelling Holy Spirit, Whose presence means that the Father reigns in her heart. The Holy Spirit dwells within her from the first moment of her existence, sanctifying and perfecting her.

Her holiness is evidence that the Kingdom of God has definitively arrived within her (Lk 17:21) and that God reigns over the entirety of her person. In the Immaculata, there are no other powers contending to rule over her in opposition to the Father. In her, the struggle that St. Paul relates in Romans 7:15-20 never existed; in her, the Father reigns with unabated delight ("you have found favor with God" — Lk 1:30). The Holy Spirit penetrates and permeates every aspect of her humanity with His presence and holiness. She *does not place any barrier* to His work; she allows Him to make her fully and completely immaculate and holy. Her holiness is a gift that she fully receives. In turn, this gift becomes her identity and her mission.

The mystery of the Immaculate Conception serves the definitive coming of the Kingdom (the Holy Spirit) through Jesus Christ, the Word made flesh in the womb of the Immaculata. The entire life of Jesus — from conception to Ascension — is for the sake of inaugurating this Kingdom by transmitting the Holy Spirit, as most powerfully realized in the Immaculata. This Kingdom is made present precisely through His gift of the Holy Spirit poured out from Christ's side on the Cross (Jn 19:34) and at Pentecost (Acts 2:1-13). This flowing of the Holy Spirit from the pierced side of Christ is the source of the mystery of the Immaculate Conception. Mary draws us to this same source in the Eucharist: to the pierced side of her Son, so that with her, we place ourselves beneath the torrent of mercy that gushes forth in the Blood and Water.

The Immaculata desires to extend this Kingdom to our hearts and lives. What Jesus accomplished in her, she desires to extend to the entire Church and to each of the Church's members by opening our hearts to the Holy Spirit. For immaculacy — the fruit of sanctification — is simply the effect of His presence. He is Himself the forgiveness and remission of all sins.[162] But in the Immaculata, He prevents sin, and that is is "more noble" than to remit sin.[163] Since immaculate holiness is the fruit of the Spirit's merciful presence, St. Maximilian speaks of the Immaculata as the one "full of mercy": filled in every aspect of her being with the Holy Spirit, she is the one permeated by Divine Mercy. She is "Mother of Mercy," for she has known Divine Mercy in a particular, unique way through her Immaculate Conception. As St. John Paul II wrote, "Mary is also the one who obtained mercy in a particular and exceptional way, as no other person has. At the same time, still in an exceptional way, she made possible with the sacrifice of her heart her own sharing in revealing God's mercy."[164]

When we beseech Jesus to forgive us our sins, we are asking Him to fill us anew with the Holy Spirit. For where sin is, He is not; where He is, sin is not. In this sense, beseeching God for mercy is a petition not for something but for Someone. Since the Holy Spirit actualizes and personifies Divine Mercy, every petition for mercy is a request for the Holy Spirit. Even the Chaplet of Divine Mercy, then, is a continual request for the Father to send the Holy Spirit to us on account of the

Passion of His Son. The Chaplet of Divine Mercy is a constant petition to the Father to fulfill this mystery in the Church: to have mercy — to pour forth the Spirit — on her sinful members, so that they too may be healed of sin and made immaculate. We are asking that the Kingdom truly come — into our hearts, into the Church, and into the world.

In November, we celebrate Christ the King, the goal of the entire liturgical year. The entirety of time, of history, of creation is the recognition of Christ, of His Kingship at His Second Coming. But the fact of His Kingship is one thing; the acknowledgment of and submission to His Kingship is another. Our work, with that of the Immaculata, is for all hearts to be able to accept, to recognize the King when He comes by accepting His will — His Spirit — within our hearts. For the goal of promoting and living the Immaculate Conception is the definitive coming of the Kingdom through the explicit acknowledgment of Christ as King of all creation and of all hearts.

This will take place at the Second Coming, when everyone shall kneel before Him, both friend and foe. But the Immaculata wants our hearts to freely and lovingly acknowledge her Son as King. Our time is a time of mercy, and a time of Mary, particularly of her Immaculate Conception. The two go together: the unprecedented abundance of Divine Mercy is poured forth on the Church to prepare her for the Second Coming. For if the Immaculata was preserved from sin to be prepared for the first coming of Jesus, the Church must be cleansed of sin to be ready for His Second Coming. The Immaculate Conception — the beginning of Mary's life — points to the end — goal — of the Church's life: when her King will come to reign over all (Rev 19:6-8).

QUESTIONS

- How does living in the time of mercy and time of Mary Immaculate affect you?
- How does the association of Kingdom and Divine Mercy with the Holy Spirit affect the way you pray (for example, the Our Father, the Chaplet)?
- How do you help spread the Kingdom and help others to acknowledge Christ as King?

PRAYER

Pray the "Prayer to the Immaculate Conception" (p. 204) and the Chaplet of Divine Mercy (p. 221).

DAY 23
IDENTITY AND MISSION

Immaculata Virginis Mariae Conceptio Sit Nobis Salus et Protectio

Saint Maximilian Kolbe, pondering the mystery of the Immaculate Conception, repeatedly asked, "Who are you, Immaculate Conception?" When Our Lady states at Lourdes that she is the "Immaculate Conception," she tells "us in the most precise and essential manner who she really is."[165] She does not state, "I was immaculately conceived," but rather, states that she *is* the Immaculate Conception. Her identity and person are marked by that first moment of her existence, just as our lives are unique because of the DNA configuration formed at the moment of our conception.

The moment of conception is also when we received both our identity and our mission. We often imagine that vocation is a term applicable to priests and religious, a specific calling within Christian life. We were chosen by God to exist, and the first aspect of surrendering to God's will is accepting His desire for us to exist with a particular purpose, with all our characteristics and limitations. There is much we did not decide, and our freedom is not absolute. At most, we can receive with gratitude what the Father has chosen and with Mary respond "yes" to what He has ordained for us. The Father, by calling us into existence, has ordained each of us to have an absolutely unique, irreplaceable, unrepeatable vocation. Saint John Henry Newman beautifully illustrates this in his prayer:

> God has created me to do Him some definite service. He has committed some work to me which He has not committed to another. I have my mission. I may never know it in this life, but I shall be told it in the next. I am a link in a chain, a bond of connection between persons. He has not created me for naught. I shall do good; I shall do His work. I shall be an angel of peace, a preacher of truth in my own place,

> while not intending it if I do but keep His commandments. Therefore, I will trust Him, whatever I am, I can never be thrown away. If I am in sickness, my sickness may serve Him, in perplexity, my perplexity may serve Him. If I am in sorrow, my sorrow may serve Him. He does nothing in vain. He knows what He is about. He may take away my friends. He may throw me among strangers. He may make me feel desolate, make my spirits sink, hide my future from me. Still, He knows what He is about.[166]

At conception, we are endowed with an unrepeatable identity and mission, which are revealed progressively throughout life. Mary names herself the "Immaculate Conception," for the name reveals the identity and mission given her at that first moment of existence. Similarly, each person is to learn to progressively receive and cooperate with the Holy Spirit in the unrepeatable manner unique to his person. The Father gently forms each one of us throughout our lives, through the many circumstances of life, to manifest and realize our identity and mission.

By prayerful meditation on the Father's choice to create us at conception, we discover, or rediscover, our vocation and identity given by the Father.[167] Moreover, the witness of gratitude for the gift of life from conception to death provides the antidote for the culture of death. Fidelity to this original and unique gift of life bears fruit in holiness that the Father desires for us. As St. John Paul II wrote, "As part of the spiritual worship acceptable to God (cf. Rom 12:1), the Gospel of life is to be celebrated above all in daily living, which should be filled with self-giving love for others. In this way, our lives will become a genuine and responsible acceptance of the gift of life and a heartfelt song of praise and gratitude to God who has given us this gift."[168]

Let us return to the question, "Who are you, Immaculate Conception?" Pondering the profound and beautiful meaning of this name, Kolbe concludes that the Holy Spirit is the original, uncreated Immaculate Conception. For the Holy Spirit is the "flowering of the love of the Father and the Son. If the fruit of created love is a created conception, then the fruit of divine love, that prototype of all created love, is necessarily a divine 'conception.' The Holy Spirit is, therefore, the 'uncreated, eternal conception,' the prototype of all the conceptions that multiply life throughout the whole universe. ... The Spirit is, then this thrice holy 'conception,' this infinitely holy, Immaculate Conception."[169]

But why, then, does the Immaculata take this name for herself? She claims this name because of her intimate relationship with the Spirit. The Immaculate Conception is not some kind of casual feature, but a part of her very nature. A woman, upon marrying her husband, takes his name, symbolizing their marital union of being one flesh. In calling herself the Immaculate Conception, Mary reveals her intimate, interior union with her Spouse, the Holy Spirit, Who dwelled personally within her from the first moment of her existence. She has her name in virtue of her spousal relationship with the Holy Spirit. While Joseph is Mary's human spouse, the Holy Spirit is Mary's divine Spouse. Mary is the transparent icon and spouse of the Holy Spirit: She is filled with His presence and grace, as in the painting on the cover.[170] In her feminine humanity, she reveals and reflects the eternal reality and origin of the Holy Spirit.[171]

Like the Immaculata, we are called to be in a sense spouses of the Holy Spirit. For that reason, this consecration is properly a consecration to the Holy Spirit, the uncreated Immaculate Conception; through the Immaculata, the created Immaculate Conception. Through her, with her, we learn how to allow the Holy Spirit to imbue our hearts with divine life so that the Kingdom fully arrives in our hearts. I purposefully used the term "consecration to the Immaculate Conception" to show its double-meaning as a consecration to the Holy Spirit through the Immaculata. For the two — joined in this mystery — can never be torn asunder or separated.

"United to the Holy Spirit as his spouse, she is one with God in an incomparably more perfect way than can be predicated of any other creature. What kind of union is this? It is above all interior; it is the union of her very being with the being of the Holy Spirit. The Holy Spirit dwells in her, lives in her, from the first instant of her existence, and he will do so always, throughout eternity. ... This uncreated Immaculate Conception conceives divine life immaculately in the soul of Mary, his Immaculate Conception."[172] This consecration moves constantly from one person, the Holy Spirit, to another, the Immaculata. In this mystery, they are inseparably united. We cannot understand Mary without the Holy Spirit, nor can we fully understand the Holy Spirit without Our Lady. Nor can we understand ourselves without both the Holy Spirit and the Immaculata, for they guide us and teach us how to allow the Father to fulfill His eternal plan in our lives.

Since the Holy Spirit is the divine conception, the divine fecundity in the Trinity, He "makes her fruitful, from the very first instant of her existence, all during her life, and for all eternity. This eternal 'Immaculate Conception' (which is the Holy Spirit) produces in an immaculate manner divine life itself in the womb (or depths) of Mary's soul, making her the Immaculate Conception, the human Immaculate Conception."[173] Her unique immaculacy becomes her identity and her mission in the Church: to guide and intercede for the Church into ever-greater participation in the redemption of Christ until the Church, too, becomes immaculate. Being imbued with divine grace throughout her existence, Mary becomes our mother. In union with the Holy Spirit, she gives birth to divine life in our hearts and fosters this life so that it reaches the full maturity of love.

The fundamental human vocation is to receive love and to give love. "Love is the fundamental and innate vocation of every human being" (*Catechism*, 2392). Our vocation is intimately tied to and connected with the Holy Spirit, Who is love in Person. Our deepest identity — like that of Our Lady — is found only in and through our union with the Holy Spirit. For we are given our earthly names by our parents; but by union with the Spirit, we encounter the name He reserves for us, describing the identity and mission for which we were created. "To the victor ... I shall also give a white amulet upon which is inscribed a new name, which no one knows except the one who receives it" (Rev 2:17).

QUESTIONS

- What is your deepest identity or name before the Lord?
- How does the Immaculata help you to discover and live your unique, unrepeatable vocation?
- How does that vocation manifest itself in love in daily life?

PRAYER

Pray the "Prayer to the Immaculate Conception" (p. 204) and the Litany of the Immaculate Conception of Mary Mother of God (#3 — p. 216).

DAY 24
WITHOUT BLEMISH

Immaculata Virginis Mariae Conceptio Sit Nobis Salus et Protectio

Just as the mystery of the Immaculate Conception looks backward to the beginning of Mary's life and forward to the end of history — the Second Coming — so, too, this mystery looks back to God's original plan and design for our lives as well as to their full maturation. The Immaculate Conception reveals God's providential care for us that gently leads us each day from *purification* toward *perfection.*

The Father's eternal plan, before the creation of the world, is that we be "holy and without blemish" in Christ (Eph 1:4). Now, this means, as stated before, that we are destined to be immaculate like Mary. The Greek word that Paul employs, *amomos*, emphasizes the negative aspect: blameless, without blemish. The Hebrew equivalent in the Old Testament, however, *tāmîm* highlights the positive side: "complete, whole, sound, unscathed, intact, free of blemish, free of physical or moral defect."[174] A different translation of this same verse in Ephesians is that the Father destined us to be "holy and whole before Him in love."[175] The Father *actively desires* your life to be *complete, whole, intact,* and *unscathed*. Even more, He has prepared and executed a plan to bring this about in His Son (Eph 1:10). That plan — for the Church to be immaculate like Mary — continues to be fulfilled in the Church through the Holy Spirit at work in the Sacraments (Eph 1:14).

In the Bible, *immaculacy* is intrinsically related to *perfection*. Now, when we think of perfection, many fearful neuroses may arise that cloud our capacity to understand what authentic perfection entails. Perfectionism places the burden of effort on ourselves, following rules, etc. We fear that God exacts perfectionism from us, and He Himself turns into both police officer and judge. That false idea of perfection empties the Gospel of its central message: that Jesus came to save — not condemn — sinners (1 Tim 1:15). So, what does Jesus mean when He enjoins all His disciples to be "perfect just as our Heavenly Father is perfect" (Mt 5:48)?

The Greek word behind Jesus' statement is *teleios*, which means "complete, perfect, mature, initiated, fully developed." Biblical perfection describes the condition of wholeness or purity, which results from cleansing persons or objects or bringing them to full measure or maturity. When perfected, a person or thing is complete and entire: *nothing is lacking*.[176] For instance, St. Paul advises the Corinthians to be *mature* in their thinking (1 Cor 14:20). Jesus Himself is made perfect, consecrated, through suffering to bring salvation to all (Heb 2:10). Love is to be perfected, for Christians are perfected and brought to full measure in love (1 Jn 2:5).[177] The Father desires that we all be perfect, namely, that we grow into full maturity after the image of His Son, as did the Immaculata. The Holy Spirit perfects us by sanctifying us, filling us with every grace necessary, so that nothing will be lacking to us.

The beloved Psalm 23 begins with this statement of faith: "The Lord is my shepherd; there is nothing I lack" (Ps 23:1). Notice the present tense. The psalmist does not state, "I *shall* lack nothing," but states that *in the present* "there is nothing I lack." How often do we instead live as if we were lacking what we needed? We perhaps lack what we want, but in Christ, we are assured of every heavenly blessing necessary to be mature in Him (Eph 1:3). When by our living faith God is our Shepherd, then our life is complete, whole, lacking in nothing that is necessary to grow in holiness and love for God and neighbor. But this requires entrusting ourselves entirely to His pastoral care — both directly through prayer and through His Church. The Immaculata is evidence of the truth of Psalm 23: by living in faith in His love, we are given all that we need, even in the darkest hours of Calvary.

Perfection, from the Latin *per + facere*, "to completely accomplish, complete, finish,"[178] refers to the complete accomplishment of the Father's design in each human heart and in the Church as a whole. Jesus' injunction to be perfect is not primarily about what we do but about allowing the Father to complete His plan in us. Christian perfection places the burden on the grace of the Holy Spirit, allowing Him to perfect us. We participate in this mystery of the Immaculate Conception when we docilely collaborate with the Holy Spirit in completing this work in ourselves and the Church, in growing toward perfection.

Now, if the Father's focus is on each one of us, our gaze ought to be not on ourselves but on His Son. By our focusing on the Lord and on the Immaculata, the Holy Spirit Himself perfects us (2 Cor 3:18)! When we give full freedom to the Holy Spirit to accomplish His work of sanctification and healing, then He will make us "complete, lacking in nothing" (Jas 1:4). For God is generous in bestowing His gifts, so that we may be intact and blameless (Jas 1:17). He will make us holy and whole in our body, soul, and spirit (1 Thess 5:23).

Saint Luke uses a unique Greek word to describe the Archangel Gabriel's greeting to Mary: *kecharitomene.* Saint John Paul II states that this becomes a sort of second name for Mary, an interpretive key that helps us to understand her: "For the messenger greets Mary as 'full of grace'; he calls her thus as if it were her real name. He does not call her by her proper earthly name: Miryam (= Mary), but by this new name: 'full of grace.'"[179] The Greek indicates that Mary was favored by God's grace not only once but continuously up to the present moment. While St. Jerome's translation into Latin (*gratia plena*, "full of grace") has stuck, a better way to translate the Greek would be "completely transformed by grace."[180] She has been completely, perfectly, enduringly endowed with grace. The Holy Spirit has been able to accomplish His work in her to the full and His work endures within her.[181] She is the image of human *perfection* in body and soul. The Church has an ancient hymn in honor of the Immaculata that utilizes a verse from Song of Songs (4:7): "You are beautiful in every way, my friend, there is no flaw in you!" The hymn sings, "*Tota Pulchra Es, Maria!* — You are all beautiful, Mary!"

Another way, then, to imagine the perfection to which the Father desires to lead us is *beauty*. Indeed, the Immaculata is the masterpiece of the Father, showing what the Father's true desire is for each of us. She is the ideal creature who never deviated from His plan. She radiates the Father's grace and mercy. She is the mirror of divine beauty, for God is the author of beauty (Wis 13:3). Everything within her is in harmony, reflecting the beauty of divine love through her human heart.

The Immaculate Conception reveals the beauty with which God desires to endow us. In a world marked by sin, it is hard to believe in genuine beauty, unmarred by the ugliness of sin and tragedy. But the Immaculata reminds us that this ideal of perfect beauty exists, not merely in ideas, but in truth, in human flesh. While we may have faith that such perfection exists in God, we may struggle to believe that it is possible in humans. But by His grace, as in the Immaculata, such beauty becomes our own. Contemplation of Mary and her beauty — similar in effect to gazing on the beauty of nature — opens our hearts to the grace of Divine Mercy.

The Holy Spirit completes this mystery in the Church and in us, so that we too, may be "completely transformed by grace." We cannot fathom how He accomplishes this work, but we do know that we require humble faith to believe that He not only can but does accomplish it within us. Our task is not to understand, but rather to trust in Him and express our fiat to His daily, silent work. By gazing on the Immaculata, we see what He is doing within us!

Now, in God's plan, perfection includes *daily growth.* Thus, I am perfect today inasmuch as I grew as God desired. For just as an acorn grows imperceptibly into a giant oak, so we too grow little by little. Mary herself also had to grow in perfection each day: She began her life full of grace but continued daily to be transformed by grace. For she was not deprived of freedom or choice; she was entirely in harmony with God through love. Though her union with God had a habitual character, she nonetheless grew as a person to the fullness of union throughout her life. In other words, she was given the acorns of all the divinely infused virtues and graces in her soul at the moment of her conception, but she, too, needed to cooperate with the Holy Spirit in her daily life so that these could reach full maturity (and grow into oaks). That she was without original sin meant that she never failed to collaborate with the Spirit and so continuously grew. Part of perfection is corresponding each day to the new grace that the Spirit offers, until, like Mary, we are entirely new creatures in Christ (2 Cor 5:17). We are no longer a mixture of old and new, of new wine and old wineskins, but entirely new (Mk 2:18-22). In the Immaculata, we see already fulfilled the cosmic renewal that comes at the Second Coming (Rev 21:5).

QUESTIONS

- Where is your life not yet whole or not complete?
- What does the word *perfection* mean to you?
- How can the beauty of our Lady open your heart to the fullness of grace?

PRAYER

Pray the "Prayer to the Immaculate Conception" (p. 204) and the Litany of the Immaculate Conception (#4 — p. 219).

DAY 25
THE POTTER AND THE CLAY

Immaculata Virginis Mariae Conceptio Sit Nobis Salus et Protectio

In Genesis 2:7, the Hebrew words used to describe creation depict God as a blacksmith or a potter, working with His hands to shape, form, and perfect us. The work of creation does not cease with the moment when we begin to exist. Rather, the Father continues to create us and mold us according to His design in Christ, so that we become ever more like the Immaculata. In an image from St. Irenaeus of Lyons, the Son and the Holy Spirit are the two hands of the Father, Whom He uses to constantly reshape and renew us by His love and grace.[182] Pouring forth the Spirit through His risen Son, the Father creates us anew (2 Cor 5:17).

The mystery of the Immaculate Conception highlights the activity of the Triune God and our docile cooperation. Unlike us, Mary makes no resistance to the work of God as the potter. As the clay, she allows herself to be formed each day by His merciful hands. Like the potter, the Father constantly forms us (the clay) into the desired shape (Is 29:16, 45:9, 64:7; Jer 18:1-23). This forming extends from conception until death. Now, since we are the clay, we do not directly see what He is doing. We only experience the constant molding — and we begin to complain, wondering what He is doing! But, "Woe to anyone who contends with their Maker. ...Shall the clay say to the potter, 'What are you doing?' or, 'What you are making has no handles'?" (Is 45:9). If God is at work, surely what He does is perfect!

The psalmist states that he was "made in secret and fashioned in the depths of the earth" (Ps 139:15). Here "depths of the earth" is figurative language that symbolizes the womb and the hidden, mysterious work that occurs there.[183] The Father quietly creates, shapes, and intricately weaves each person from the womb onward. The reality of the dark night helps to elucidate this divine pedagogy of forming each person secretly, even unbeknownst to the person.[184] Such moments of darkness and hiddenness are, in fact, privileged moments when the Father desires to shape each person, similar to a doctor doing surgery while the patient is under anesthesia.[185]

We often do not cooperate, for we lack faith and trust, doubting His intentions and wondering what His plan is. The Immaculata's Heart was not injected with this venom of suspicion that doubts the Father's good intentions toward us (*Catechism*, 397). Thus, she was able to live her *fiat* even in the darkest moment of Calvary — and she teaches us to do the same. For the Father's work is completed in our heart only through our free consent. God created us without us but will not save us without us, without our participation.[186] Our part is to allow the Father to bring that to full completion, as He did in the Immaculata.

Now, Mary does not state, "I will do your will," but rather says, "May it be done to me" (Lk 1:38). She uses the passive to indicate that she is receptive, allowing God to actively fulfill His Word in her. But she is not merely passive. In the Greek, the verb (*genoito)* is in the optative mood, which expresses her *active desire* for this to be accomplished. She is eager for His plan to be fulfilled in her, and she surrenders her will to Him for that to happen.. Christ likewise prays in the Garden not that He may accomplish the Father's will, but that the Father's will may be fulfilled (*ginestho*). Both Jesus and Mary illustrate the docility required for the Father to have complete freedom within our hearts. Mary's femininity reveals this receptivity called *docibilitas*: the capacity to learn and be formed by the Holy Spirit. That docility — manifest in active desire — is the work of the Spirit within our hearts. For He ignites that active desire for the Father's creative activity to be fully accomplished in our hearts through His intercession with "inexpressible groaning" (Rom 8:26).

Sin is thus *resistance* to the creative, formative work of the Father's "hand," the Holy Spirit. For this reason, the daily examen — in the style of St. Ignatius of Loyola — is profoundly important. Traditional examinations of conscience focus on clear transgressions of the Commandments. After a certain point, such examinations may cease to be helpful when, by God's grace, we may no longer be falling into mortal sin. The daily examen provides time to see where the Holy Spirit is at work and so learn where we need to grow in cooperation with Him. Hence, the sins we notice in the examen may not be ones we see on a list; but we recognize the ways we fail to give our "yes" to His Spirit and the ways we succeed in imitating Mary.[187]

As in learning to dance, we master our collaboration only by trial and error with constant practice. Just as athletes not only participate in a game but also review a record of it afterward, so we need to both try our best and then review how well we succeeded. This develops the virtue of prudence, which guides our actions to be in accord with His will. Sometimes we forget that Mary not only began her life "full of grace" but grew in that grace each day of her life. It was not a foregone conclusion that she would do so, for Adam and Eve were created immaculate but did not persevere in grace.

The Immaculata, as our Mother, wants to imprint *docibilitas* into our own hearts, so that the Holy Spirit can accomplish great work in us, as in her. This conscious cooperation with the Holy Spirit begins in Baptism (even if only through the faith of the parents) and is strengthened in Confirmation. The path to cooperating with the Holy Spirit's transformative work in the heart requires engaging and entering into the depths of one's heart (Lk 5:4).

Now, we are used to thinking that the change from mortal sin (darkness) to sanctifying grace (light) is dramatic (as in chiaroscuro paintings). But there are also infinite gradations in light — its intensity and purity. In a strange paradox, the Immaculata *grew more in grace* than sinners during her earthly life: having never opposed the work of the Spirit, she permitted Him to fully transform her (2 Cor 3:18). Like St. Paul, we are called to press forward constantly, without looking at what we have already attained (Phil 3:13). The only limit to what the Spirit can do within and through us is our trust in Him.

Because she is docile to this gentle but constant work of the Holy Spirit to shape her as He pleases, she is an entirely new creation in Christ, radiant with His grace and dazzling with His glory. She reveals what happens when one surrenders unconditionally to His constant creative work. She never tried to invent her own self, to create her own self. Rather, she lived in harmony with God's plan for her. In Mary, there is no division between who she is and what God desires her to be. Mary's *humility* — living according to her true self — is at odds with our current secular world. We are told to define ourselves: to create ourselves to be who we want to be. Yet this often yields not peace but anxiety, worry, doubt, depression, and despair. These emotions manifest a growing chasm between who we currently are and who we are called by God to be. When we live separated from the true self, that *God desires,* then we experience inner tension that takes away peace of heart. For our identity is found only within Christ and the Father's plan in Him.

The Immaculata reflects the grace of her Son, and hence her evangelical virtues not only reveal her but reveal the work of His grace within her. In Our Lady, we see what the Spirit is capable of accomplishing within us. Our part is to continue the daily surrender to His work until we are perfected, until we shine in spotless splendor like the Immaculata.

QUESTIONS

- Where do you sense the Father at work to form and perfect you?
- Where do you struggle with the formative work of the Spirit — between your idea for yourself and who He is creating you to be?
- How can you incorporate an examen into your prayer routine, to grow in collaboration with the Spirit?

PRAYER

Pray the "Prayer to the Immaculate Conception" (p. 204) and the Chaplet of the Ten Evangelical Virtues (p. 223).

DAY 26
THE TRINITY

Immaculata Virginis Mariae Conceptio Sit Nobis Salus et Protectio

In the Immaculata, the Father announces a new era of grace for humanity. The Immaculata is for us an epiphany of the merciful love of the Trinity: She reveals the love, the Spirit, that the Father desires to inject into human hearts through faith in His Son. The Immaculata is the one who has — more than any other creature — known and experienced the mystery of the Trinity. Through this particular gift of grace, she has access to the fullest participation in the interior life of the Trinity. She has a unique bond with each of the Divine Persons, and she invites us into these relationships, teaching us how to live in communion with the Trinity after her example. She is the Tabernacle of the Spirit, Mother of the Word, and Daughter of the Father. The Immaculata is the vessel through which the Trinity meets human history, touching and forming it from within. She opens our hearts so they too may be the vessels where the Trinity touches our history and transforms our lives from within.

Enjoying that unique intimacy, she helps us the most to know and love the Trinity, for she is closer than anyone else to the Trinity. Together with her, we discover the mystery of the Triune God. By union with the Immaculata, we come to know and love each Person of the Trinity as she does. The Immaculata is thus the *Mystagogue* — one who leads us more deeply into the mystery of the Triune God. She helps us to discover the true face of God and to plunge into the depths of His love, as the image of God is often falsified. As described above regarding spiritual combat, Satan purposefully distorts our image of God. God is depicted as a strict Father, in accordance with the logic of human justice, but with no mercy. He is not immediately accessible through confident trust, and thus is reachable only through the saints. Christ is "only" God; His humanity recedes into the background. We thus have no immediate relationship with Him. Even the Immaculata is removed from our grasp; she is the queen apart from sinners.

But, as mother, she reminds us that divine love desires to draw near, embrace, and accompany us. The Immaculata is an icon of the merciful action of God. In her Immaculate Conception, the three Divine Persons are revealed: the admirable initiative of the Father; the salvific action of the Spirit; and the perfect redemption of Christ. She visibly manifests the infinite love of God; His selflessness, with which He has chosen each person before the creation of the world; and the holiness He desires to grant each person. She reveals the Spirit's work of grace by which He fashions in her an image of humanity fully redeemed, the effigy of the Church without stain or wrinkle.[188]

Gazing in this manner on the Immaculata leads to profound awe, which praises God for the work He has accomplished in her. In theological words, our adoration of the Trinity (*latria* in Greek) is because of this great work He realized in Mary. In the Liturgy of the Mass for the Immaculate Conception, the preface begins with praise, not of Mary, but of the Father.[189] Similarly, in preparation for December 8, St. Faustina prayed 1,000 Hail Mary's in praise of God "for having accorded this great privilege to Mary" (*Diary*, 1412). We offer supreme veneration (*hyperdulia* in Greek) to the Immaculata for His divine work in her.

Honoring the Immaculata is thus oriented toward worshipping and adoring the Father, Who in His Spirit is at work within our hearts. With Mary, we learn to glorify God. We do not pass from devotion to Mary to praise of God; rather, we join with her in authentic spiritual worship of God. We seek the Father with her, for without her Son we would have no way of accessing the Father. Our love for and devotion to the Immaculata do not pass through her unchanged as if through a lifeless channel. Rather, we — and our love — are ennobled by the grace with which she is full. She enriches the imperfection of our love with her perfect love. Our hearts are united with hers, and so the dim fire of love in our hearts is ignited by the blaze of love in her Immaculate Heart. Our love for God is inflamed by her love: she offers our acts of love to Jesus as though they were hers — without stain, immaculate. What we offer to the Immaculata is not merely then handed by her to the Father. Rather, in and through her, our imperfections are healed, cleansed by her perfection.

She assumes what we offer her as our own, and she presents our offering with all that is hers: all her holiness. But by our entrusting them to the Immaculata, these imperfect acts of love assume what would otherwise be lacking: immaculate purity. As St. Maximilian Kolbe explains:

> The soul offers to the Immaculate its acts of love, not as an object delivered to any mediator, but in property, in full and exclusive property, because it understands that the Immaculate offers such acts to Jesus as though they were hers; that is to say, she offers them to Jesus without stain, immaculate. Jesus then offers them to the Father. This way, the soul becomes more and more of the Immaculate, just as the Immaculate is of Jesus, and Jesus is the Father's.[190]

By joining our prayer to that of the Immaculata, we let her lead us toward a doxological spirituality. Doxology is an expression of praise to God, so a doxological spirituality is one based in glorifying and praising God. Our very existence is for the glory of the majesty of God (Eph 1:12). The purpose of our lives is not merely to do God's will but to glorify and praise God in all that we are and do. God does not have low self-esteem, nor does He need our praise. As one preface of the Liturgy states, "For, although you have no need of our praise, yet our thanksgiving is itself your gift, since our praises add nothing to your greatness but profit us for salvation."[191] Praise opens us to the beauty of His reality, just as gazing on mountains leads to awe and wonder before their majesty. There is no other goal beyond this, for God created us to praise Him, that is, to savor the glory of His beauty.

We do not, however, always live in praise. More likely, if we were to keep a mental record of our thoughts, we are filled with complaints, anger, and sadness. Granted, we do live in a world that provides many reasons for such emotions. But the Immaculate Conception teaches us to place our foundation in the beauty, goodness, and love of God, so that — no matter what is happening in this valley of tears — we always have a reason for joy. In this sense, praying the psalms — as in the Liturgy of the Hours — is helpful. For there is always one psalm of praise each day, reminding us that — even in our greatest lament and deepest pain — there is always cause for glorifying God.

This frees us from being bound by our sorrow and our pain. While we need not invalidate our suffering or imagine that we are not suffering, praising God amid our suffering reminds us that the last word always is His grace and mercy. As St. John of Avila stated, one "Blessed be God!" can be more meritorious in a time of desolation than hundreds in moments of consolation.[192] By anchoring ourselves through faith in His goodness, we stand firm on an unchanging foundation amid trials. Jesus told St. Faustina: **"Most dear to Me is the soul that strongly believes in My goodness and has complete trust in Me. I heap My confidence upon it and give it all it asks"** (*Diary*, 453).

I remember an exorcist sharing thoughts about singing — during the exorcism — the *Sanctus* from Mass: "Holy, Holy, Holy is the Lord." In Isaiah 6:3 (see also Rev 4:8), the seraphim repeat one to another this hymn of praise to the Triune God. The demons, by choosing to rebel, have ceased their praise of God and instead blaspheme Him. Sin, in this light, is intrinsically related to ceasing to praise God. Part of our examination of conscience can thus be to find those moments when we cease praising God, for that shows when we have lost contact with His goodness amid the evil of this life.

The Immaculata is known for her Magnificat, which she sang in response to Elizabeth's praise of her faith. Amid the domination by Rome and the many horrible events of her own time, she nonetheless could see God at work, performing great works both within her and in the world. Her faith enabled her to see His work and so spontaneously led to praise. By anchoring herself always in His goodness, she remained free from the sin of this world. She invites us to sing her song with her: singing of what He is accomplishing in us and around us!

QUESTIONS

- How can you live a doxological spirituality in your daily life?
- When do you cease to praise God? Where do you doubt or lose contact with His goodness?
- How do you experience the Immaculata leading you into a deeper relationship with the Persons of the Trinity? Which Person do you know the least?

PRAYER

Pray the "Prayer to the Immaculate Conception" (p. 204) and the Litany of the Blessed Virgin Mary (#1 — p. 212).

DAY 27
GRATITUDE

Immaculata Virginis Mariae Conceptio Sit Nobis Salus et Protectio

The Immaculate Conception leads not only to verbal praise of God but to a doxological life, whereby the goal of what we do and how we live is simply His glory (1 Cor 10:31). But this is not produced by sheer effort of the will. The Immaculate Conception reveals that everything in our lives is a selfless, gratuitous gift of the merciful God. When we view everything in this light — that God is constantly trying to love us and reveal His love to us in every way possible — then gratitude is the natural result.

Saint Ignatius of Loyola provides the "Contemplation to Attain Divine Love" at the end of the *Spiritual Exercises*. It is worthwhile to use this as an examen of conscience, so as to ask ourselves how aware we are of His magnanimous love and to arouse a spirit of grateful praise. For without taking time to examine and remember His gifts, it is easy to forget them, and when we forget, we more easily fall away from God. It is not without reason that Moses emphasizes to the Israelites 16 times in Deuteronomy: "Remember!" When we remember all that God has done and is doing, then we find cause for joy even amid current trials and difficulties.

When we lose sight of His many gifts, our gratitude dwindles, and so our praise ceases. Saint Ignatius, in one of his letters, noted that ingratitude is the source of all sin, for our entire lives are meant to be a response of love to the God Who always loves us first — each and every day. "It seems to me in the light of the Divine Goodness, although others may think differently, that ingratitude is the most abominable of sins and that it should be detested in the sight of our Creator and Lord by all of His creatures who are capable of enjoying His divine and everlasting glory. For it is a forgetting of the gracious benefits and blessings received. As such it is the cause, beginning, and origin of all sins and misfortunes. On the contrary, the grateful acknowledgment of blessings and gifts received is loved and esteemed not only on earth but in heaven."[193] While one might look to those things that are more visibly evil (wars, abuse, etc.), all these have their origin in the lack of gratitude toward our good Father.

The examen helps us to see — as the Immaculata saw — the great things that God accomplishes each day. Her Magnificat expresses her capacity to see all that God is doing. Moreover, she desires to share this spirit of grateful praise with us. As St. Ambrose wrote: "May the soul of Mary be in each one of you to proclaim the greatness of the Lord. Let the spirit of Mary be in each one of you to rejoice in God. ... The soul that has been able to reach this state proclaims the greatness of the Lord just as Mary did and rejoices in God its Savior just like her ... And thus the soul itself has some share in [God's] greatness and is ennobled."[194]

Now, such gratitude is a hallmark of our relationship with God because He always initiates the relationship. Everything that we have, all that we are, even our duty toward Him and others, comes from His absolute, gratuitous gift of love. He always loves first, and our love is always a response (1 Jn 4:10). Seen in this light as a gift, our relationship with Him becomes less of a burden or duty and more of a joy and privilege. By contemplating this mystery, we grasp how our relationship with God is a gift that invites us to form deeper bonds of love with Him. God explains the tenderness of His love through Hosea: "When Israel was a child I loved him ... it was I who taught Ephraim to walk, who took them in my arms; ... I drew them with human cords, with bands of love; I fostered them like those who raise an infant to their cheeks; I bent down to feed them" (11:1-4).

Not only are we obligated to conversion, but the joy of this gift of love leads to deepening and caring for bonds of friendship and love with God as with a best friend (Jn 15:15). Living the Immaculate Conception thus entails not only forming a deeper bond with the Immaculata but entering, with her, more deeply into the mystery of the Trinity, to be immersed in grateful love. The Greek *baptizein* means "immerse," and so the Immaculate Conception beckons us to fulfill our Baptism by being immersed anew — as was Mary — in His love.

In this light, being a Christian is primarily a *gift*, which "unfolds in the dynamic of living and acting in and around the gift."[195] In a secular world where religion is reduced to obligation, we are called to bear witness to the gift and joy of being Christian, inviting others to receive and live within the gift of the Holy Spirit. Moreover, we encounter our deepest identity — as did Simon before Jesus when he received the name Peter — by experiencing for ourselves the "gift of the saving love of God in a personal encounter with Christ Jesus in the power of the Holy Spirit." Experiencing that saving love, as did Mary, "manifests itself in a life of joy, love, praise, gratitude, and humility."[196] Only a deep receptivity for the divine gift can sustain a life of self-giving service to others. In imitation of Immaculata, we are to give freely what we have freely received (Mt 10:8).

Modern, western culture has been described as "liquid," meaning that it is shapeless, formless, and ever-changing.[197] The presumption is that nothing truly lasts, for nothing has any definitive solidity. This is seen in a lack of any definitive commitment among many persons. Man feels ever more lost and alone, and needs the support that love offers. As St. John Paul II stated, "Man cannot live without love. He remains a being that is incomprehensible for himself, his life is senseless, if love is not revealed to him, if he does not encounter love, if he does not experience it and make it his own, if he does not participate intimately in it."[198] In other words, without the Holy Spirit, offered to us in Jesus Christ, life is empty and meaningless. Now, to believe in this love is to believe in the Holy Spirit. This, in turn, means believing in Divine Mercy, the specific way such divine love has been revealed in the face of the evil of this world. We experience the Spirit of love as mercy — as balm for broken hearts: as strength to prevent us from succumbing to temptations, particularly despair. When we lack a real awareness of being loved by God, then the result is either practical atheism, searching for substitutes for love; or neo-paganism, with contemporary idols such as money, career, power.

The Immaculate Conception teaches us that the foundation of our existence is the solidity of His love, and that this foundation does not change, for it does not depend on us. Since we did not cause Him to love us, we cannot cause Him to stop loving us. We can reject His love, but we cannot make Him stop loving us. Thus, the Immaculate Conception enables us to construct our lives on the only solid foundation: the love that the Father has for us, which is given to us in the Holy Spirit (Rom 5:5). But that construction is complete only when, like the Immaculata and her Son, we too make a complete gift of ourselves. "This likeness reveals that man, who is the only creature on earth which God willed for itself, cannot fully find himself except through a sincere gift of himself."[199] The Immaculata teaches us how to direct our hearts' love back toward the Father, Who is infinite love.

Through her, our love reaches Jesus, and with Him, reaches the Father. All our love terminates — that is, has its goal — in the Father.

Living by His grace entails recognizing that the foundation of our everyday reality is the self-giving love of the Father. Rather than anxiously trying to hold it all together so that our projects and plans succeed (as if it all depended on us), we can breathe and relax as beloved sons and daughters (knowing that it all depends ultimately on Him). Our response, then, is not so much an act of the will, though this is included, but a spontaneous love flowing from our hearts. Just as the Father does not first exist and then decide to love, so, too, our very existence becomes love. As St. John Paul II wrote in *Dominum et Vivificantem*, the Holy Spirit is the "personal love" between the Father and Son in the Trinity. He is the uncreated "Love-Gift." In the Holy Spirit, "the intimate life of the Triune God becomes totally gift, an exchange of mutual love between the divine Persons and that ... through the Holy Spirit God exists in the mode of gift. It is the Holy Spirit who is the personal expression of this self-giving, of this being-love" (n. 10).

The Holy Spirit is the personal expression of the intimate life of the Trinity, whereby God "exists in the mode of gift." By dwelling in us, the Holy Spirit enables us to exist in the mode of gift. Love then becomes not only one specific moment, among many, but rather becomes our very existence through living in self-giving. We develop the capacity to live in love always, no matter the circumstance or our mood. This happens because the Holy Spirit — as uncreated gift — is the living font of all gifts to creatures — in terms of both creation (existence, the natural world) and grace (salvation offered in Christ).[200] In the Holy Spirit, God opens Himself to creation, bending over it, infusing it with His love. This grace — the effect of the Spirit's presence — is the fullness that fills the emptiness of our hearts. God's perfect love becomes a pure gift for our hearts: one we do not merit, nor deserve. In theology, this is called His *prevenient grace*, that is, "grace that comes before" anything we do. His prevenient grace comes before our cooperation and, in fact, enables us to cooperate with Him. This prevenient grace is most visible in the Immaculate Conception, since the Father bestowed this grace of the Spirit before anything Mary could do — before she even existed.

But her entire life was a return in thanksgiving for this gift. The Immaculata teaches us to live a doxological spirituality by remembering God's deeds, praising Him for His goodness, and reciprocating His gift by our grateful love.

QUESTIONS

- How often do you remember God's goodness, presence, and work in your life?
- What is your solid foundation, and where do you experience life as liquid?
- How do you experience the Holy Spirit as the "personal love" of the Father for you?

PRAYER

Pray the "Prayer to the Immaculate Conception" (p. 204) and the Litany of the Holy Spirit (#3 — p. 209).

DAY 28
GOD'S LOVE

Immaculata Virginis Mariae Conceptio Sit Nobis Salus et Protectio

The Immaculate Conception consists essentially in the gift of the Holy Spirit to Mary since the first moment of her existence. Through the Sacraments, we receive the same Spirit, albeit later. In possessing the Holy Spirit, we receive every possible gift, for He is the source of all gifts. But — being filled "to the brim" (Jn 2:7) with such gifts — we are enabled by the Spirit to respond with giving of ourselves. This leads to the final part of the consecration. If first the Holy Spirit bestows His gifts on us, He thereby enables us to make a response of self-giving love to God. He makes us capable of giving ourselves — in imitation of Jesus — entirely to the Father, in obedience and gratitude. Only then is life "complete": when our response to His love is complete. Heaven is definitive precisely because it is the place where our response of love to Him is irrevocable.

The Immaculata teaches us to respond to His love with our love, for "love is paid by love alone."[201] In her, the response is complete; in us, incomplete. The fullness of grace and salvation does not exclude but includes our human freedom and cooperation. Her Immaculate Conception led her to stably cooperate with grace, so that every gift she received enabled her to give of herself in love. The Holy Spirit draws us into Mary's response: With Mary, He leads us to a life of self-giving love — a life in harmony with God and neighbor. This is our life's journey: to enter more deeply into His mystery of the Trinity, throughout life, in the Church.

Transformed by grace, Mary is a new creation, directly created by the Holy Spirit. By her love, she draws us into the orbit of her grace-filled life and leads us into harmonious cooperation with the Spirit in daily striving for holiness by giving of ourselves in love. Just as there are myriads of stars, snowflakes, animals, and persons, there are myriads of ways to give of ourselves in love and so become saints. As many people as exist, so many ways are there to become a saint! We need not copy others — whether the Immaculata or other saints. Rather, the Immaculata leads us to give our unique, unrepeatable "yes" to the Father and give Him the fullness of our love.

When we learn to live in His grace — receiving His love and giving of ourselves in love in return — we live in profound joy, as did the Immaculata, who exclaimed: "My spirit rejoices in God my savior" (Lk 1:47). Sometimes, we imagine joy to be an emotion or experience that happens to us on good days. Such joy is largely out of our control, a sort of accident of fate. Now, emotional happiness depends on many circumstances beyond our control. But what if joy were not an accidental emotion that happened to us, but rather is the fruit of our own choice? Just as we experience joy that flows from attaining what we have planned (for example, an academic degree, marriage), so too we experience joy in fulfilling our deepest calling to love. Authentic joy is always within our grasp, because the Holy Spirit never ceases to pour forth His gifts of love.

In the Christian sense, joy depends in large measure upon our receptivity to His grace and our willingness to give of ourselves in return. When we are in the presence of what we love, we experience joy; or we rejoice because of the well-being of one we love (for example, when a friend is doing well). Now, we are always in the presence of God, Whom we love, and He is Himself always blissful. By loving Him, we experience a profound, stable joy. When we possess and abide in God, our joy does not depend on external circumstances or anything else that can change. Rather, we are in touch with the font and source of joy. When we experience sorrow or trials, by drawing near to God, we receive consolation. Undoubtedly we will experience sorrow; but when we open our suffering to God, His grace at work within us brings joy even amid pain.

Our joy is complete only inasmuch as our love is complete. Not only was the Immaculata passively touched by God's love; she actively loved God. Only then is our joy complete, and only then is it on a firm foundation. To be "confirmed in grace" means to be confirmed in joy, that is, the joy both of being loved by God and of loving God in return.

Saint Faustina, in the last paragraph of her *Diary*, highlighted these two fundamental axes of the spiritual life: "I am thoroughly enwrapped in God. My soul is being inflamed by His love. I only know that I love and am loved. That is enough for me" (*Diary*, 1828). That is enough for us, also: to know that we are at least trying to love, and to have faith that we are irrevocably loved by the Father.

Our joy is complete only when we live fully the first commandment: when we love God with all that we are (Dt 6:4-6). Wherever there is a lack of joy, there is a part of our hearts that is yet to be filled with love. To experience the joy we desire, we ought to ask for an increase of love: our capacity to be loved and to love God and neighbor in return. When we truly love God with all that we are, then we will experience the joy of the Immaculata and of the saints: a joy that knows no limit, for our love then knows no limit. This is a joy that is not conquered or removed by suffering but paradoxically increased for we can love God *more* in suffering.

Saint Faustina relates her own experience of this paradoxical joy, which was noticeable to a fellow sister:

> Great love can change small things into great ones, and it is only love which lends value to our actions. And the purer our love becomes, the less there will be within us for the flames of suffering to feed upon, and the suffering will cease to be a suffering for us; it will become a delight! By the grace of God, I have received such a disposition of heart that I am never so happy as when I suffer for Jesus, whom I love with every beat of my heart.
>
> Once, when I was suffering greatly, I left my work and escaped to Jesus and asked Him to give me His strength. After a very short prayer, I returned to my work filled with enthusiasm and joy. Then, one of the sisters … said to me, "You must have many consolations today, Sister; you look so radiant. Surely, God is giving you no suffering, but only consolations." "You are greatly mistaken, Sister," I answered, 'for it is precisely when I suffer much that my joy is greater; and when I suffer less, my joy also is less.' However, that soul was letting me recognize that she does not understand what I was saying. I tried to explain to her that when we suffer much we have a great chance to show God that we love Him; but when we suffer little we have less occasion to show God our love; and when we do not suffer at all, our love is then neither great nor pure. By the grace of God, we can attain a point where suffering will become a delight to us, for love can work such things in pure souls" (*Diary*, 303).

We may be like the sister who did not understand how this is possible. In fact, we may have heard many times that the saints experienced joy in suffering. We may wish to share in such joy, but we often are bitter and frustrated. There can be several reasons for this difference. We may unconsciously associate suffering with punishment and so interpret pain as a sign of God's displeasure with us (much as children associate punishment with their parents' disapproval). The saints held firm in their belief in God's love, even when their suffering seemed to question that love. Whatever the deeper reason may be for our lack of joy, the path to experiencing such joy remains the same: holding our pain before the One who loves us and accompanies us always.[202]

We need not act as if we were joyful, feigning a smile and pretending things aren't all that bad. The joy the saints experience is precisely that God's merciful love meets them time and again in their misery and pain, to touch, heal, console and sustain them. This joy, then, does not presuppose an absence of suffering; but rather, it is the joy that flows from suffering that is assuaged, alleviated by the One who is love itself. For the Immaculata — filled with grace and joy — is also the sorrowful mother. More than any other saint, she plumbed the depth of sorrow on Good Friday and Holy Saturday. Yet she also encountered joy — unhinged by any sorrow — on Easter. She experienced the truth of Jesus' statement to His disciples:

> Amen, amen, I say to you, you will weep and mourn, while the world rejoices; you will grieve, but your grief will become joy. When a woman is in labor, she is in anguish because her hour has arrived; but when she has given birth to a child, she no longer remembers the pain because of her joy that a child has been born into the world. So you also are now in anguish. But I will see you again, and your hearts will rejoice, and no one will take your joy away from you (Jn 16:20-22).

The Immaculata shares with us her joy, teaching us how to rejoice in loving God, even amid suffering.

QUESTIONS

- Where do you struggle with sorrow or with a lack of joy?
- How conscious are you throughout the day of God's love for you, and how do you consciously love Him in return?
- What emotions do you experience in times of suffering and desolation?

PRAYER

Pray the "Prayer to the Immaculate Conception" (p. 204) and the Litany of the Immaculate Conception (#2 — p. 214).

DAY 29
FULLY AND ENTIRELY HAPPY

Immaculata Virginis Mariae Conceptio Sit Nobis Salus et Protectio

In Greek, there is an etymological connection between the words *charis*, "grace" and *chara*, "joy." The effect of being full of grace — like the Immaculata — is to be full of joy. To be transformed by grace is to be transformed by joy. The Immaculate Conception, the beginning of Mary's life, harks back to the very beginning: creation in Genesis. The *Catechism* teaches, in its first paragraph, that God — infinitely perfect and blessed in Himself — created us to share in His own "blessed life." In other words, God created us to share in His eternal joy. Saint Thomas Aquinas states that "God is happiness by His essence."[203] That might challenge our idea of God, for we may more easily associate God with solemnity or seriousness. But God is an overflowing font of joy and created us so as to bestow that joy on us and so make us deeply happy.

That is the goal of the Immaculate Conception: to make Our Lady fully and entirely happy by filling and transforming her with grace and so enabling her to love in response. The Immaculata always remains in the joy and delight of the Father. As revealed in her, God has the same goal for each of us. God desires to infuse our lives — from conception onward — not only with His supernatural grace but with authentic joy. For the goal of the Holy Spirit's work in our lives is to bring about such deep, authentic joy. He Who is the source of all grace is also the font of enduring joy. Moreover, there is no greater joy than that of redemption: We are irrevocably loved, even amid our worst sin. This joy leads us, like Mary, to sing our Magnificat, for we are recipients of His mercy that "is from age to age" (Lk 1:50).

This utter joy is caused by knowing – not only in our minds but in our hearts and in the core of our being – that we are totally, irrevocably loved as we are. Sometimes we experience this joy emotionally, but sometimes it is a joy that is profoundly spiritual and is deeper than a passing emotional experience. That is the joy of the saints in Heaven, a joy we are privileged to share already now. But this joy is tasted only by the humble, who seek it not in their own accomplishments or strength, but only in His love. Seen in this light, the purpose of cleansing us from all sin is not merely to free us from moral fault but to remove the source of all unhappiness.[204] For if grace is the source of joy, then sin is the ultimate font of suffering and pain. The Father desires to free us from sin, not because He is a perfectionist, but because He wants to dry our tears and assuage our pain, whose root cause is original sin.

If sin (whether of our own or of others) is the cause of sadness, then Satan is a thief of joy. He constantly works to burden us with and drown us in misery and shame. Because Satan exists without grace, he also lives without joy. Not possessing joy himself, he is driven by his envy to steal joy from those who do possess it. This is one reason St. Ignatius of Loyola recommends preparing for desolation while in consolation.[205] While we ought to be grateful for the joy of consolation when it is given by the Holy Spirit, we also ought to be aware that any joy will be a target of Satan's tactics. He is a thief who sabotages authentic joy and proposes ephemeral substitutes for spiritual joy.

As sinners we live not always in joy, but in a certain survival mode, a bland maintenance of the status quo. Sometimes, we become so caught up in our routine that we forget that we are called to live in joy. We are burdened and tired, even exhausted and so we live from a place — not of grace and joy — but of frustration, bitterness, and pain. In short, our busy lives mean that we live in a sort of spiritual desert and desolation, without even recognizing it. We arrive at the end of the day dried up interiorly, feeling empty inside. Then we may try to remedy that gnawing emptiness through human comforts.

Since the joy of the Lord is our strength (Neh 8:10), we are truly weak when joy is dried up. We need to be sensitive to when this drying up occurs (I'm not speaking of the dark night here). Such common desolation arises from lack of a contemplative lifestyle that would be attentive to the presence of God. When we lose sight of His presence in faith, we also lose the source of joy and strength. Saint Ignatius of Loyola, well known for his apostolic spirituality, was nonetheless attentive when he entered desolation. In his journal, he recounts how he paused his planned activity to care for his interior life and resolve the desolation first.[206] While we may not always be able to do the same because of pressing tasks, it is important to take stock — through a daily examen — of our joy or lack of joy, of consolation and desolation. Such spiritual sensitivity requires a greater ability to be present to oneself, to one's bodily emotions and interior. Both the examen and keeping a journal can be of great help.

Eucharistic adoration also helps us to grow in sensitivity to the Holy Spirit, the "soul's delightful guest," (as we sing in the *Veni Creator Spiritus*). He remains constantly present in the human heart, though often forsaken and abandoned amid our myriad of tasks (*Catechism*, 1378-1379). When we abandon Him, we feel this distance as a lack of joy. Then, without the joy of His grace, our heart shrivels like a plant without water. For attentiveness to joy is not merely about emotional sensitivity, but about attentiveness to the Holy Spirit, its source. A lack of spiritual joy — on good and bad days — signals greater distance from the Holy Spirit.

Filled with the Holy Spirit herself, the Immaculata is attentive to our lack of joy flowing from the Spirit. At Cana, she pointed out to her Son, "They have no wine" (Jn 2:3). She prompted her Son to perform His first miracle to ensure joy at a wedding. Similarly, she brings our needs before her Son, asking Him to fill the emptiness of our hearts and our lives with new wine — the Spirit that comes from His pierced heart. But, as the Immaculata instructed the servers, we too are to "do whatever He tells" us (Jn 2:5). For joy is found only in God's will, not apart from it. By obedience and love, we tap into the joy that fills her heart, so that we experience the best wine that Jesus reserves for those who persevere in loving Him.

This perseverance is key, because living by His grace does not mean that at the first moment we will experience joy. Grace first brings about our (heart-wrenching, tearful) conversion. Only through persevering obedience to His will (as in filling the jars at Cana with water) do we begin to tap into the joy that is offered to us in grace (as with tasting the wine that Jesus provided). In other words, the path to the enduring joy of the Resurrection is always the Cross that crucifies our flesh and its desires. At times, it seems that God's grace may be opposed to our desire for joy. But if, with the Immaculata, we persevere at the Cross, then we will experience the true new wine of the Spirit that pours forth from the pierced side of Jesus. And, as happened at Cana, the best wine is always reserved for later.

The Immaculate Conception beckons us to return to that holy beginning, to that fundamental purpose and desire of God for each of us: to share in His immaculate joy that never fades. Without joy, life becomes drudgery, reduced to pushing through our obstacles and trials, willing it and exhausting ourselves. The Immaculata comes to our help, for she is the model of one interiorly present to the Holy Spirit within her heart, and so always full of joy. The Holy Spirit enables us to joyfully persevere, rooted in the truth that we are *always, forever loved* and so able to love.

So, if you find yourself sorrowful, empty, like the jars at Cana: turn to Our Lady, ask for her intercession, and obey her Son. Through her and with her, you will taste the best wine of authentic joy: the delight of His love, which is hidden yet powerfully present even in the darkest of moments.

QUESTIONS

- When do you notice yourself as without joy, and how do you remedy that?
- How often do you bring your empty jars to Our Lady?
- How do you experience Satan as a thief of joy?
- How aware are you of the Spirit as your "soul's delightful guest"?

PRAYER

Pray the "Prayer to the Immaculate Conception" (p. 204) and the Litany of the Immaculate Conception of Mary, Mother of God (#3 – p. 216).

DAY 30
DEEP JOY

Immaculata Virginis Mariae Conceptio Sit Nobis Salus et Protectio

As at Cana, the Immaculata wants to provide — through her Son — an abundance of new wine of the Father's love in our hearts. She has tasted this wine since the first moment of her existence, and she wants us as her children to share in her joy. For the Holy Spirit is the new wine that brings non-alcoholic intoxication but sober inebriation in deep joy. Saint John of the Cross, in the *Spiritual Canticle*, speaks about this wine of perfect love: "In the inner wine cellar I drank of my Beloved, and, when I went abroad through all this valley, I no longer knew anything, and lost the herd that I was following."[207] His imagery is similar to Song of Songs 2:4: "He brought me to the banquet hall, and his glance at me signaled love." (The Latin version, which St. John of the Cross used, translates "banquet hall" as "the cellar of his wines.")

When we drink of our Beloved — of His deep love — then we became inebriated with His love. We lose the herd of distractions that we so often follow, namely, substitutes that never fully slake our thirst for this infinite love. Mary directs us to this wine of love, just as Jesus promised the Samaritan: "Whoever drinks the water I shall give will never thirst" (Jn 4:14).

Apparently, the effect of the Holy Spirit on the Apostles at Pentecost was so perceptible that people in the street thought that they were drunk at 9 in the morning (Acts 2:13)! When we speak of spiritual joy, sometimes we imagine it as unfelt or as some sort of non-bodily experience. But the Holy Spirit has a manifest effect on our lives, similar to intoxication. In this vein, St. Paul exhorts the Ephesians (5:18) to be not drunken with alcohol but rather filled with the Holy Spirit. As some seek alcohol to relieve tension or stress, so Christians are to find their consolation and joy in the Spirit. The Pentecost sequence, *Veni Sancte Spiritus*, sings: "In our labor, rest most sweet; grateful coolness in the heat; solace in the midst of woe."[208]

Saint Augustine similarly warns that we ought to rejoice in the Lord — not in the world.[209] For we can find passing joy in things that lead us away from God. We need to be careful, then, about where and how we search for joy. For Christians, our path in this life toward Heaven entails finding more and more joy in the Holy Spirit, Who strengthens our communion with God and with each other. In this way, we are able to be joyful because of His presence, even when the external circumstances of life are difficult.

The lack of joy is both an emotional and a moral challenge, for the vice of *acedia* is manifest in a lack of joy. *Acedia* is often translated as "laziness" or "sloth," but it is not merely lack of diligence in daily work. Rather, it is a lack of joy in the presence of God, who loves us. Joy is the fruit or effect of love. In turn, this joy then provides motivation to fulfill our duties, the first of which is to love our neighbor, beginning with those closest to us (e.g., family and community). Without that joy flowing from love, we lack strength for our duties, because joy enables us to persevere amid obstacles. In this sense, acedia does become sloth, inasmuch as a lack of joy ultimately leads to inability or lack of desire to work.[210]

While *acedia* is not a common word, burnout and depression are commonly used. Both of these imply a lack of joy, though they are on opposite ends of a spectrum. They are manifest in the incapacity of a person to be motivated to engage life wholeheartedly. Now, clinical depression can have various causes which are not reducible to sin; but the wounds and tragedies of life which weigh upon us can, through the help of professionals and priests, find healing in this life or the next. For now, I am referring to the lack of joy that is a result of *acedia*, which is manifest not only in laziness but also in excessive work or busyness devoid of the joy that the Holy Spirit brings. Laziness and overwork both arise from a lack of embracing the real cross that Jesus offers: being loved and loving in return.

Now, Jesus does invite us to bear His Cross. It is true that He Himself wept at the tomb of Lazarus (Jn 11:35), and many psalms express lament and sorrow. But when we are with Jesus, every sorrow will be turned into joy, for our pain is assuaged by His love and mercy. Thus, the Cross that Jesus invites us to bear is always accompanied by grace and hence by joy, even amid our suffering. Even more, it is important to remember that the essence of the Christian life is not suffering in itself but the love that bears suffering.

Only in this sense do the saints write about "joy in suffering" or "perfect joy" in sharing the Cross. They are not masochists but rather madly in love with God, and the Cross provides the tinder to inflame their love. While the path to joy involves the Cross, only joy can provide the strength for persevering amid our trials. Too much sorrow and sadness can be a foretaste of death and so prevent us from moving forward on the spiritual journey. For joy gives us emotional energy to advance, even amid trials, whereas sadness leads us to stay still and focus on ourselves.

After the return from exile, the Jews listened to Ezra read the book of the Law. They were reduced to tears, as they recognized how they and their forefathers had not kept the Law and so had brought disaster — the exile — on themselves. But Nehemiah exhorts them: "Today is holy to the LORD your God. Do not lament, do not weep! ... Go, eat rich foods and drink sweet drinks, and allot portions to those who had nothing prepared; for today is holy to our LORD. Do not be saddened this day, for rejoicing in the LORD is your strength!" (Neh 8:9-10). Apparently, there was so much weeping that the Levites had to quiet the people: "Silence! Today is holy, do not be saddened" (verse 11). Here, the connection between *holiness* and *joy* is explicit: a day holy to the Lord is a day that is joyful. Granted, there are days when sorrow and fasting are proper, such as Good Friday; they are preparations for the holiest of days, such as Easter, when joy abounds. All penance and sorrow are but a preparation, in the Christian sense, for the abounding joy of the Holy Spirit within and among us.

There is a story of St. Teresa of Avila asking the Lord in prayer to save her from "sour-faced saints." Too often, holiness is depicted as solemn, serious, with no spontaneity or joy. But if one looks at the natural world — and how even animals play joyfully — one finds a reflection of the joy of God. Authentic holiness is manifest in deep, human joy that is capable of expressing God's love, even in the worst moments and tragedies. The Immaculata herself is a woman full of grace and filled with joy. Those who have seen her with their own eyes speak of the great joy they experienced in her presence and how they wished they would never have to leave her! Indeed, this joy is a foretaste of the joy of Heaven, where we are definitively, forever, loved by God irrevocably. The deeper the joy, the more profound our participation in Heaven.

Filled with joy at being so loved by God, the Immaculata wants to share that joy with us. The nature of joy is that it is fully experienced only by being shared. In turn, just as she shares her joy with us, we are called to share that joy with those who are sorrowful, those who do not know the Father's love. In this manner, we evangelize — we share the Good News — that joy, not sorrow, has the last word, for His love is stronger than sin, death, and Satan. In this, we are joyful in hope (Rom 12:12), for even while we do not yet see this total victory over sorrow, we remain firm in hope. We see in the Immaculata that this victory has already occurred, and through her, it will happen in each of us and in the entire Church.

QUESTIONS

- How do you experience the Holy Spirit as comfort, solace, and refreshment?
- How does *acedia* manifest itself in your life?
- How do you see the Immaculata as a woman of joy?

PRAYER

Pray the "Prayer to the Immaculate Conception" (p. 204) and the Litany of the Immaculate Conception (#4 — p. 219).

DAY 31
PERFECT RECIPROCITY

Immaculata Virginis Mariae Conceptio Sit Nobis Salus et Protectio

In the Trinity, the Holy Spirit is love in Person. In His Person, He is the synthesis between the initiative of the Father's love toward the Son and the grateful response of the Son to the Father. He is the interchange of the mutual love between the Father and Son. Similarly, He is poured forth into our hearts as a pure gift: "The love of God has been poured out into our hearts through the holy Spirit that has been given to us" (Rom 5:5). The Holy Spirit is the expression of the Father's love for each one of us, gathered together in the name of His Son. At the same time, the Holy Spirit also enables us — like the Son — to make a full return of love to the Father, in the same measure we have received.

This perfect reciprocity — of receiving love from the Father and returning that same love to the Father — is visible in Jesus as well as in the Immaculata. Jesus, though, is a Divine Person, whereas the Immaculata is a human person. Thus, in her, we find the fullness of the Father's love for His creation, as well as all of creation's love flowing back to the Father. In her Immaculate Heart, Heaven and earth are joined: the love of Heaven with all the love of creatures. As St. Maximilian Kolbe stated, "So it is that in this union heaven and earth are joined; all of heaven with all the earth, the totality of eternal love with the totality of created love. It is truly the summit of love."[211] The Immaculata gives forth to the Father the fullness of love in the name of all creation, gathering our partial, imperfect love in union with her perfect love. The Immaculata is the vertex or highest manifestation of this love, from creatures, returning to God. In union with hers, our love rises to the Father through Jesus.

The Immaculata is able to give this full response of love because the Holy Spirit, Who is divine love, dwells within her. If the Holy Spirit is the love of the entire Trinity, then all of that love is found in her. By the grace of her Immaculate Conception, she is rendered capable of returning that love most perfectly. And she actually does return that love, not only on her own behalf, but on behalf of all creation. In Mary, according to St. Maximilian, Heaven meets earth and all of uncreated love (the Holy Spirit) meets with all created love (the response of the human heart).

This is what the Father desires from us: immaculacy not only as absence of sin, but also as participating in this summit of love. For if the Father's objective in creation is for us to share in His eternal beatitude, our sharing in that bliss depends on our choice to return His love. If He always loves us first, His love nonetheless arouses a full response of love within our hearts, just as happened in the Immaculata. Thus, the goal of creation is for creation to return to God voluntarily through love. Jesus will return and bring us into His Kingdom, back to the Father. We voluntarily choose to return to the Father with Jesus, to go back to Him, like the prodigal son, there to remain, to live, to stay in our true home of love.

With the Immaculata, we give our fiat of consent to the Holy Spirit to enter our hearts and kindle in them the fire of His love. The Father wants devotion to the Immaculate Heart so that our hearts will be filled with His divine love — the Holy Spirit — and so make a return to Him of all the love of our human hearts. When our hearts are united with hers — immaculate and blazing with love — then creation reaches its goal and we fulfill our deepest vocation. He created us to know Him and love Him, and we find our rest only when our hearts attain this summit of love with the Immaculata. That summit of perfect reciprocity of love is the inner reality of Heaven. We already now begin to experience Heaven — eternal life — inasmuch as we join the Immaculata in her summit of love.

That is the essence of consecration to the Immaculate Conception: being united with her response of love, that is, with the same Holy Spirit that fills her. In and through the Immaculata, one is able to love Jesus "in a way incomparably more perfect than he himself might strive to do with any other means."[212] Just as any grace from the Father flows through Jesus and the Immaculata to the soul, so no response rises to the Father except through her and Jesus. In union with her, we are able to achieve the easiest and most sublime holiness, rendering the greatest possible glory to God, by allowing our own hearts to be ever more of the Immaculata.

This living participation in the summit of love is in a sense the second page of the mystery of the Immaculate Conception. The first page was the theological debate during the course of centuries, that finally produced its proclamation as a dogma in 1854. This second page is revealed in the transformation of hearts, of dedicated disciples burning with the joy of heroic charity. For the evidence of this mystery is the presence of the Holy Spirit, love itself, within our hearts, capable of returning love in imitation of the Immaculata. Washed in Baptism, we are filled with the same Holy Spirit that fills her heart. That Spirit works in and through the Immaculata to communicate supernatural love, so that we — together with her — may partake in the interchange of love in the Triune God.

But this flame of love grows only through the wood of the Cross. The more wood, the greater the flame, and the more intense the love of the Spirit — if we but allow Him to consume our pain and heartache. For at the Cross alone do we grow — through suffering — to give a full response of love. Like St. John, we are called to stand near the Cross with the Immaculata, learning to love as Jesus has loved us (Jn 13:34). Hence, the disciple who lives this mystery is capable — and desirous — of living as an *oblatio*. This Latin term refers to the sacrificial offering, the oblation, placed on the altar at Mass. It is used twice in the first Eucharistic prayer: "Therefore, Lord, we pray: graciously accept this oblation [*oblationem*] of our service, that of your whole family." Thereafter, the priest prays: "Be pleased, O God, we pray, to bless, acknowledge, and approve this offering [*oblationem*] in every respect; make it spiritual and acceptable, so that it may become for us the Body and Blood of your most beloved Son, our Lord Jesus Christ."

First and foremost, *oblatio* refers to the sacrifice of Jesus, Who offers Himself in loving obedience to the Father in this Sacrament. But our full and active participation in the Mass entails the capacity to present ourselves with Jesus on the altar as a sacrificial offering, an *oblatio,* to the Father. Only when we offer ourselves in love — offering *all the love of our human hearts* — is our participation complete. For just as Jesus desired to associate the Immaculata in a unique manner with His sacrificial death on Calvary, so through the Eucharist, Jesus associates us — the Church — with His sacrificial death. In other words, through the Eucharist we are enabled — with Jesus and the Immaculata — to participate in this full return of love to the Father. For the essence of Jesus' sacrifice — and of our own — is returning to the Father all the love He has poured forth on us in the Spirit. No one has participated in that sacrifice of love so deeply as the Immaculata, and she initiates us into the mystery, so that we, too, become an *oblatio* with her Son.

QUESTIONS

- How do you understand active participation in the Eucharist?
- How can you turn to Our Lady in moments of sacrifice and suffering, to be strengthened to offer yourself as an *oblation of love* to the Father?
- When do you have a foretaste of heavenly bliss as an interchange of love?

PRAYER

Pray the "Prayer to the Immaculate Conception" (p. 204) and the Litany of the Blessed Virgin Mary, Immaculately Conceived (#1 – p. 212).

DAY 32
ESSENCE OF SACRIFICE

Immaculata Virginis Mariae Conceptio Sit Nobis Salus et Protectio

I use the Latin word *oblatio* purposely because of St. Stanislaus Papczyński. When he departed from his first religious congregation (the Piarists), he pronounced his *Oblatio* on December 10, 1670. As a priest, he purposely chose this term to unite himself to Christ in His sacrificial offering at Mass. Through the *Oblatio*, St. Stanislaus desired to freely and totally give, offer, and consecrate himself to the Most Holy Trinity and to the Immaculata. The intention of this consecration is to enable us to participate in his *oblatio* by making our own *oblatio*, a total self-offering in union with the Immaculata and Jesus for the salvation of souls. The natural result of participating in the Immaculate Conception is our personal sinlessness *for the sake of* offering ourselves in burning love to the Father.

Saint Stanislaus lived his *oblatio* by his life of prayer, by his pastoral ministry, and particularly by his founding of the Congregation of Marian Fathers. His self-giving was quiet and humble, unnoticed largely by history and the Church until his recent beatification and canonization. But a more popular example of *oblatio* — of ardent charity — is that of St. Maximilian Kolbe. When a prisoner escaped from the Auschwitz concentration camp, the German guards — to discourage any further escapes — drew a number of innocent persons from among the remaining prisoners. When the guards called on a Polish man — a father and husband — St. Maximilian Kolbe voluntarily offered himself to die in this man's place. The Germans accepted, and Kolbe suffered for two weeks underground in a bunker, naked, and without any food or drink. After the other called-up prisoners had died, on August 14, he died as a result of an injection of carbolic acid into his arm — while praying to the Immaculata. It is no coincidence that St. Maximilian, so devoted to the Immaculata, would offer himself as did Jesus — as an oblation for the salvation and life of another.

The essence of our sacrifice, then, is not suffering in itself, but the loving fulfillment of His will. As St. Paul forcefully reminds us: we can do any number of good deeds, but without love, they prove to be "nothing" (1 Cor 13:1-3). Moreover, in Heaven we shall fulfill His will without any difficulty. In fact, the fulfillment of His will becomes our delight and joy there. On earth, as sinners, we experience suffering simply as part of what happens when we surrender our will to His will. Thus, the Cross itself — pain — is not what the Father desires. Rather, He desires our obedience and love, which takes the form of the Cross in a sinful world. This is important to keep in mind because in the Catholic sense the praise we offer to God — in living a doxological spirituality — is inseparable from sacrificial worship. That is, there is no authentic praise of God without sacrifice: without our participation in the one sacrifice of Christ, in imitation of the Immaculata who suffered with her Son for our salvation.

The Immaculate Conception is an invitation to strive for ever-greater holiness by living the fullness of our Baptism, which is found in the Eucharist. Like the Immaculata, we were embraced by God's love at the beginning of our lives: and like her, we are to grow in His grace, until we mature to the full measure of love He desires of us. The purpose of creation, of redemption, and of sanctification was and remains for us to participate in God's intimate life of love: to be loved by Him and return that love in full by loving our neighbor. Sin obscured this love, but through the Cross, the Holy Spirit enables us — in union with the Immaculata and Jesus in the Eucharist — to make this return of love to the Father. The Immaculata attracts all hearts to herself by way of her motherly heart. Through her, Holy Spirit inspires our hearts with greater love for the Father.

"We must constantly strengthen the love for the Immaculata in souls, tighten the bond of love that exists between her and souls, so that they may become one with her — become her herself; so that She herself may live and love (act) in them and through them. Just as she is of Jesus and of God, so each soul will become of Jesus and of God through her and in her, in a much more perfect way than either without her or not through her, if that were even possible. Then souls will love the Most Sacred Heart of Jesus as they have never loved Him before, because, like her, and in ways they have never experienced before, they will plunge into the mysteries of love: the Cross and the Eucharist. Through her, God's love shall kindle the world, set it on fire, and lead to the assumption' of souls through Love."[213]

As the Father's love descends to us through the Son in the Person of the Spirit, so in that same Spirit, our love ascends to the Father through the Son. The initiative of the Father in giving us His love finds its equal response in the Holy Spirit in our hearts. Love is repaid by love alone, and the Immaculate Conception points out that the only way to respond to God in full is to love Him in full, to make an oblation of ourselves in love to the Father, a holocaust of love in the fire of the Spirit. We sinners imperfectly reciprocate such love with love; but Jesus and the Immaculata teach us how to offer such love perfectly back to the Father. That is the sacrifice He desires: total love.

Such love does involve emotions but cannot be reduced to emotions. It consists primarily in the fulfillment of God's will that leads to the union of one's will with His. "Such love is not reducible to memory or understanding, much less to pious imagination or sentiment. The essence of love is the union of wills. Understanding, imagination and sentiment all have their place, but they are placed at the service of the will, the true seat of love. The nobility of the human will is its capacity, aided by divine grace, to love God in a divine way."[214] As St. Maximilian Kolbe wrote, "The essence of our love for God will always lie not in experiencing sweetness, not in remembering, not in thinking, understanding, imagining, but only in fulfilling the Will of God in every moment of our lives and surrendering completely to such Will."[215] The *oblatio* may thus take the form of everyday, mundane tasks — simple or complex duties that are part of our state of life. It may even be hidden from our own experience, so that we do not feel love for God in what we do. We may even feel repugnance, but love moves us to give even that as our offering. As Jesus taught St. Faustina:

> **I will not spare My grace, that you may be able to fulfill what I demand of you. I will now instruct you on what your holocaust shall consist of, in everyday life, so as to preserve you from illusions. You shall accept all sufferings with love. Do not be afflicted if your heart often experiences repugnance and dislike for sacrifice. All its power rests in the will, and so these contrary feelings, far from lowering the value of the sacrifice in My eyes, will enhance it. Know that your body and soul will often be in the midst of fire. Although you will not feel My presence on some occasions, I will always be with you. Do not fear; My grace will be with you"** (*Diary*, 1767).

This is the holocaust that God desires: the complete and total fulfillment of His will, which is nothing other than loving as Jesus has loved us (Jn 13:34-35). As sinners, we have a tendency to fall away from love and act merely on instinct and self-interest. But, by cooperating with the Holy Spirit, we can relinquish our self-will — that is, those parts of our will that are opposed to God's will. At times, this will be difficult, and courage will be required, as we are afraid of letting go of what we want for fear of missing out. But Jesus encouraged St. Faustina: **"Be afraid of nothing; love will give you strength and make the realization of this easy"** (*Diary*, 372).

Now, we show our devotion to the Immaculata precisely through accomplishing the will of God. For her will is in perfect harmony with the will of God. Thus, to please her, we need only fulfill His will; for in fulfilling His will, we fulfill hers, and vice versa. Saint Maximilian went a step further, stating that we give greater glory to God in seeking to fulfill His will by fulfilling her will. For in doing so, we recognize and revere the perfect work of the Holy Spirit in her, just as we praise and admire the masterpiece of an artist. Our "food," then, is to fulfill the Father's will, which is given to us through the gentle touch of the Immaculata.

The essence of holiness — and immaculacy — is found in this quiet fulfillment of God's will, of being led by the Holy Spirit: "I understood that all striving for perfection and all sanctity consist in doing God's will. Perfect fulfillment of God's will is maturity in sanctity; there is no room for doubt here. To receive God's light and recognize what God wants of us and yet not do it is a great offense against the majesty of God. Such a soul deserves to be completely forsaken by God. It resembles Lucifer, who had great light, but did not do God's will" (*Diary*, 666).

As St. Faustina points out, there is no room for compromise here. Either we grow in imitation of the Immaculata in loving fulfillment of the Father's will, or we face the alternative of imitating Lucifer, who did not fulfill His will. In this life, either we grow more like the Immaculata, or we become deformed like Satan — even if only through our mediocrity and indecision. But, as Jesus reminded St. Faustina, there is no limit to the number of times that He forgives us, for He knows that we fall even as we strive to grow in holiness (*Diary*, 1488). Our part, like the just one who falls seven times a day, is to rise anew with trust in His mercy (Pr 24:16).

As stated above, the goal of our participation in the Immaculate Conception is to become an oblation in union with Jesus and the Immaculata to the Father. Such an *oblation* is necessarily a *holocaust* — a wholly burned offering. But what kind of fire consumes this holocaust? Saint Thérèse of Lisieux, in her self-offering to Merciful Love, identifies the fire — that once consumed the holocausts of the Old Testament — with the spiritual fire of love that is the Holy Spirit. In other words, the earthly, material fire that once consumed the holocausts offered to God symbolized the Holy Spirit, Who is the spiritual fire of pure, burning love. As St. John Paul II wrote: "The Old Testament on several occasions speaks of 'fire from heaven' which burnt the oblations presented by men. By analogy one can say that the Holy Spirit is the 'fire from heaven' which works in the depth of the mystery of the Cross. Proceeding from the Father, he directs toward the Father the sacrifice of the Son, bringing it into the divine reality of the Trinitarian communion."[216]

In thinking of Calvary, we often focus on the Son, offering Himself to the Father. But the entire Trinity is present, which means that the Holy Spirit is equally active in our redemption at Calvary. He consumes the sacrifice of the Son, burning His offering with love, as represented in the Fire atop the Sacred Heart of Jesus. Similarly, our self-offering reaches the Father not by our force of will or merit of holiness, but by our surrendering ourselves to the consuming fire of the Holy Spirit, so that all that we are may be transformed into love through Him. Just as earthly fire purifies metals of dross, so the Holy Spirit purifies us of sin and makes of us an acceptable offering to the Father. The Immaculata invites us to enter into this fire of Calvary, assuring us that — just as the burning bush was burning but not consumed (see Exodus 3) — we will not be obliterated but transformed into an offering of pure love to the Father. She teaches us to open our hearts to His presence and love, so that — as He transforms bread and wine into the self-offering of Christ — He transforms us into a living sacrifice.

Jesus invited St. Faustina to present herself as an offering — of the will: "Today, the Lord said to me, **I demand of you a perfect and whole-burnt offering; an offering of the will. No other sacrifice can compare with this one. I Myself am directing your life and arranging things in such a way that you will be for Me a continual sacrifice and will always do My will. And for the accomplishment of this offering, you will unite yourself with Me on the Cross**" (*Diary*, 923).

Now, this self-offering on the Cross was preceded by prayer. Saint John Paul II also wrote about Jesus:

> The Son of God Jesus Christ, as man, in the ardent prayer of his Passion, enabled the Holy Spirit, who had already penetrated the inmost depths of his humanity, to transform that humanity into a perfect sacrifice through the act of his death as the victim of love on the Cross. He made this offering by himself. As the one priest, "he offered himself without blemish to God": In his humanity he was worthy to become this sacrifice, for he alone was "without blemish." But he offered it "through the eternal Spirit," which means that the Holy Spirit acted in a special way in this absolute self-giving of the Son of Man, in order to transform this suffering into redemptive love."[217]

Jesus offered Himself to the Father because He was immaculate, without blemish. The Eucharistic prayer — after the Consecration — describes the offering as "unblemished" or immaculate. Being herself immaculate, Mary was able to participate most fully in His self-offering. All the previous steps have been necessary: purification from sin; penance and spiritual combat; growth in prayer to imbue our hearts and humanity with the Spirit; and finally the self-offering of ourselves to the Father in the Holy Spirit, for the salvation of many hearts. For only with the Holy Spirit is suffering redemptive. All men and women suffer, but not all suffer in a redemptive manner. Only those who, like the Immaculata, make a voluntary self-offering of it allow the Spirit to transform suffering into redemptive love — for our salvation and that of others.

QUESTIONS

- Where do you need to grow in harmony with the Father's will?
- How do you experience suffering as redemptive?
- Where do you experience the Holy Spirit as the consuming fire of love?

PRAYER

Pray the "Prayer to the Immaculate Conception" (p. 204) and the Litany of the Holy Spirit (#1 — p. 205).

DAY 33
MERCIFUL LOVE

Immaculata Virginis Mariae Conceptio Sit Nobis Salus et Protectio

Jesus' own *oblatio* of Himself to the Father was both an act of love for Him in obeying His will and an act of mercy toward sinners. Similarly, by uniting ourselves — as the Immaculata united herself — to His *oblatio,* not only do we offer the love of our hearts to the Father, but that very love becomes mercy for those most in need. Indeed, the more we direct our gaze in praise and love toward our Heavenly Father, Who is "rich in mercy" (Eph 2:4), the more we are filled with that mercy and so are able to gaze on others with eyes of mercy and love.

Just as Jesus could see and adore the Father and so be merciful toward sinners, we too adore Him and in so doing are imbued with His mercy toward His lost children. In fact, only such joy and praise lead us to embrace everyone, living in solidarity with others by discovering them as our brothers and sisters in Christ. For faith — strengthened by praise — enables us to see the image of God in them, even when that image is disfigured by sin. When we do not recognize His face in that of our neighbor, we lack living faith, since we do not recognize the living image of God. Only by contemplating Christ — crucified and yet risen — do we recognize Him in our neighbor.

Merciful love, given to man from God, provokes an answer from man toward God. That is, the gift is not something man then "possesses" apart from God; the gift is precisely the Holy Spirit, Who is our bond with God. The gift thus is the foundation of our relationship with Him and the Communion of Saints, our capacity to form relationships with other people, receiving them as a gift, and offering ourselves as a disinterested gift of self to them. Sin, in the context of interpersonal relationships, means a rejection of other persons, since they do not correspond to our idea of who or what they should be: we do not want to accept them as they are, with his good and bad qualities. But each person is both a gift and a duty, representing the will of God, Who desires that we accept others and help them with love to find their own face — their own dignity and identity of being loved by God — through our love for them. The gift of His merciful love is expressed, then, through interpersonal dialogue and communion.

For there is an inner logic of mercy. The Immaculata experienced mercy — more than all of us, because of her Immaculate Conception — and responded to it with merciful love toward her suffering Son and toward sinners. Just as the Immaculate Conception calls forth a deeper bond with God, so it leads to a deeper bond with our neighbor. The measure of her mercy was the love of her Immaculate Heart. The deeper one's own experience of mercy, the more fruitful the apostolate of mercy for others becomes. Thus, contemplating the Immaculata leads us not only to admire her graceful beauty but to discover the face of the God Who is merciful love. This teaches us thanksgiving for His marvelous work, which includes every person we meet.

The Immaculata, as we know, knew no sin. So, her holocaust of love — in union with Jesus — was directed entirely for our salvation. She invites us — in imitation of her — to offer ourselves for the salvation of others. For there is nothing more precious than eternal life: and for a brief moment of suffering, we gain eternity for others. At the Cross, we see in her the icon of merciful love that reveals itself in solidarity. Mary's response to being the recipient of abundant Divine Mercy was to be with Jesus in His suffering. But she also reveals this merciful solicitude toward others: in the mystery of the Visitation and at the wedding of Cana.

The Immaculata — full of mercy — is the model apostle of Divine Mercy: having experienced it, she shows it to others. In her, we admire the beauty and depth of Divine Mercy present amid God's people.

That *nearness* — through compassion, empathy, and understanding — is best described as feminine, maternal sensitivity, which is possible only through her immaculacy of heart. She reveals that the closer we are to God, the more we draw near to our neighbor, particularly to the poor and the sinner. The more we are filled with divine love, the more our sensitivity to our neighbor grows and our compassion is the deeper and purer. The Immaculata is not only *for* but *with* her neighbor. It is easier for us to be *for* rather than *with* others, among them; it is easier to do something *for* them rather to than help them grow by accompanying them *with* patient, merciful love. But when we are merely *for* others, then the dialogue of mercy becomes a monologue, and the other person only a recipient; then, mercy is philanthropy, not Divine Mercy.

This reflects Pope Francis' constant appeal to us to accompany others in their lives and their suffering. Just as a mother's love means she is constantly present in the life of her children, so the Immaculata manifests mercy in the particular form of her constant, though subtle, presence. It is often easier for us — in a busy world — to do something *for* others rather than to *be with* others. We would rather fix a problem and then leave, so as to move on with our lives, than truly be present to and with another person. But there are many human issues that cannot be fixed. The most painful human suffering — loneliness — is healed only by being with others, just as Jesus is with us. Only then does our love raise others to the level of personhood: they are not merely machines, nor problems, but persons, worthy of love, time, and attention.

Saint Stanislaus Papczyński founded a religious congregation to honor the Immaculate Conception. He provided many devotional practices, including the Rosary and the Little Office of the Immaculate Conception. But St. Stanislaus implied that the primary path to living and expressing devotion to the Immaculata is in and through community life, through mutual, fraternal love. Saint Stanislaus in his *Rule of Life* wrote an entire chapter on love, stating that one who departs from mutual love departs from life itself.[218] For the farther we are from love, the farther we are from the Spirit, Who is Lord and giver of life. We witness to the power of the Immaculate Conception — which is the Person of the Holy Spirit — in our ability to live in mutual love in a community. The Holy Spirit forms us as people capable of communion, reviving the life of the early Church, which was of one heart, one mind, one soul (Acts 2:42-47; 4:32-34).

The primary way that we express such devotion to the Immaculata is through restoring relationships with others: through gratuitous, stable bonds of love.[219] Saint Paul instructs the Romans to *owe nothing to anyone, except love* (Rom 13:8). In this way, we live as the Communion of Saints. We construct the Church bit by bit so that she will be immaculate. This mystery enables us to remain always in love: Even when others mistreat us or do not love us, we are always able to love. For in human relationships, we are not always already loved in return. But the mystery of the Immaculate Conception teaches us the gratuity inherent in love. The Father does not love us so as to receive in return. Only by experiencing His utter gratuity, His free initiative in loving us, can we learn to take that step with others in broken, human relationships. For this reason, faith is necessary to restore our human relationships.

We no longer expect or demand from others the unconditional love that is possible only from God the Father. Instead, we share it freely with others. In this manner, we recover the lost harmony of paradise. Before the fall, Adam and Even enjoyed *original justice*: the state in which every relationship (between God and man, between man and woman, between man and creation) was *whole, integral, holy.* What does it mean for a relationship to be whole, except for it to be filled with, guided by, and sustained by love? But we face so many relationships where there are violations of love or where love is absent. Drawing from the inexhaustible font of love, we can see those as are opportunities to "put love where there is no love."[220]

All sin is a rupture of communion. We are created not to be isolated (as happens in hell) but to be persons in relationships, with God and with others (as in the Communion of Saints in Heaven). The rupture of communion occurs through the introduction of hatred or negligence into a relationship that ought to exist. Mary, then, is the one who is completely capable of entering into a relationship not only with God but also with others. That she is free of sin means that she has an utter capacity to live in relationship, to live in love with and for others. Her Immaculate Conception reveals the utter gratuity of the Father's love. It is without precedent; He takes the first step. So, too, are we called to love others without precedent, to imitate the Father's love.

The Immaculata displays this love in her attention to the lack of wine at Cana: The couple did not have to ask for help; she already came to their aid. All of Jesus' moral injunctions to love our neighbor have their root in bearing the Father's image: not on the basis of the other's response, but simply loving as He does.

The Immaculata thus teaches us a form of mercy that is capable of forming and sustaining relationships with others. This requires patience, love, and endurance that go beyond doing service to others. It requires a commitment of love. This is what people most need: healthy relationships. Indeed, sin is corrected above all by the reestablishment of relationships in love. We are called to help the sinner above all by providing ourselves, giving of ourselves, giving our time and love.

By sharing Mary's immaculacy, we are to be marked by sensitivity, and tenderness, becoming icons of the merciful love of God. For immaculacy entails living not only in communion with God but also in communion with others. The Immaculate Conception entails openness toward God and neighbor, bearing fruit in concern for harmony with our neighbors, accepting them in love, creating trust and a sense of security — just as a mother does in her home with her children. And what is this, other than extending the peace of Heaven — and of the Immaculate Heart — to earth?

QUESTIONS

- Where you do struggle to put "love where there is no love"?
- How can you unite being *for* others with being *with* others?
- How can you imitate the Immaculata's nearness, sensitivity, and tender compassion in your relationships?

PRAYER

Pray the "Prayer to the Immaculate Conception" (p. 204) and the Litany of the Immaculate Conception (#2 – p. 214).

DAY 34
DIVINE MERCY, DIVINE PROVIDENCE

Immaculata Virginis Mariae Conceptio Sit Nobis Salus et Protectio

In the face of the contemporary culture of death — where other persons' value is based only on their productivity — the Immaculate Conception is an inspiration for defending the dignity of every human person. In the Gospels, Jesus was particularly concerned with those most vulnerable and in need of help. To be devoted to the Immaculate Conception entails not only healing what has already been wounded in others but, even more, defending and protecting from harm the dignity of the unborn, the dying, the crippled, and even the worst of sinners.

Through the prism of the Immaculate Conception, Divine Mercy is revealed not only as forgiveness of sins but also as protection from sin. Adam's first task was to "cultivate and care for" the Garden (Gen 2:15). Because we all have grown up after the fall, we are used to the necessity of asking for forgiveness and healing what is broken. But the Immaculate Conception looks not only to repair what is broken but to protect what is whole and innocent. Adam failed at this task, and so the first problem in the Garden was not merely Eve's talking with the serpent, but also, that the serpent got into the Garden at all.

All of us are called to be like Jesus, the second Adam, willing to offer our lives for our neighbors, to protect them from Satan and from sin. Perhaps not without reason Mary Magdalene mistook the Risen Jesus for a gardener (Jn 20:15). He is a *true gardener,* Who protects what is entrusted to Him. In this sense, we need to remember well that we must be careful about not only sins of commission but of omission. Adam's first sin was omitting to protect and guard the garden — and hence failing to protect Eve and all of us, his children. We are obliged, then, by charity, not only to forgive others and help others when their need is apparent. We have the duty to foster beauty and goodness — both in ourselves and in others. We must remember: Satan is envious of the gift of grace given to us, and he desires to steal it through tempting us to sin. Thus, as St. Peter warns, we are to be on guard against Satan, who prowls "looking for [someone] to devour" (1 Pet 5:8).

Divine Providence, then, as revealed in our Good Shepherd, not only guides us in our lives along the path to Heaven but also protects us from sin and harm. The Immaculate Conception reveals that the Father has always been at work since our conception, not only to heal but to protect us. This love that creates us at conception is present throughout our life. He constantly watches over us, protecting the beauty of our hearts and preserving our innocence from harm, as He did with the Immaculata. We are called to do the same in loving our neighbors: protecting the beauty of their hearts and preserving their innocence from harm.

The Immaculate Conception reminds us that our dignity depends on the free choice by the Father to create us in and for love. The ultimate value of each person depends not on that person's own actions or worth, but on the love of God, Who never stops loving even the worst of sinners. The Immaculate Conception is an impetus for creating a civilization of love, where all human relationships are based on such prevenient love, and mercy takes the form not merely of providing service to others but of enabling them to enter into relationships with God and neighbor, and of finding harmony and happiness in life.

But we can love others in this manner — protecting them, nourishing them, guiding them to beauty, goodness, and the fullness of life — only if we ourselves have first been loved by God the Father in this way. When the Immaculate Conception is little known, then we can live in the illusion that we are loved by God because of what we have done, that somehow we have merited His love. This is a serious obstacle to building and protecting a civilization of love. What ensues is a sort of hypocrisy: covering over who we truly are and pretending to be someone else, so that we can be loved. At its root is a lack of faith in God's prevenient love: a lack of faith that He has chosen to love us on His own, without taking into account our merits or demerits. When that faith is lacking, then we must prove our worth (as we must do in the world), and hypocrisy quickly ensues: a division between who we really are and who we appear to be — to ourselves and others.[221] Humility is truth because there is no disparity between appearance and reality: who we imagine ourselves to be and the truth of who we are.

Hypocrisy signals disbelief in being loved *for who we are,* and belief only in being loved for *what we do*. This leads to *narcissism*, whereby we tend to focus upon ourselves and our own growth, on knowing the right things to say or do in order to "be loved." In the religious context, such hypocrisy is exhibited by using religious practices to cover over weaknesses, problems, or sins, a tendency for which Jesus condemned the Pharisees (Mt 23:1-36). Despite the pious practices, the wounds remain unhealed. Such hypocrisy is unconscious — rarely does a Christian set out to be a Pharisee — but for that reason, it can be all the harder to detect in oneself. In their blindness and denial, hypocrites are psychologically similar to addicts who, because they cannot see themselves clearly or objectively, deny that they are addicted. The danger for those who are entrenched in religion is that, paradoxically, they can use even the good things of God to avoid entering their own pain and areas in need of healing.

Hypocrites or narcissists lack interior surrender to the Holy Spirit; they do not surrender to being loved *as they are*. That belies the work of His grace to heal and love us for who we are. Ironically, the areas we find difficult to love in others are likely to be those areas of our own hearts where we feel unloved or unlovable. Thus, love of neighbor is perhaps the best way to rid ourselves of any hypocrisy: for this is the litmus test of the grace of God at work to love us, and to inspire us to love others.

This problem arises from a subtle division between faith and the everyday reality of one's life. There are, as it were, two tiers of life: the spiritual and the human.[222] For us, consecrating ourselves to the Immaculate Conception, we must face a danger: devotion to the Holy Spirit and the Immaculata may have little or no effect on our human life or relationships. But grace is meant to transform all that we are, not merely provide a new outfit.

An example of this danger has been provided by a questionnaire about humility that was given to a group of Catholics. Most admitted that they were not very humble. They then attended a lecture on humility and were given the same questionnaire again. Their answers now indicated that they had apparently grown in humility. Actually, nothing had actually changed in them to prove that they grew in humility. They simply *felt* humbler because they had learned more about humility. That is a danger in this consecration as well: by reading the book and making the consecration, one may feel more devoted to the Immaculata, or even more desirous of growing in holiness. But actually growing in holiness is quite different: it requires the daily task of eliminating the difference between who we imagine ourselves to be or who we appear to be and who we really are. Loving our neighbor reveals to us how great a gap exists, and so is a good test of how we live this mystery.

The Immaculata, as entirely transformed in the grace of Christ, "is the image of the new man capable of a relationship with God and others, the beginning of the new People of God and the seed of a new humanity."[223] This radical *newness of life* is essential, for otherwise we can still parade our false self under the external regalia of the new self.[224] Our faith and everyday life — as they were for Mary — are to be one piece. To use percentages, this means that the Immaculata was entirely, 100 percent transformed by grace. In union with the Immaculata, we are like the Apostles at Pentecost, recipients of the same Holy Spirit, Who desires to transform each of us 100 percent. This mystery leaves no room for complacency: the Father is not content with His sons' and daughters' being *mostly* healed. In Christ, He desires the *complete* healing and transformation of each sinner. We are called to witness to the fact that we are not merely touched up or patched together (Mk 2:21-22); rather, we are an entirely new creation (Gal 6:15; 2 Cor 5:17), a new man in Christ (Rom 6:4-6; Col 3:10).

Redemption is not about simply repairing what is broken, but rather about dying with Christ to rise to an entirely new life that is immaculate. This complete transformation is most manifest by analogy with the mystery of Transubstantiation, by which the bread and wine are entirely transformed into the Body and Blood of Christ (*Catechism*, 1376). What the Holy Spirit accomplishes in the Eucharist, He desires to accomplish in us: to transform us into His Body, the Church. Participation in the Eucharist is important so that we will not only be Christian in name but, by the Spirit, be transformed into Christ, into His Body. Hence, the priest invokes the Holy Spirit twice in every Eucharistic prayer: both to transform the bread and wine into the Body and Blood of Christ, and to transform us into the mystical Body of Christ, the Church. And that Church — by her very nature — is holy and immaculate, for she is the new creation of the Spirit, Who is at work to make us reflect the model of the Immaculata.

As Catholics, we hear the word *Transubstantiation* in reference to the Eucharist. But St. Maximilian Kolbe speaks of being *transubstantiated* into the Immaculata. What does it mean to be transubstantiated into the Immaculata, if not to be more like her, to imitate her virtues, to become like her in every aspect of our being? Kolbe wrote: "Let us disappear in her! May she alone remain, and we in her, a part of her. … She alone must instruct each one of us at every moment, lead us, transform us into herself, so that we may no longer live, but she may live in us, just as Jesus lives in her and the Father in the Son."[225] The key here is to remember that one can switch between the Holy Spirit and the Immaculata: She lives within us through the Holy Spirit, Who forms in us those attitudes and virtues she possesses, so that we may share her immaculacy.

To be transubstantiated means belonging to her without limits: "We belong to her, to the Immaculate. We are hers without limits, most perfectly hers; we are, as it were, herself ... We have heard of persons who are obsessed, possessed by the devil, through whom the devil thought, spoke, and acted. We want to be possessed in this way, and even more, without limits, by her: may she herself think, speak, and act through us. We want to belong to such an extent to the Immaculate that not only nothing else remains in us that isn't hers, but that we become, as it were, annihilated in her, changed into her, transubstantiated into her, that she alone remains, so that we may be as much hers as she is God's."[226]

She enters into hearts that are open, and in taking "full possession of them, she may give birth to sweet Jesus, who is God, that he might grow in them in age and perfection."[227] By transubstantiation into Mary, we are more intimately united to God the Father. Through her, the created Immaculate Conception, we are more thoroughly united to the uncreated Immaculate Conception. For Mary, through the complete transformation of her entire person by the work of grace, was — using St. Maximilian's analogy — "transubstantiated," as it were, into the Holy Spirit.

The point of transubstantiation into the Immaculata is that our very being becomes conformed ever more into hers — pure, holy, immaculate. Just as the Holy Spirit is capable of transforming the gifts on the altar into Christ, so He is capable of transforming us into Mary. For by becoming like the Immaculata, we are enabled to have Christ formed within us, as He was within her.[228] Such transubstantiation into the Immaculata entails aiming in one's life for a vertex of sanctifying grace, for a maximal point of view in terms of holiness. In other words, the focus of our lives is to give God a full response of love in union with Mary. That is possible only when, like the Immaculata, we participate intimately in the Cross, both through the Eucharist and in our actual life through suffering.[229]

As St. Maximilan Kolbe wrote, "Let us devote ourselves to her completely without any limitation, to be her servants, her children, her unconditional possession and her property, so as to become, somehow, herself living, speaking, acting in this world. … The Immaculata wants to show in us and through us the fullness of her mercy: We do not want to be a hindrance."[230]

QUESTIONS

- How, like Christ the Good Shepherd, do we tend, protect, and guide others?
- How is hypocrisy present in our lives?
- What does it mean for you to be *transubstantiated* into the Immaculata?

PRAYER

Pray the "Prayer to the Immaculate Conception" (p. 204) and the Litany of the Immaculate Conception of Mary, Mother of God (#3 — p. 216).

DAY 35
THE BODY OF CHRIST

Immaculata Virginis Mariae Conceptio Sit Nobis Salus et Protectio

The Immaculata personifies the future glory of the Church, the Bride of Christ. She symbolizes the hope that the Church will one day be resplendent with the beauty of holiness. Revelation 21:9-27 relates the amazing splendor of the New Jerusalem. We need to gaze on the Immaculata, seeing in her our destiny, because it is easy to lose hope. If one watches the news, the Church seems irreparably marred by the sins of her members, including her own priests and bishops. More and more people dissociate themselves from the Church, with all her stains, to be "spiritual" or "nondenominational." Others, seeing the gravity of problems since Vatican II, want to return to the Church of past eras. But we are called to love the Church as she is today. For we love not the idea of the Church, but rather the Church in her living yet sinful members. Moreover, because of the intrinsic connection between the Immaculata and the Church, the more we love Our Lady, the more we love the Church — and vice versa.

The litmus test for our devotion to the Immaculata is our love for the Church, our working and sacrificing ourselves so that she may become immaculate. Blessed George Matulaitis experienced this deep union of love for Mary and for the Church: his zeal for the Church was fueled by his love for the Immaculata. As he wrote in his spiritual journal, copying the words of the Psalmist: "If I forget you, Mother Church, let my right hand wither."[231] Now, Blessed George was not blind to the problems in the Church of his time. In fact, as bishop of Vilnius, he lived amid continual problems. Yet his love for the Church — filled with sinners — was undying and faithful. Just as we profess our devotion to the Immaculata, so, too, we need to express our devotion to the Church — not because she is perfect, but so that, by our love and devotion, she may become perfect and immaculate. Now, the Church is already holy because of Jesus, whose love for her makes her such, and we love her because she is the chosen Bride of Christ. But those dusty corners are the places where our love for the Church moves us to become dishrags that clean her. In other words, our love for the Church participates in Christ's love for the Church, who continuously washes her and cleanses her through His Word and Sacraments (Eph 5:25-27).

As humans, we are fond of constructing buildings. Yet the Temple of Jerusalem, with its glorious splendor, has no stone left (Mk 13:2). Even the cathedrals of Europe, with all their beauty, are often empty. Church growth is often measured by building projects and statistics of Baptisms. Yet God asks in Isaiah (66:1) whether we can build Him a temple. The only temple the Lord approves is the "afflicted" person of "crushed in spirit" who "trembles" at His word (Is 66:2). The temples or cathedrals we are to construct are human hearts, immaculate like the Immaculate Heart of Mary. The living stones of the Church alone last, not the buildings, since there is no temple but God alone in the heavenly Jerusalem (Rev 21:22-27).

The Immaculata is the new Ark of the Covenant. The Father created her as a dwelling place for His Son. Her Immaculate Heart is a temple of the Holy Spirit. Similarly, our devotion to the Holy Spirit is measured by our working so that many hearts open themselves to Him and become temples of His presence. The Church — composed of hearts burning with love for Jesus — is the only enduring temple. For the Church as the Body of Christ is composed of living stones, built on Jesus, her foundation (1 Pet 2:4-6; Eph 2:20). The growth of the Church is judged not by the construction of buildings but by the development of human hearts as temples of the Holy Spirit.[232]

This leads us to a key question: how can the Church of today ever become like Our Lady, resplendent with glory and grace? That chasm is bridged by the intense purification of the Holy Spirit. The beauty of the New Jerusalem is preceded by several chapters of plagues, woes, and catastrophes. However, we have our own part to play, as well, in such cleansing of the Church. Blessed George wrote: "If I may ask, Lord, let me be but a dish rag in your Church, a rag used to wipe up messes and then thrown away into some dark and dirty corner. I want to be used up and worn out in the same way so that your house may be a little cleaner and brighter. And afterwards, let me be thrown away like a dirty, worn-out dish rag."[233]

We may not have large roles to play in renewing the Church. Unlike Blessed George, the majority of us will never be an archbishop.

But like him, we can be a dishrag, able to be used by the Lord wherever He wishes, to clean up some hidden corner of the Church — which may be our family, our parish, or our workplace. This requires humility and a spirit of sacrifice, whereby our love for the Church is stronger than self-love. The key is placing ourselves in the hands of the Lord, allowing Him to use us as He wishes, as Blessed George prayed:

> My God, let me be used in Your vineyard, in Your field as manure, as fertilizer, so that Your harvest would be richer and the fruit more abundant. Let me be despised, used up, and worn out so that Your glory may increase and so that I may be of some use to the growth of Your Church … O God, grant that Your will be done in all things. Here I am, take me and do with me what You will; let me be a docile instrument in Your hands. May Your glory increase, may Your Kingdom grow, may Your will be done! Grant, that as I renounce myself more and more, I may love You more and more.[234]

What does this look like in everyday life? An example may help. The late Br. Leonard Konopka, MIC, told a story of his early years in the Marians. He helped construct the National Shrine of The Divine Mercy. The entirety of the interior is painted, sometimes in places where the human eye cannot see. He shared how, humanly speaking, it "made no difference," but he learned to paint those hidden corners of wood with gold leaf with the same dedication. For God sees all those details, and our work is to please God, not men (Col 3:23, Eph 6:7).

Each of us is entrusted with our little corner of the Church. For many, it may be their homes, families, workplaces, and parishes. For others, it may be larger, through a specific apostolate in the Church. But whatever the size of our corner may be, the task remains the same: to pour ourselves out in self-sacrificial love, so that the Church entrusted to us will be a bit more like the Immaculata. Now, this can be discouraging, particularly when there is a lack of apparent results. Or we may clean up a dusty corner, only to find it dusty again after a few days. Any gardener knows the patience required to continually uproot weeds that persistently return!

In such moments of discouragement, we need our devotion to Our Lady. In her, we see that our efforts will not fail: They will yield results. Adrienne von Speyr, in her writings, indicates that Jesus Himself was strengthened in His Passion to die for sinners by seeing in Our

Lady, the Immaculata, the fruit of His death.[235] So, too, we know that our sacrifices will bear fruit, just as the death of Christ bore fruit in her. Gazing on the Immaculata amid our labors reminds us of the reason for work: We have experienced the tender love of God in her and so want to make that same love present in the Church. In Mary, in her one person, we see the future of the Church.

In gazing on the Immaculata, we find the consolation and support to give ourselves entirely, knowing that our self-gift will never be in vain (Is 49:4). In her, we are assured that our total self-offering will indeed bear fruit in the Church. The Immaculata is the assurance of the efficacy of all our sacrifices and apostolic endeavors, as she was the first fruit of the Paschal Mystery. In her, we gain the loving courage necessary to *give all, without reserve,* in imitation of Christ, who Himself, gazing upon the Immaculata, was also strengthened by her in His Passion.

By gazing on her, we also are reminded that the Church is our mother, and as a mother, she deserves our undying love. The Church is not merely the institution, but the temple of living stones, of living members. Thus, just as loving the Immaculata means loving her person (and not merely ideas or doctrine about Our Lady), so, too, loving the Church means loving the living stones of which she is composed. "Children, let us love not in word or speech but in deed and truth" (1 Jn 3:18). To build and love the Church means to love each of her members, one moment at a time, in our daily life. We build the Church by building relationships — to be with others in the Church, not merely to be for others. Then, we actively work for the Church to grow to be a bit more like the Immaculata and the New Jerusalem of Revelation. And each time we love others, we prove our love to the Immaculata, our mother.

QUESTIONS

- What stains of the Church scandalize you?
- How can you pour forth love, precisely there, to cleanse and sanctify the Church?
- How do you express your responsibility and love for the Church?

PRAYER

Pray the "Prayer to the Immaculate Conception" (p. 204) and the Litany of the Immaculate Conception (#4 — p. 219).

DAY 36
THE GIFT OF GRACE

Immaculata Virginis Mariae Conceptio Sit Nobis Salus et Protectio

The Marians recite proper prayers after evening prayer. One invocation — to our Renovator, Blessed George Matulaitis — petitions that we serve Christ and the Church "after the example of Mary Immaculate and St. Paul the Apostle."[236] Rarely are St. Paul and the Immaculata found mentioned together: Mary is more contemplative, Paul eminently apostolic. Yet, as we know, both were *radically touched* and *healed* by grace: Mary in the moment of her conception, and Paul in his conversion. Both fully received the gift of grace and poured forth that gift in sharing it with others: Mary through her participation in her Son's death and her prayerful presence in the early Church, and St. Paul through his evangelization to the nations.

Saint Paul, the Apostle to the Nations, is an example of how the *gift, fully received,* urges us on in Christ to *fully share it* with all (2 Cor 5:14-21). Such evangelization is not so much an obligation (1 Cor 9:16), but rather the effect of the joy of the Gospel, which leads to sharing with all the gift freely received: "The joy of the gospel fills the hearts and lives of all who encounter Jesus. Those who accept his offer of salvation are set free from sin, sorrow, inner emptiness and loneliness. With Christ joy is constantly born anew."[237] This same joy appears in the parables of the pearl of great price and the treasure hidden in the field (Mt 13:44-46), a joy that outweighs all earthly joy.[238] A characteristic of one devoted to this mystery is the joyful proclamation of the Gospel: sharing joyfully with others the gift received.

Such joy is the effect of the Gospel: of knowing and receiving the eternal love of our Father. But such love is repaid by love alone: whether in active work or in suffering, we are called to give of ourselves in love. There is thus no opposition between contemplation and activity.[239] The two are complementary, like night and day and like sleep and work. Through the lens of *gift,* we glimpse that there is no opposition between prayer and activity. For if in prayer the gift is received, then in activity that same gift is shared. There is no opposition between Martha and Mary, between the Immaculata and St. Paul, between being contemplative and being active. The more one learns to surrender to the Holy Spirit in contemplative prayer, the more one's activity is empowered and guided by Him.

The more He fills one's activity, the more fruit it will bear, for He is the source of all fecundity, since He is the Lord and giver of life. The key, whether in prayer or activity, is collaboration with Him. Only then can we bear abundant fruit (Jn 15:5). Prayer is necessary in learning to cooperate with the interior work of the Spirit so as to cooperate with His external work in the vineyard of the Church for the salvation of souls. Only if the Gospel has truly been *Good News* for us can we proclaim the Gospel of the Kingdom as saving news for others. Gratitude for our own healing and salvation will propel us to tirelessly proclaim the Kingdom and the mystery of the Immaculate Conception. Mary's self-offering with her Son is the mature fruit of the Immaculate Conception: the fullness of love she has received is poured out as the fullness of love for the Father and for us sinners.

Saint Paul was zealous to spread the Gospel because of his own continued experience of God's love. Only when we live in God's love, are convinced of it, and experience it anew each day, can we proclaim it with conviction to others. Then, we speak not as a teacher conveying information but as a witness of His love. The Immaculate Conception confirms that each person finds meaning only in this context of God's gratuitous, merciful love. The Immaculata is thus a sign of hope, encouraging us to trust in this merciful love, which is not merely something but the Person of the Holy Spirit. And she, the Immaculata, is the visible face of this Spirit of love. We, in turn, are called to be visible faces of this love to others, and also to incarnate that love as Jesus did. But even Jesus could do this only in and with the Immaculata.

Saint Maximilian Kolbe is known for his eminently apostolic life, filled with work. But he was also a man of profound prayer and union with the Immaculata, and through her, with the Spirit. Similarly, St. Stanislaus Papczyński was transformed in holiness through his years of hidden contemplation and suffering during the transition from being a Piarist and founding the Marians. He endured much suffering over the course of years, that were similar to a dark night. This transformed the well-known preacher and confessor into a canonized saint. His time of deeper contemplation opened his heart to mystical visions of Purgatory and enabled him to perform the many miracles reported by the faithful in and around Góra Kalwaria. This led him to *greater — not less — activity in the Lord's vineyard.* Apostolic work is not merely being busy with tasks, but seeking the salvation of souls in union with the Holy Spirit, in obedience to the Father's will.

Like John, we learn to stand next to Christ Crucified with the Immaculata. With her, we are washed anew by His Blood and Water. Having remained with Mary in prayer, like the disciples until the descent of the Spirit at Pentecost, we can each be sent forth and proclaim the Risen Lord. Only when the instruction of the Lord to stay in Jerusalem for those nine full days (Acts 1:4) has been obeyed can we be disposed to receive the fullness of the Spirit. For Christ called His apostles first to be with Him and only then to be sent out (Mk 3:14). This is the proper order, since no one sends himself into the world to accomplish his own tasks. Rather, we wait for the Lord to send us forth — from contemplative adoration to apostolic work. Otherwise, we are like soldiers running off into battle but without yet knowing our mission.

The transition from love *received* to love *shared* is not merely a moral commandment that requires more effort in making sacrifices. Becoming an *oblatio* does not mean simply gritting one's teeth. Rather, an *oblatio* includes all that has come before: praise, gratitude, and joy leading one to a total gift of self in love. But this requires allowing one's "I" to be absorbed into that of Christ (Gal 2:20). "Only by letting ourselves be repeatedly cleansed, 'made pure', by the Lord himself can we learn to act as he did, in union with him."[240] Only by being immersed daily in His mercy can our hearts be transformed and rendered capable of sharing that same mercy with others.

Our consecration does not end with ourselves. Rather, we are to kindle this love for the Immaculata in the hearts of all, so that all — individually and together — burn with such love. For Jesus Himself came to "set the earth on fire" (Lk 12:49). The goal is for all of creation to be enveloped in, imbued with the love of God — the Holy Spirit — and so impelled by the Spirit to return to the Father with that very same love with which He first loved us. Remember, the essence of *oblatio* is not suffering, not pain, but self-giving love. For the Trinity exists in this mode of self-giving, and to enter into Heaven requires us to participate in that mode of self-giving love. This is the inner logic behind Jesus' requirement that we lose our life in order to gain it: We possess only what we give to another in love (Mt 10:39).

We anticipate losing our life by becoming entirely hers, handing over the rights of ourselves — and of our lives — to her. "And then we are hers, of the Immaculata, hers without limits, most perfectly hers; we are almost herself."[241] Total consecration to the Immaculata entails consciously, willingly, deliberately, and unconditionally cooperating with her.[242] Saint Maximilian "resolved to let [himself] be guided always by her, anywhere and in everything, and thereby return unceasingly to peace and to love."[243]

Those who have consecrated themselves "will strive, above all, to consolidate their will with that of the Immaculata, or rather to love her as ardently as possible and then to light this fire around themselves, each according to their means." [244] If this is accomplished, then the Immaculata will become "the Queen of the whole world and of each person individually." [245] Saint Maximilian wanted not only himself but all persons to know the Immaculata:

> Immaculate, Queen of Heaven and earth, I know I am unworthy to approach you, to fall on my knees before you with my face to the ground, but because I love you so much, I dare beg you to be good enough to deign to tell me who you are. For I wish to know you more and more, endlessly more, and love you more and more ardently, with boundless zeal. Also, I wish to reveal to other souls who you are, that an ever increasing number of souls may know you ever more perfectly and love you ever more ardently, so that you become the Queen of all the hearts that beat and will beat on earth at any time, and that as soon as possible, as soon as possible.[246]

QUESTIONS

- How do you balance receptivity — imitating our Lady — with activity — imitating St. Paul?
- Do you experience joy in evangelizing or sharing the Good News about Jesus?
- How do you reveal the love of God, Whose maternal face is that of Mary?

PRAYER

Pray the "Prayer to the Immaculate Conception" (p. 204) and the Litany of the Blessed Virgin Mary, Immaculately Conceived (#1 — p. 212).

DAY 37
AN *OBLATIO* FOR THE CHURCH

Immaculata Virginis Mariae Conceptio Sit Nobis Salus et Protectio

In order to make the Church immaculate, Jesus chose to suffer and to die on the Cross. For without the purifying love and fire of the Holy Spirit, apostolic work and the sweat of hard labor are incapable of making the Church immaculate. As St. Faustina wrote, "O my Jesus, I know that, in order to be useful to souls, one has to strive for the closest possible union with You, who are Eternal love. One word from a soul united to God effects more good in souls than eloquent discussions and sermons from an imperfect soul" (*Diary*, 1595). Jesus instructed her, **"You will save more souls through prayer and suffering than will a missionary through his teachings and sermons alone"** (*Diary*, 1767). This goal — making the Church immaculate — needs to be kept in mind with all apostolic endeavors: for it is the same goal for which Christ died on the Cross. The *only* way for the Church to be made immaculate is to participate in the one way Jesus accomplished this (Eph 5:24ff): to wash the Church in the bath of our own blood.

For only the Precious Blood has the power to "cleanse our conscience" (Heb 9:14) and make the Church immaculate, precisely because it has, so to speak, been fully oxygenated by the Holy Spirit, by love.[247] We need, then, not only to actively work to build relationships and so build the Church. We need also to imitate Our Lady and participate in the Passion of Jesus. Indeed, in the Old Testament, the word "immaculate" was largely used in the context of liturgical norms for animal sacrifices. While we no longer need to offer unblemished lambs in sacrifice, we offer the one unblemished Lamb in the Eucharist. Having been washed in Baptism and Confession, we are invited to offer ourselves with Him as an *oblatio* for the Church.

Hebrew *tāmîm*, "immaculate," describes either physical perfection (i.e., a spotless animal or complete, physical beauty) or moral perfection (a blameless or innocent person). The word appears often in Leviticus,

Numbers, and Ezekiel: Both the animals offered as sacrifices and the priest who offers them must be *tāmîm* (Lev 22:20, 21:16; Dt 15:21). This requirement is fulfilled in the perfect moral blamelessness of Christ, which enables Him to be the eternal High Priest (Heb 4:15, 7:26, 9:14). Jesus is also the immaculate victim,[248] capable of offering Himself in a *pure sacrifice of love* to the Father for our healing and salvation. For us to participate in Jesus' sacrificial worship of the Father, we too must fulfill this requirement.[249]

Today, purity is often associated with morality, particularly in terms of sexual purity. However, in the Jewish mind set, purity was associated with divine worship. Objects, persons, and animals were purified and restored to their whole or unblemished state, and the animals to be sacrificed were to be immaculate. Only then could they be fit to enter God's presence in divine worship. This connection is perhaps clearest in the need for Confession before reception of the Eucharist: Purity is not merely a moral requirement, but a need for proper participation in the liturgy and divine worship.

As we have seen earlier, such purification is a necessary preparation for consecration. When Jesus petitions the Father, "Consecrate them in the truth" (Jn 17:17), He is asking the Father not only to make us holy but to render us "fit for divine worship."[250] To be fit to render worship to God, we must be immersed in the cleansing bath of Jesus' truth. This is Jesus pouring forth *His love to the point of death* (Jn 13:1;15:13). Jesus' purifying Word is more than a human word. His word is the truth, the reality, of His self given in love (Jn 14:6).

This love *unto death* is symbolized by the precious Blood (Rom 5:9; 3:25; Eph 1:7.) that washes the Church clean of every stain and that preserved Mary from all sin. The difference between the Immaculata and the rest of sinful humanity is how the Holy Spirit sanctifies us. The Holy Spirit preserved Mary from all sin at the moment of her conception, whereas He cleanses us from all sin at Baptism. But all purification and sanctification, as well as Mary's preservation from sin, flow from the gift of the Spirit coming forth from the pierced side of Jesus (Jn 19:34).[251] The Passion of Christ reached its full effect in Mary from the first moment of her existence; through her intercession, we too can allow His Passion to reach its full effect in cleansing us of all sin. The manner is different, but the goal is the same: to render the Church immaculate and so capable of worshipping the Father in "Spirit and truth" (Jn 4:23).

To make the mystery of the Immaculate Conception present and active in the Church, we are called to imitate Jesus: to be capable of being crucified, with our hearts pierced, so as to give all we have, and in doing so, to give the Holy Spirit anew to the Church *through our own self-giving unto death* so that she may be holy, immaculate, "without spot or wrinkle" (Eph 5:25-27; Rev 21:2).[252]

Mary exemplifies full participation — receptive and active — through her cooperation in the Paschal Mystery. Both St. Peter (1 Pet 4:13) and St. Paul (Col 1:24) write of suffering as participation in this mystery, to complete it and make it present at each stage of the Church's pilgrimage throughout history. Blessed George Matulaitis speaks of the efficacy of such suffering, even in the absence of any apostolic work: "If you are seriously ill and bedridden, do not worry that you cannot work. You already have something to do — to bear the pain and discomfort of your illness patiently and peacefully ... Suffering in the spirit of Christ is very worthwhile. Our Savior never accomplished so much as when he appeared to be doing nothing — on the cross."[253]

If the mystery of the Immaculate Conception were oriented solely toward our own healing, then it could easily lead us to be self-centered and self-preoccupied. The goal of such healing purification is divine worship. Now, this does not mean attending liturgical services the entire day. Rather, by restoring us to full health and wholeness, the Father desires us to live a life of sacrificial, self-giving, gratuitous love. He created us *in love* for the sake of our learning to love *as He loves.* Like the Son, we are loved so much by the Father that we not only receive His love but are made *capable of loving as He does.* Only then are we truly His sons and daughters.

This is *true health*: love *in imitation of Jesus.* Healing thus restores our capacity first to receive love: and when we fully, deeply receive His love, we are made capable of giving love. As with ordinary breath, we are called both to *inhale* His breath of love and then to *exhale* it around us, on all we meet, through sacrifice — making holiness, by breathing forth the Spirit. All true, authentic sacrifice is oriented toward this sharing of love; hence Jesus quotes Hosea: "For it is loyalty that I desire, not sacrifice" (Hos 6:6). God Himself does not need ritual sacrifice. Rather, the sacrifice He desires is that of pouring forth the love we have received from Him to those who do not know or do not have that love. We can never fully repay Him for the love that He gives us. Rather, we can in a sense "repay" Him only by sharing that love with those who most need it. Jesus offers His parable on the Last Judgment: that we are judged primarily on our self-giving love for others, that is, our pouring forth of His love as He has poured it forth upon us — without measure, freely, and gratuitously (Mt 25:31-46).

The Immaculata reveals this reciprocity of fully receiving and fully giving love. We are able to give only in the manner and in the measure with which we have received: if we receive partially, we can give partially. If we receive fully, then we can share fully. Mary, who received the overflowing abundance of love, fully shared that love by suffering with her Son during His Passion and through her continued life of sacrificial love during the first generation of the Church.

For that reason, the goal of this consecration is to imitate St. Stanislaus Papczyński in his oblation. The English derives from the Latin *oblatio,* "offering, sacrifice, offering of the Eucharistic elements." Hence, the definition is: "the act of making a religious offering," and more specifically, "the act of offering the Eucharistic elements to God." An oblation is "something offered in worship or devotion."[254] Saint Stanislaus, in referring to his self-offering as an *oblatio* connects his total self-giving with that of Christ in the Eucharist, so that he may become, with Christ, a sacrificial offering to the Father. But who has associated herself more to the sacrifice of Christ than the Immaculata?

This mystery then leads to what is called the "co-redemption" — Mary's unique, intimate participation in the one sacrifice of Christ, to "make up [together with St. Paul] what is lacking in the sufferings of Christ" (Col 1:24). The goal of this mystery is to ensure the capacity to live in self-giving, sacrificial love for the Church. That is a paradoxical image of health: the capacity to give of oneself, like Christ, upon the Cross!

QUESTIONS

- How do you imagine health and healing connected with self-giving love in your life?
- How do you find yourself associated with the oblation of Christ in daily life?
- How does the Liturgy of the Mass extend into daily worship?

PRAYER

Pray the "Prayer to the Immaculate Conception" (p. 204) and the Litany of the Immaculate Conception (#2 — p. 214).

DAY 38
PLEASING FRAGRANCE

Immaculata Virginis Mariae Conceptio Sit Nobis Salus et Protectio

The Immaculate Conception reveals the gift of the Father's prevenient love for us at the beginning of our existence. The fulfillment of this mystery is in being drawn into the Immaculata's gift of love to the Father in union with Jesus. Saints — like St. Stanislaus and St. Maximilian — provide examples of offering oneself as a spiritual holocaust of pleasing fragrance to the Father. As Jesus instructed St. Faustina:

> **My child, you please Me most by suffering. In your physical as well as your mental sufferings, My daughter, do not seek sympathy from creatures. I want the fragrance of your suffering to be pure and unadulterated. I want you to detach yourself, not only from creatures, but also from yourself. My daughter, I want to delight in the love of your heart, a pure love, virginal, unblemished, untarnished. The more you will come to love suffering, My daughter, the purer your love for Me will be** (*Diary*, 279).

Now, Jesus Himself sought comfort from His Apostles during His Agony (Mt 26:37). Jesus' instruction to St. Faustina highlights the need to seek comfort in our pain *according to His will.* One translation of "Paraclete" is "Comforter," for the Holy Spirit *comforts us in all our afflictions* (2 Cor 1:4). Jesus emphasizes the need to remember that Satan proposes apparent remedies that assuage pain temporarily, but which lead to greater spiritual harm. Our pain and suffering is sacred to our heavenly Father, who desires to embrace it as a fragrant offering of incense that is consumed by the fire of our love. But we must be careful not to adulterate our suffering with worldly comforts that lead to rancid odors. If our *oblatio* is to be immaculate, then the fragrance must be unadulterated, that is, one of pure love: "virginal, unblemished, untarnished." *This* is the kind of love that is pleasing to the Father, the love manifested by Jesus and Mary at Calvary in their self-offering for our salvation.

As stated previously in regard to sacrifice, this *oblatio* may not look glorious on a daily basis. As a Dominican explained to us in seminary, ecstasy comes from the Greek *ek-stasis* — "to stand outside" — in this case, to stand outside oneself. While ecstasy is often associated with a state of bliss, actual ecstasy in the Christian sense means loving another and so going forth from oneself to be with another. Hence, a mother who is changing her baby's diaper at 2 a.m. is in "ecstasy" — standing outside her own wants and needs, to attend to those of her baby. *Oblatio* in daily life is a bit like ecstasy: a quiet, hidden, but continuous self-offering in the monotony of daily duties and burdens. As one theologian (Father Jean-Baptiste Lacordaire) wrote: "The martyrs had already immolated themselves a hundred times in their hearts before they were sacrificed in reality."[255] Martyrdom is the fruit of a multitude of hidden sacrifices that the Father "who sees in secret" notices and rewards (Mt 6:6).

Saint Faustina uses a beautiful but simple image to describe this reality. While the exterior remains the same, the interior is radically transformed — just as in the Eucharist. Hence, St. Faustina describes herself as a host: "Jesus, hide me; just as You have hidden Yourself under the form of the white Host, so hide me from human eyes, and particularly hide the gifts which You so kindly grant me. May I not betray outwardly what You are effecting in my soul. I am a white host before You, O Divine Priest. Consecrate me Yourself, and may my transubstantiation be known only to You. I stand before You each day as a sacrificial host and implore Your mercy upon the world. In silence, and unseen, I will empty myself before You; my pure and undivided love will burn, in profound silence, as a holocaust. And may the fragrance of my love be wafted to the foot of Your throne. You are the Lord of lords, but You delight in innocent and humble souls" (*Diary*, 1564).

In the Mass, the appearance of bread and wine remains after the consecration. Under a microscope, everything would look the same. But by faith, we know that everything is now different, for what looks like bread and wine is actually the Body and Blood of Christ. Similarly, the Holy Spirit leaves the outward appearance of our lives, but He transforms the interior, what is unseen, so that it is love.

The Immaculate Conception serves as the foundation of Mary's role as "co-redemptrix." While that title is controversial among theologians, its meaning remains true: She participated in a unique way in the sacrifice of Christ at Calvary. By her offering of herself in union with Jesus, the unmerited gift of her Immaculate Conception becomes in turn a gift for all. At Calvary, she now participates actively in sharing what she first received.[256] The Immaculata is the pattern for all Christians. Having been washed and cleansed of sin through a pure gift of salvation from the Father in Christ (Eph 2:8), Christians are to share with others this same gift, making it available through their own self-sacrifice in imitation of Jesus (1 Jn 4:11-12).

Saint Rafael Arnaiz (1911-1938), a Trappist oblate who had to leave the monastery three times and died shortly after entering for the fourth time, stated that the best of all devotions is the Cross. For him, as for St. John of the Cross, the Cross is the place of being fully consumed by love: of both receiving love and responding fully with love.[257] Any devotion that does not lead to this consummation of love is not authentic, and even this consecration loses its value if it leads away from this best of all devotions.[258] Hence, this consecration leads us to *oblatio:* to placing ourselves before the Father, in imitation of the Immaculata beside her Son, as immaculate victims for the salvation of souls. For the essence of this mystery is the self-giving love that is the Person of the Holy Spirit, Whose visible face is the Immaculata.

Only by *oblatio* are we truly immaculate: not only because we have no stain of sin but because we positively are filled with love. Saint John Chrysostom observes that by practicing charity we become irreproachable, immaculate before our God and Father. "It is charity, it is love, which makes us blameless." [259] But this charity is not purely human affection, by which we love one person but show indifference to others. Charity has no such restrictions but embraces all. Saint John Chrysostom continues: "Good land does something more than give back the grain put into it; and therefore the soul should not limit itself to doing what is laid down, but should go further [...]. Two things make for virtue — avoiding evil and doing good. Fleeing from evil is not the be-all of virtue; it is the beginning of the path that leads to virtue. One needs, in addition, to have an ardent desire to be good and to do good."[260]

The total self-gift in love is the essence of this mystery: God, Who gives of Himself in the Holy Spirit to Mary, enables her to make a complete gift of herself in turn through union with Christ. In a similar manner, each baptized Christian, having received more fully each day the self-gift of the Holy Spirit, is enabled by Him to imitate the

Immaculata in the total gift of self for Christ and the Church. In so doing, we make the Church immaculate.

By standing daily with Mary at the Cross, we stand with her beneath the Blood and Water, allowing Jesus to cleanse us of all sin: "On the other hand, man cannot live by oblative, descending love alone. He cannot always give, he must also receive. Anyone who wishes to give love must also receive love as a gift. Certainly, as the Lord tells us, one can become a source from which rivers of living water flow (cf. Jn 7:37-38). Yet to become such a source, one must constantly drink anew from the original source, which is Jesus Christ, from whose pierced heart flows the love of God (cf. Jn 19:34)."[261] We are called to offer ourselves — with Christ — as an *oblatio* to cleanse others of sin, living Jesus' words: "This is my body, my blood." At Mass, we are to unite ourselves with Christ — like the Immaculata — for the sake of the Church (Eph 5:25-27).

Christians both as a whole and individually are the temple of the Holy Spirit (*Catechism*, 797-798).[262] Christians ought to be pure *constantly*, for they are constantly in the presence of God, the Holy Spirit Who dwells within. Our worship should never cease, for we are a "holy priesthood" enabled to make spiritual sacrifices pleasing to God (1 Pet 2:5 and *Catechism*, 1324).[263] Such spiritual worship is centered on the self-offering of Jesus, Who died for our sins and was "raised for our justification" (Rom 4:25). Our spiritual worship through sacrifices entails offering ourselves in union with Christ to the Father (*Catechism*, 1368).[264] This worship extends beyond the Mass, for we are to present our bodies "as a living sacrifice, holy and pleasing to God" (Rom 12:1). This entails an entire life of self-giving love, which is true worship of the Father (Jn 13:34; worship in spirit and truth).

Jesus' immaculate self-offering, in communion with Mary, enables Him to communicate the Holy Spirit to "all flesh" (Joel 3:1; Acts 2:17). By union with Jesus' one sacrifice, we participate in communicating this gift of the Spirit to others. The fruit, then, for us living the mystery of the Immaculate Conception is to cooperate with the Holy Spirit, so that He can bring to completion the redemptive work of Christ in the Church and the world.

QUESTIONS

- How do you work and suffer to complete the work of Christ?
- How can you live self-giving love — ecstasy — as the essence of this mystery?
- What kind of human comforts do you seek and how can you seek the divine comfort of the Spirit?

PRAYER

Pray the "Prayer to the Immaculate Conception" (p. 204) and the Litany of the Immaculate Conception of Mary, Mother of God (#3 — p. 216).

DAY 39
IMMACULATE CONCEPTION

Immaculata Virginis Mariae Conceptio Sit Nobis Salus et Protectio

All Marian devotion — including the Immaculate Conception — leads to the Eucharist. Just as the Immaculate Conception prepared Mary to receive the Son in the Incarnation, so it leads us to receive Him in the Eucharist. For by our entrusting of ourselves to the Immaculata, she leads us to the pierced side of her Son at Calvary. She leads us, as it were, to stand beneath the rays of the Divine Mercy Image. Through us, she wants to lead others to these same rays of mercy that pour forth from the Eucharist (*Diary*, 336, 344, 657).

In order for Jesus to return, the bride must be immaculate, like Mary. Just as Jesus came by way of Mary, so He will return by way of Mary. Purification, as stated above, has to do with being able to enter into the presence of God. Immaculacy of heart enables us to stand before the Son of Man when He returns, just as Mary "stood" by her Son at Calvary (Lk 21:36; Jn 19:25). We end this consecration, then, by preparing for the coming of Jesus: His Real Presence in the Eucharist and His Second Coming, Parousia. Are we ready for judgment? Are we waiting, ready for His coming?

This Sacrament makes the entire event of Calvary present to us. By His death, Jesus "offered himself unblemished to God" so as to "cleanse our consciences" from sin, making us likewise unblemished to serve the living God (Heb 9:14). Washed in Baptism, cleansed anew through Confession, and united to Him in the Eucharist, Jesus presents Christians to the Father as "holy without blemish, and irreproachable before him" (Col 1:22). Growing in immaculacy of heart requires, at a minimum, Sunday (if not daily) participation in the Eucharist, for in this Sacrament, He offers Himself to the Father so that we may be blameless and unblemished.

In this manner, as Christians we fulfill St. Peter's injunction to make every effort to remain "without spot or blemish" in Christ as we await the Day of the Lord (2 Pet 3:14). That Day is the summit of love — the union of human and divine love. It is the Second Coming, the consummation of the marriage banquet. This is the vertex of love, whereby love received is fully returned: The Church will return the love of her Bridegroom. Then, the "great mystery" (Eph 5:32) of the marriage of Christ and the Church will be complete.

But not only are we to be ready for that day, but we are to be "unblemished and exultant, in the presence of his glory" (Jude 24). That may seem like an impossible task, but remember that it is God who "is able to keep you from stumbling and to present you unblemished" (Jude 24). By continual praise — by living a doxological spirituality — we are able to advance confidently toward that final day of encounter with Jesus in His Second Coming, just as we joyfully approach Him in the Eucharist each day. Making use of the Sacrament of Reconciliation enables us to live that spirituality of praise, for even there we confess — profess — not only our sins, but above all, His abundant mercy. In this way, we anticipate the Day of Judgment: we already endure the weight of His justice by the voluntarily admission of our sins and so receive merciful pardon in response.

Immaculacy is our direct preparation for the Second Coming. An immaculate heart is one that is actively waiting for and preparing for the definitive coming of the Kingdom. Such a vigilant heart is necessary, as Jesus states that we must not be caught up in the worries and trials of life (Lk 21:34). It is far too easy to become content, somnolent, and stupefied by this world. Indeed, St. Peter described the attitude of some who scoffed at the idea of the Second Coming, stating that everything was continuing in the world as it had been for centuries. Such scoffers are still present, and they live as if the Judge will never come (2 Pet 3:3-6)!

An immaculate heart is zealous in imitating our Father, Who is blameless in His ways and perfect in His love. Like a bride awaiting her bridegroom, we are zealous to be ready to meet Christ. The saints witness to this: They strove to be freed from all sin throughout their life and looked forward to their death, not dourly, but as the precise moment when they would be able to definitively enter into the Kingdom of Heaven. There is no better way to await that terrible but great day than by remaining with Our Lady. But this entails the daily practice of inviting Our Lady to help us prepare for each Holy Communion, so that we may receive Him as she did in the Incarnation. She helps us to receive the fullness of His love in Holy Communion, so that we can also return the fullness of love to Him. But not only are we concerned about our own hearts; we are to prepare as many hearts as possible to be immaculate, ready, waiting, eager for Jesus to come: Both in the Eucharist and in the Second Coming. For Jesus wants to come, not to punish, but to be received by the hearts of many, as Mary received Him so generously and warmly.

Only in the Eucharist, then, is this mystery complete: for there, the vertex of love is consummated already in a Sacrament; there, the bride meets the Bridegroom; there, like the Immaculata, we receive Jesus when He comes. But in the Eucharist, we are not merely passive but also active participants, offering ourselves, with Mary, in the self-offering of Christ. In so doing, we prepare ourselves, our families, and the Church for the final coming of Christ. And that is where we end the consecration: in living every day more profoundly the mystery of the Immaculate Conception in and through the Sacrament of the Eucharist. There, we receive mercy, and we commit ourselves anew to sharing that same mercy with others, particularly with the poor, with sinners, with the neglected.

Now, when or how does our consecration take place? As the priest consecrates the Eucharist, he invokes the Holy Spirit on the bread and wine. After we proclaim the mystery of faith, he then invokes that same Spirit on us, to become the Body of Christ, an offering pleasing to the Father. There, we are consecrated with Christ in His oblation to the Father. But remember: Christ did not offer Himself to the Father without the Immaculata, and His sacrifice was consumed, consecrated by the Spirit.

So, too, the heart of this consecration is not the formula of prayer that follows, but rather the Sacrament of the Eucharist itself, and our deepened participation in it. For we often focus on participation as a matter of what we are doing at Mass. But our activity at Mass ought to be a deeper, more intimate union with Jesus in His self-offering to the Father, in imitation of the Immaculata. The prayer that follows, then, is an aid to this central moment of Mass. It is, as it were, an additional — silent — prayer for the moment of the Offertory, when we place ourselves on the paten with the bread, when we pour ourselves into the chalice with the wine.

This prayer is to help us live the consecration of Mass more deeply, not just today on December 8, but each day. For this consecration has as its goal living this oblation each day. There, we are made anew unblemished by Christ, and there, we offer ourselves with Him for the Church to be made unblemished.

I, (name), surrender every aspect of my being to the Holy Spirit through the hands of the Immaculata: my interior — heart, soul, intellect, memory, will, emotions, mind, spirit — and my exterior: my body, possessions, activities, and reputation. I surrender anything else I am or possess, leaving absolutely nothing for myself. Even when I want to hold onto something as my own, I now surrender it to You, asking You without reserve to take dominion over all I am. Imbue every aspect of my being, my life, with Your grace and love.

Holy Spirit, make me ever more like the Immaculata; transubstantiate me into her living image: free of all sin, even the smallest, and overflowing with Your grace and love. Make of me a saint, an icon, your Pneumatophore. *Purify me of everything that is not of You. Indicate the path of penance I must walk, and strengthen me in the spiritual battle. Deepen my prayer, so that I may be consumed and transformed by You, the living flame of love.*

Holy Spirit, thank You for loving me and pouring forth Your love into my heart. Make of me an oblation, a holocaust of love, so that I may return Your love with love. Consume me in Your spiritual fire, in union with Jesus and the Immaculata, so that I may be an unblemished, immaculate oblation pleasing to the Heavenly Father.

Holy Spirit, prepare me, as You prepared the Immaculata, to receive Jesus when He comes — in the Eucharist, in my neighbor, and at the Second Coming. Make use of me, of my life, as You wish, so that the Church may be immaculate, purified, and ready for the Second Coming. Help me to be not only for others but with others, so that together, with one voice, we may fulfill Scripture:

The Spirit and the bride say, "Come." Amen! Come, Lord Jesus!

DAY 40
EPILOGUE

Where do we go from here?

Like the liturgical year, which revisits the same mysteries of our faith, we find ourselves going in a circular direction. But, we hope, it is not merely circular, but spiral: for each time we revisit the same mysteries of our faith, we enter a bit more deeply into their reality. My hope is that this consecration pushes you a bit further along the spiral of living our faith. For we are never done — in this life — with growth in holiness, purification, prayer, living in praise, and oblation.

Just as a tailor works to make a suit so that it can be worn, this consecration is "over" in one sense, but now it is to be lived, to be shared, and to be deepened. I would encourage you, then, to continue in this spiral growth through joining the Association of Marian Helpers (MICPrayers.org), which is the equivalent of a third order of the Marians of the Immaculate Conception. If you desire a more intense association with Marian spirituality, you can also join the Confraternity of the Immaculate Conception. You can find information on how to join in the last pages of the book.

Philo, a Jewish philosopher who lived in Egypt around the time of Christ, describes virtues as "faultless" or immaculate victims that are offered in sacrifice to God.[265] Our devotion to the Immaculata is proved by our imitating her evangelical virtues, which we offer as an *oblatio*, a sacrifice of "faultless victims" in worship to the Father. Ever striving to grow in virtue in daily life is part of this *oblatio*.[266] A daily practice, already touched upon during this consecration, which you can take up to honor her Immaculate Conception, is the recitation of the Chaplet of the Ten Evangelical Virtues.

May the Immaculate Conception — both the Holy Spirit and the Immaculata — help you to wear with dignity your white baptismal garment until you appear — shining in spotless splendor — among the saints in Heaven!

APPENDIX I
CONSECRATION SCHEDULE

You can use this consecration in preparation for any major Marian feast day, most of which are listed below. The first date is the consecration date, which is "day 39", so the starting date is 38 days before the consecration date.

SOLEMNITY	CONSECRATION DATE	STARTING DATE
Mary, Mother of God	**January 1**	November 24
Presentation of the Lord	**February 2**	December 26
Our Lady of Lourdes	**February 11**	January 4
The Annunciation	**March 25**	February 16 (leap year) or 15 (non-leap year)
Our Lady of Fatima	**May 13**	April 5
The Visitation	**May 31**	April 23
Our Lady of Mount Carmel	**July 16**	June 8
The Assumption	**August 15**	July 8
The Queenship of Mary	**August 22**	July 15
The Nativity of Mary	**September 8**	August 1
Our Lady of Sorrows	**September 15**	August 8
Our Lady of the Rosary	**October 7**	August 30
Mary, Mother of Mercy	**November 16**	October 9
Immaculate Conception	**December 8**	October 31

APPENDIX II
PRAYERS

Prayer to the Immaculate Conception by Pope St. John Paul II

Immaculate Conception, Mary, my Mother.
Live in me. Act in me. Speak in and through me.
Think your thoughts in my mind. Love through my heart.
Give me your dispositions and feelings.
Teach, lead, and guide me to Jesus.
Correct, enlighten, and expand my thoughts and behavior.
Possess my soul. Take over my entire personality and life.
Replace it with yourself.
Incline me to constant adoration and thanksgiving.
Pray in me and through me.
Let me live in you and keep me in this union always.[267]

Prayer to the Queen of Heaven and Earth

O Glorious Queen of Heaven and earth, Virgin Most Powerful, you who have the power to crush the head of the ancient serpent with your heel, come and exercise this power flowing from the grace of your Immaculate Conception. Shield us under the mantle of your purity and love, draw us into the sweet abode of your heart, and annihilate and render impotent the forces bent on destroying us. Come, Queen of the Holy Angels and of the Most Holy Rosary, you who from the very beginning have received from God the power and the mission to crush the head of Satan. We humbly beseech you, send forth your holy legions, that under your command and by your power, they pursue the evil spirits, encounter them on every side, resist their bold attacks, and drive them far from us, harming no one on the way, binding them immobile to the foot of the Cross to be judged and sentenced by Him as He wills. Amen.

LITANIES

The purpose of praying these litanies is to aid us in gazing upon the Holy Spirit and the Immaculata. Each of the invocations is like a facet of the diamond, through which we see a bit more the beauty of the diamond itself. Take your time in reciting the litanies, allowing the invocations to enter your mind and remain in your heart. Notice if there are particular titles or petitions that stir up certain emotions. Pray over those, carry them in your heart throughout the day, in imitation of Our Lady herself who "kept all these things, reflecting on them in her heart" (Lk 2:19).

Litany to the Holy Spirit

Lord, have mercy on us. *Lord, have mercy on us.*
Christ, have mercy on us. *Christ, have mercy on us.*
Lord, have mercy on us. *Lord, have mercy on us.*

God the Father of Heaven, *Have mercy on us.*
God the Son, Redeemer of the world, *Have mercy on us.*
God the Holy Spirit, *Have mercy on us.*
Holy Trinity, One God, *Have mercy on us.*
Divine Essence, one true God, *Have mercy on us.*
Spirit of truth and wisdom, *Have mercy on us.*
Spirit of holiness and justice, *Have mercy on us.*
Spirit of understanding and counsel, *Have mercy on us.*
Spirit of love and joy, *Have mercy on us.*
Spirit of peace and patience, *Have mercy on us.*
Spirit of longanimity and meekness, *Have mercy on us.*
Spirit of benignity and goodness, *Have mercy on us.*
Love substantial of the Father and the Son, *Have mercy on us.*
Love and life of saintly souls, *Have mercy on us.*
Fire ever burning, *Have mercy on us.*
Living water to quench the thirst of hearts, *Have mercy on us.*

From all evil, *Deliver us, O Holy Spirit.*
From all impurity of soul and body, *Deliver us, O Holy Spirit.*
From all gluttony and sensuality, *Deliver us, O Holy Spirit.*
From all attachments to
the things of the earth, *Deliver us, O Holy Spirit.*
From all hypocrisy and pretense, *Deliver us, O Holy Spirit.*
From all imperfections and deliberate faults, *Deliver us, O Holy Spirit.*
From our own will, *Deliver us, O Holy Spirit.*
From slander, *Deliver us, O Holy Spirit.*
From deceiving our neighbors, *Deliver us, O Holy Spirit.*
From our passions and disorderly appetites, *Deliver us, O Holy Spirit.*
From our inattentiveness to
Thy holy inspirations, *Deliver us, O Holy Spirit.*
From despising little things, *Deliver us, O Holy Spirit.*
From debauchery and malice, *Deliver us, O Holy Spirit.*
From love of comfort and luxury, *Deliver us, O Holy Spirit.*
From wishing to seek or desire anything
other than Thee, *Deliver us, O Holy Spirit.*
From everything that displeases Thee, *Deliver us, O Holy Spirit.*

Most loving Father, *Forgive us.*
Divine Word, *Have pity on us.*

Holy and divine Spirit, *Leave us not until we are in possession of the Divine Essence, Heaven of heavens.*

Lamb of God, Who takest away the sins of the world,
Send us the divine Consoler.

Lamb of God, Who takest away the sins of the world,
Fill us with the gifts of Thy Spirit.

Lamb of God, Who takest away the sins of the world,
Make the fruits of the Holy Spirit increase within us.

Come, O Holy Spirit, fill the hearts of Thy faithful,
And enkindle in them the fire of Thy love.

Send forth Thy Spirit and they shall be created,
And Thou shalt renew the face of the earth.

Let us Pray.

O God, Who by the light of the Holy Spirit instructed the hearts of the faithful, grant us by the same Spirit to be truly wise and ever to rejoice in His consolation. Through Jesus Christ Our Lord, Amen.[268]

2

Litany of the Holy Spirit

Lord, have mercy on us. *Lord, have mercy on us.*
Christ, have mercy on us. *Christ, have mercy on us.*
Lord, have mercy on us. *Lord, have mercy on us.*

Father all powerful, *Have mercy on us.*
Jesus, Eternal Son of the Father, Redeemer of the world, *Save us.*
Spirit of the Father and the Son, boundless life of both, *Sanctify us.*
Holy Trinity, *Hear us.*
Holy Spirit, Who proceedest from the Father and the Son, *Enter our hearts.*
Holy Spirit, Who art equal to the Father and the Son, *Enter our hearts.*

Promise of God the Father, *Have mercy on us.*
Ray of heavenly light, *Have mercy on us.*
Author of all good, *Have mercy on us.*
Source of heavenly water, *Have mercy on us.*
Source of heavenly consuming fire, *Have mercy on us.*
Ardent charity, *Have mercy on us.*
Spiritual unction, *Have mercy on us.*
Spirit of love and truth, *Have mercy on us.*
Spirit of wisdom and understanding, *Have mercy on us.*
Spirit of counsel and fortitude, *Have mercy on us.*
Spirit of knowledge and piety, *Have mercy on us.*
Spirit of the fear of the Lord, *Have mercy on us.*
Spirit of grace and prayer, *Have mercy on us.*
Spirit of peace and meekness, *Have mercy on us.*

Spirit of modesty and innocence, *Have mercy on us.*
Holy Spirit, the Comforter, *Have mercy on us.*
Holy Spirit, the Sanctifier, *Have mercy on us.*
Holy Spirit, Who governest the Church, *Have mercy on us.*
Gift of God, the Most High, *Have mercy on us.*
Spirit Who fillest the universe, *Have mercy on us.*
Spirit of the adoption of the children of God, *Have mercy on us.*

Holy Spirit, *Inspire us with horror of sin.*
Holy Spirit, *Come and renew the face of the earth.*
Holy Spirit, *Shed Thy light in our souls.*
Holy Spirit, *Engrave Thy law in our hearts.*
Holy Spirit, *Inflame us with the flame of Thy love.*
Holy Spirit, *Open to us the treasures of Thy graces.*
Holy Spirit, *Teach us to pray well.*
Holy Spirit, *Enlighten us with Thy heavenly inspirations.*
Holy Spirit, *Lead us in the way of salvation.*
Holy Spirit, *Grant us the only necessary knowledge.*
Holy Spirit, *Inspire in us the practice of good.*
Holy Spirit, *Grant us the merits of all virtues.*
Holy Spirit, *Make us persevere in justice.*
Holy Spirit, *Be Thou our everlasting reward.*

Lamb of God,
Who takest away the sins of the world, *Send us Thy Holy Spirit.*

Lamb of God,
Who takest away the sins of the world,
Pour down into our souls the gifts of the Holy Spirit.

Lamb of God,
Who takest away the sins of the world,
Grant us the Spirit of wisdom and piety.

Come, Holy Spirit! Fill the hearts of Thy faithful!
And enkindle in them the fire of Thy love.

Let us pray.

Grant, O merciful Father, that Thy Divine Spirit may enlighten, inflame and purify us, that He may penetrate us with His heavenly dew and make us fruitful in good works, through our Lord Jesus Christ, Thy

Son, Who with Thee, in the unity of the same Spirit, liveth and reigneth forever and ever. Amen."[269]

3

Litany of the Holy Spirit

Lord, have mercy on us!	*Lord, have mercy on us!*
Christ, have mercy on us!	*Christ, have mercy on us!*
Lord, have mercy on us!	*Lord, have mercy on us!*
Christ, hear us!	*Christ, graciously hear us!*
Heavenly Father,	*Have mercy on us!*
Son and Redeemer,	*Have mercy on us!*
Holy Spirit,	*Have mercy on us!*
Blessed Trinity, one God,	*Have mercy on us!*
Holy Spirit, Love of the Father and the Son,	*Have mercy on us!*
Holy Spirit, Happiness of the Father and the Son,	*Have mercy on us!*
Holy Spirit, Cause of the mystery of the Incarnation,	*Have mercy on us!*
Holy Spirit, Divine Spouse of the Immaculate Virgin Mary,	*Have mercy on us!*
Holy Spirit, Crown of the redemptive work of Jesus,	*Have mercy on us!*
Holy Spirit, Guide of Holy Mother the Church,	*Have mercy on us!*
Holy Spirit, Guardian of the Holy Father's teachings,	*Have mercy on us!*
Holy Spirit, Sun of divine grace,	*Have mercy on us!*
Holy Spirit, Dispenser of divine virtues and gifts,	*Have mercy on us!*
Holy Spirit, Spirit of our understanding and knowledge,	*Have mercy on us!*
Holy Spirit, Spirit of piety and reverential fear,	*Have mercy on us!*
Holy Spirit, Spirit of courage and fortitude,	*Have mercy on us!*
Holy Spirit, Source of all virtues,	*Have mercy on us!*
Holy Spirit, Master of perfection,	*Have mercy on us!*
Holy Spirit, Joy of the angels,	*Have mercy on us!*
Holy Spirit, Hope of the patriarchs,	*Have mercy on us!*
Holy Spirit, Inspiration of the prophets,	*Have mercy on us!*
Holy Spirit, Teacher of the apostles,	*Have mercy on us!*

Holy Spirit, Strength of the martyrs, *Have mercy on us!*
Holy Spirit, Strength of confessors of the faith, *Have mercy on us!*
Holy Spirit, Chastity of Virgins, *Have mercy on us!*
Holy Spirit, Pledge of the unity of all Saints, *Have mercy on us!*
Holy Spirit, Forgiver of sins, *Have mercy on us!*
Holy Spirit, Risen Life of all humanity, *Have mercy on us!*
Holy Spirit, Light and Joy of eternal life, *have mercy on us!*
Be merciful! *Have mercy on us, Holy Spirit!*
Be merciful! *Hear us, Holy Spirit!*

From all error of faith, *Save us, Holy Spirit!*
From all sins, *Save us, Holy Spirit!*
From the spirit of pride, *Save us, Holy Spirit!*
From the spirit of uncleanness, *Save us, Holy Spirit!*
From the spirit of hatefulness, *Save us, Holy Spirit!*
From the spirit of falsehood and pretense, *Save us, Holy Spirit!*
From the neglect of your inspirations, *Save us, Holy Spirit!*
From the resisting of recognized truth, *Save us, Holy Spirit!*
From the pride of taking
Your mercy for granted, *Save us, Holy Spirit!*
From the fear of losing divine mercy, *Save us, Holy Spirit!*
From obstinacy and lack of repentance, *Save us, Holy Spirit!*
From sudden and unhappy death, *Save us, Holy Spirit!*
From eternal damnation, *Save us, Holy Spirit!*

We, poor sinners, *We beseech You, hear us!*
We ask You to support the Holy Father and
all Bishops as they govern the Church; *We beseech You, hear us!*
We ask You to send holy priests
to the Church; *We beseech You, hear us!*
We ask You to sanctify all holy orders
and members of the Church, *We beseech You, hear us!*
We ask You to bless the work of all
Catholic catechists and teachers, *We beseech You, hear us!*
We ask You to powerfully protect
the Catholic missions, *We beseech You, hear us!*
We ask You to guide back to Christ's fold,
as soon as possible, all who have wandered
far from Him, *We beseech You, hear us!*
We ask You to keep away sadness and doubt, *We beseech You, hear us!*

We ask You to preserve the unity of the Church, *We beseech You, hear us!*
We ask You to direct all our thoughts
and desires towards Heaven, *We beseech You, hear us!*
We ask You to keep us all in Your love, *We beseech You, hear us!*
We ask You to receive us all
into everlasting happiness, *We beseech You, hear us!*

Lamb of God, You take away the sins of the world, *Spare us, O Lord!*
Lamb of God, You take away the sins of the world, *Hear us, O Lord!*
Lamb of God, You take away the sins of the world, *Have mercy on us!*

Send us Your Spirit, and we will be renewed,
And You will renew the face of the earth.

Let us pray.

Holy Spirit of God, whom the Lord had promised to His Church and whom He graciously sent to us on the day of Pentecost: Be the constant welcome Guest of our hearts! Protect and increase in us Your graces; kindle the fire of the hidden divine virtues in our hearts!

Adorn us, Your temples, with Your sevenfold gifts; allow the Spirit of Love to radiate to our brothers and sisters. Help us to build the kingdom of our Lord Jesus Christ through prayer, through the witness of our lives and our apostolate. We ask this through our Lord Jesus Christ who lives and reigns with You and the Father, forever and ever. Amen.[270]

Litany of the Blessed Virgin Mary, Immaculately Conceived

Lord, have mercy *Lord, have mercy.*
Christ, have mercy *Christ, have mercy.*
Lord, have mercy *Lord, have mercy.*

God the Father of Heaven, *Have mercy on us.*
God the Son, Redeemer of the world, *Have mercy on us.*
God the Holy Spirit, *Have mercy on us.*
Holy Trinity, one God, *Have mercy on us.*

Holy Mary, Mother of God, *Pray for us.*
Ark of Noah and Jacob's Ladder, *Pray for us.*
Burning Bush, flaming with God's infinite love, *Pray for us.*
Ark of holiness and God's exalted Throne, *Pray for us.*
Tabernacle created by God Himself, *Pray for us.*
Tabernacle formed by the Holy Spirit, *Pray for us.*
Most holy Temple of God, *Pray for us.*
Queen entirely perfect and beautiful, *Pray for us.*
Queen never stained by original sin, *Pray for us.*
Rose ever blooming, Lily among thorns, *Pray for us.*
Ever-blossoming Plant of grace, *Pray for us.*
Wood never corrupted by the worm of sin, *Pray for us.*
Fountain ever clear, sealed by the Holy Spirit, *Pray for us.*
Treasure of immortality, *Pray for us.*
Child of grace and Vessel of election, *Pray for us.*
The one and only Daughter of Life, *Pray for us.*
Virgin undefiled, *Pray for us.*
Virgin immaculate, *Pray for us.*
Virgin ever blessed, *Pray for us.*
Virgin full of grace, *Pray for us.*
Virgin free from all contagion of sin, *Pray for us.*
Virgin radiant like the dawn, *Pray for us.*
Most beautiful Paradise of innocence, *Pray for us.*
Most beautiful Paradise of immortality, *Pray for us.*
Most beautiful Paradise of delights, *Pray for us.*

Abode of the grace of the Holy Spirit, *Pray for us.*
More honorable than the Cherubim, *Pray for us.*
More glorious than the Seraphim, *Pray for us.*
Unsurpassable in beauty and loveliness, *Pray for us.*
Pillar of integrity and of innocence, *Pray for us.*
Holy Mary, Mother of God most pure, *Pray for us.*
Holy Mary, Mother of God most prudent, *Pray for us.*
Holy Mary, Mother of God most humble, *Pray for us.*
Holy Mary, Mother of God most faithful, *Pray for us.*
Holy Mary, Mother of God most devout, *Pray for us.*
Holy Mary, Mother of God most obedient, *Pray for us.*
Holy Mary, Mother of God most poor, *Pray for us.*
Holy Mary, Mother of God most patient, *Pray for us.*
Holy Mary, Mother of God most merciful, *Pray for us.*
Holy Mary, Mother of God most sorrowful, *Pray for us.*

Lamb of God, You take away the sins of the world, *Spare us, O Lord.*
Lamb of God, You take away
the sins of the world, *Graciously hear us, O Lord.*
Lamb of God, You take away the sins of the world,
Have mercy on us.

By your Immaculate Conception,
O Mary, *May my body be pure and my soul holy.*

Let us pray.

Thou art all fair, O Mary, and the original stain is not in thee. Thou art the glory of Jerusalem. Thou art the joy of Israel. Thou art the honor of our people. Thou art the advocate of sinners. O Mary, Virgin most prudent, Mother most compassionate, pray for us, intercede for us, with Jesus Christ our Lord. Amen.[271]

Litany of the Immaculate Conception

God the Father, Source of all sanctity, *Have mercy on us.*
God the Son, uncreated Sanctity, *Have mercy on us.*
God the Holy Ghost, Spirit of Sanctity, *Have mercy on us.*
Most sacred Trinity, one God, *Have mercy on us.*

Holy Mary, immaculate, *Pray for us.*
Virgin of virgins, immaculate, *Pray for us.*
Holy Virgin, by predestination immaculate, *Pray for us.*
Holy Virgin, in thy conception immaculate, *Pray for us.*
Holy Virgin, after thy conception immaculate, *Pray for us.*
Daughter of the Father, immaculate, *Pray for us.*
Mother of the Son, immaculate, *Pray for us.*
Spouse of the Holy Ghost, immaculate, *Pray for us.*
Seat of the most Holy Trinity, immaculate, *Pray for us.*
Image of the Wisdom of God, immaculate, *Pray for us.*
Dawn of the Sun of justice, immaculate, *Pray for us.*
Living ark of the body of Christ, immaculate, *Pray for us.*
Daughter of David, immaculate, *Pray for us.*
Guide to Jesus, immaculate, *Pray for us.*
Virgin, triumphing over original sin, immaculate, *Pray for us.*
Virgin, crushing the head of the serpent, immaculate, *Pray for us.*
Queen of Heaven and earth, immaculate, *Pray for us.*
Gate of the heavenly Jerusalem, immaculate, *Pray for us.*
Dispenser of graces, immaculate, *Pray for us.*
Spouse of Saint Joseph, immaculate, *Pray for us.*
Star of the world, immaculate, *Pray for us.*
Impregnable tower of the Church Militant, immaculate, *Pray for us.*
Rose amid thorns, immaculate, *Pray for us.*
Olive of the fields, immaculate, *Pray for us.*
Model of all perfection, immaculate, *Pray for us.*
Cause of our hope, immaculate, *Pray for us.*
Pillar of our faith, immaculate, *Pray for us.*
Source of Divine Love, immaculate, *Pray for us.*
Sure sign of our salvation, immaculate, *Pray for us.*

Rule of perfect obedience, immaculate, *Pray for us.*
Pattern of holy poverty, immaculate, *Pray for us.*
School of devotion, immaculate, *Pray for us.*
Abode of chaste modesty, immaculate, *Pray for us.*
Anchor of our salvation, immaculate, *Pray for us.*
Light of Angels, immaculate, *Pray for us.*
Crown of Patriarchs, immaculate, *Pray for us.*
Glory of Prophets, immaculate, *Pray for us.*
Lady and Mistress of Apostles, immaculate, *Pray for us.*
Support of Martyrs, immaculate, *Pray for us.*
Strength of Confessors, immaculate, *Pray for us.*
Diadem of Virgins, immaculate, *Pray for us.*
Splendor of all Saints, immaculate, *Pray for us.*
Sanctity of all Christians, immaculate, *Pray for us.*
Companion of devout souls, immaculate, *Pray for us.*
Joy of those who hope in thee, immaculate, *Pray for us.*
Health of the sick, immaculate, *Pray for us.*
Advocate of sinners, immaculate, *Pray for us.*
Terror of heretics, immaculate, *Pray for us.*
Protectress of all mankind, immaculate, *Pray for us.*
Patroness of those who honor thee, immaculate, *Pray for us.*

Lamb of God, Who takest away the sins of the world:
Spare us, O Lord.
Lamb of God, Who takest away the sins of the world:
Graciously hear us, O Lord.
Lamb of God, Who takest away the sins of the world:
Have mercy on us.

In thy Conception, O Virgin Mary, thou wast immaculate.
Pray for us to the Father, Whose Son, Jesus, conceived of the Holy Ghost, thou didst bring forth.

Let us pray.

O Almighty and Eternal God, Who didst prepare for Thy Son a worthy habitation, by the Immaculate Conception of the Blessed Virgin Mary: we beseech Thee that, as Thou didst preserve her from every stain of sin, through the merits of the pre-ordained atonement of Jesus Christ, so Thou wouldst grant that we also may come without spot to Thee. Through the same Jesus Christ our Lord. Amen.[272]

3

Litany of the Immaculate Conception of Mary, Mother of God

Lord, have mercy on us. *Lord, have mercy on us.*
Jesus Christ, hear us. *Jesus Christ, hear us.*
Jesus Christ, hear us. *Jesus Christ, graciously hear us.*

God the Father, who prepared a worthy dwelling place
for Thy Son through the Immaculate Conception,
Have mercy on us.
God the Son, who redeemed Thy Mother
by the anticipated application of Thy merits, *Have mercy on us.*
God the Holy Spirit, who vivified Mary from
Her immaculate Conception, *Have mercy on us.*
Holy Trinity, who predestined Mary in
Her immaculate Conception before all time, *Have mercy on us.*
O Mary, conceived without sin,
beloved Daughter of the Eternal Father,
Pray for us who have recourse to thee.
O Mary, conceived without sin,
most worthy Mother of the Son of God,
Pray for us who have recourse to thee.
O Mary, conceived without sin,
most pure Virgin and Spouse of the Holy Spirit,
Pray for us who have recourse to thee.
O Mary, enriched with all the supernatural gifts
from your immaculate Conception,
Pray for us who have recourse to thee.
O Mary, who alone among all creatures was
preserved from original sin, *Pray for us who have recourse to thee.*
O Mary, adorned in your immaculate Conception
with the fullness of the most signal graces,
Pray for us who have recourse to thee.
O Mary, to whom the prerogative of
thy immaculate Conception gives preeminence
over all that is created, *Pray for us who have recourse to thee.*

O Mary, who, from the time of your entry into the world,
has always appeared like the sun as it advances in its career,
Pray for us who have recourse to thee.
O Mary, who by Your immaculate Conception
was preserved from the threefold concupiscence,
Pray for us who have recourse to thee.
O Mary, all beautiful and without blemish,
Pray for us who have recourse to thee.
O Mary, shrine of Wisdom incarnate,
Pray for us who have recourse to thee.
O Mary, Mother of good counsel,
Pray for us who have recourse to thee.
O Mary, Mother of good hope, *Pray for us who have recourse to thee.*
O Mary, Mother of good help, *Pray for us who have recourse to thee.*
O Mary, Mother of grace, *Pray for us who have recourse to thee.*
O Mary, Mother of sweet consolation,
Pray for us who have recourse to thee.
O Mary, Mother of beautiful love,
Pray for us who have recourse to thee.
O Mary, dawn of the most beautiful days,
Pray for us who have recourse to thee.
O Mary, lily of purity whiter than snow,
Pray for us who have recourse to thee.
O Mary, new Eve, who crushed the head of the serpent,
Pray for us who have recourse to thee.
O Mary, whose Immaculate Conception is the glory and happiness
of the triumphant and militant Church,
Pray for us who have recourse to thee.
O Mary, who floods the hearts of Your children with joy,
Pray for us who have recourse to thee.
O Mary, whose name is full of sweetness and blessing,
Pray for us who have recourse to thee.
O Mary, model of the life of faith, hope, and love,
Pray for us who have recourse to thee.
O Mary, impregnable tower to the enemies of our salvation,
Pray for us who have recourse to thee.
O Mary, Mother of Jesus and ever Virgin, Immaculate Mother,
Pray for us who have recourse to thee.
O Mary, Virgin and Mother, blessed above all women,
Pray for us who have recourse to thee.

O Mary, depositary and dispenser of the graces which
Jesus grants to Christians, *Pray for us who have recourse to thee.*
O Mary, hope and consolation of the afflicted,
the sick and the dying, *Pray for us who have recourse to thee.*
O Mary, most powerful and most liberal protector
of those who call upon you, *Pray for us who have recourse to thee.*
O Mary, who, after Jesus, are all the joy and happiness of
the poor children of Adam, *Pray for us who have recourse to thee.*
O Mary, radiant gateway to the glory
and delights of paradise, *Pray for us who have recourse to thee.*
O Mary, rainbow of glory and splendor
of the blessed in Heaven, *Pray for us who have recourse to thee.*
O Mary, whose heart was flooded with an ocean of sorrow
at the foot of the Cross, *Pray for us who have recourse to thee.*
O Mary, conceived without sin,
Draw us with the fragrance of your virtues, and lead us to Heaven.

Lamb of God, who taketh away the sins of the world,
Have mercy on us.
Lamb of God, who taketh away the sins of the world,
Have mercy on us.
Lamb of God, who taketh away the sins of the world,
Have mercy on us.

You were conceived without sin, O Virgin Mary!
Pray for us to God the Father, whose Son You begot.

Let us pray.

O God, who by the Immaculate Conception of the most holy Virgin Mary prepared for Thy Son a worthy dwelling place in her virginal womb, and who also preserved her from all stain for the honor of this same Son, deign, we beseech Thee, to grant us the grace, through her intercession, to purify us from all sin, to preserve us from all relapse, and to help us to imitate her virtues, so that we may attain the happiness of possessing Thee for ever. Through our Lord Jesus Christ. Amen.[273]

Litany of the Immaculate Conception

Lord, have mercy on us. *Christ, have mercy on us.*
Lord, have mercy on us. Christ, hear us. *Christ, graciously hear us.*

God, the Father of Heaven, *Have mercy on us.*
God, the Son, Redeemer of the world, *Have mercy on us.*
God, the Holy Ghost, *Have mercy on us.*
Holy Trinity, one God, *Have mercy on us.*

Holy Mary, *Pray for us.*
Holy Mother of God, *Pray for us.*
Mother, most pure, *Pray for us.*
Mother, entirely perfect, *Pray for us.*
Mother, most dear to God, *Pray for us.*
Mother, never stained with the least blemish, *Pray for us.*
Mother, more beautiful than beauty, *Pray for us.*
Mother, more lovely than loveliness, *Pray for us.*
Mother, more holy than holiness, *Pray for us.*
Mother, surpassing all integrity and virginity, *Pray for us.*
Holy Virgin, by predestination immaculate, *Pray for us.*
Holy Virgin, in thy conception immaculate, *Pray for us.*
Holy Virgin, after thy conception immaculate, *Pray for us.*
Holy Virgin, ever immaculate, *Pray for us.*
Holy Virgin, radiant with divine splendors, *Pray for us.*
Holy Virgin, full of the glory of God, *Pray for us.*
Holy Virgin, seat of all divine graces, *Pray for us.*
Holy Virgin, ever blessed, *Pray for us.*
Holy Virgin, never in darkness, always in light, *Pray for us.*
Holy Virgin, chosen before the ages, *Pray for us.*
Holy Virgin, adorned with all the gifts of the Holy Ghost, *Pray for us.*
Holy Virgin, abounding in delights, *Pray for us.*
Holy Virgin, leaning on thy Beloved, *Pray for us.*
Impregnable tower before the enemy, *Pray for us.*
Garden enclosed on all sides, *Pray for us.*
Resplendent city of God, *Pray for us.*
Gate of the heavenly Jerusalem, *Pray for us.*

Most august temple of God, *Pray for us.*
Exalted throne of God, *Pray for us.*
Ark of holiness, built by Eternal Wisdom, *Pray for us.*
Lily among thorns, *Pray for us.*
Plant ever green, *Pray for us.*
Land entirely intact, *Pray for us.*
Most beautiful paradise of innocence, *Pray for us.*
Fountain ever clear and sealed by the Holy Ghost, *Pray for us.*
Rose ever blooming, *Pray for us.*
Queen and Light of Angels, *Pray for us.*
Queen and Lady of Patriarchs, *Pray for us.*
Queen and Glory of Prophets, *Pray for us.*
Queen and Mistress of Apostles, *Pray for us.*
Queen and Crown of Martyrs, *Pray for us.*
Queen and Strength of Confessors, *Pray for us.*
Queen and Diadem of Virgins, *Pray for us.*
Queen and Splendor of all Saints, *Pray for us.*
Queen conceived without original sin, *Pray for us.*
Queen assumed into Heaven, *Pray for us.*
Queen of the Most Holy Rosary, *Pray for us.*
Queen of peace, *Pray for us.*

Lamb of God, Who takest away the sins of the world,
Spare us, O Lord.
Lamb of God, Who takest away the sins of the world,
Graciously hear us, O Lord.
Lamb of God, Who takest away the sins of the world,
Have mercy on us.

In thy Conception, O Virgin Mary, thou wast immaculate.
Pray for us to the Father, Whose Son Jesus conceived of the Holy Ghost, thou didst bring forth into the world.

Let us pray.

O Almighty and Eternal God, Who didst prepare for Thy Son a worthy habitation, by the Immaculate Conception of the Blessed Virgin Mary: we beseech Thee that, as Thou didst preserve Her from every stain of sin, through the merits of the pre-ordained atonement of Jesus Christ, so Thou wouldst grant that we also may come without spot to Thee. Through the same Jesus Christ our Lord. Amen.[274]

Chaplet of Divine Mercy

The Chaplet of Divine Mercy is recited using ordinary Rosary beads of five decades. The Chaplet is preceded by two opening prayers from the *Diary of Saint Maria Faustina Kowalska* and followed by a closing prayer.

Make the Sign of the Cross.

Opening Prayers:

O Jesus, eternal Truth, our Life, I call upon You and I beg Your mercy for poor sinners. O sweetest Heart of my Lord, full of pity and unfathomable mercy, I plead with You for poor sinners. O Most Sacred Heart, Fount of Mercy from which gush forth rays of inconceivable graces upon the entire human race, I beg of You light for poor sinners. O Jesus, be mindful of Your own bitter Passion and do not permit the loss of souls redeemed at so dear a price of Your most precious Blood. O Jesus, when I consider the great price of Your Blood, I rejoice at its immensity, for one drop alone would have been enough for the salvation of all sinners. Although sin is an abyss of wickedness and ingratitude, the price paid for us can never be equalled. Therefore, let every soul trust in the Passion of the Lord, and place its hope in His mercy. God will not deny His mercy to anyone. Heaven and earth may change, but God's mercy will never be exhausted. Oh, what immense joy burns in my heart when I contemplate Your incomprehensible goodness, O Jesus! I desire to bring all sinners to Your feet that they may glorify Your mercy throughout endless ages (*Diary of Saint Maria Faustina Kowalska*, 72).

You expired, Jesus, but the source of life gushed forth for souls, and the ocean of mercy opened up for the whole world. O Fount of Life, unfathomable Divine Mercy, envelop the whole world and empty Yourself out upon us.

(Repeat three times) O Blood and Water, which gushed forth from the Heart of Jesus as a fount of mercy for us, I trust in You!

Our Father, Hail Mary, Apostles' Creed.

Eternal Father, I offer you the Body and Blood, Soul and Divinity of Your Dearly Beloved Son, our Lord, Jesus Christ, in atonement for our sins and those of the whole world.

On the 10 Small Beads of Each Decade:

For the sake of His sorrowful Passion, have mercy on us and on the whole world.

Repeat for the remaining decades, saying the "Eternal Father" on the "Our Father" bead and then 10 "For the sake of His sorrowful Passion" on the following "Hail Mary" beads.

Conclude with (repeat three times): Holy God, Holy Mighty One, Holy Immortal One, have mercy on us and on the whole world.

Concluding prayers:

Eternal God, in whom mercy is endless and the treasury of compassion — inexhaustible, look kindly upon us and increase Your mercy in us, that in difficult moments we might not despair nor become despondent, but with great confidence submit ourselves to Your holy will, which is Love and Mercy itself.

O Greatly Merciful God, Infinite Goodness, today all mankind calls out from the abyss of its misery to Your mercy — to Your compassion, O God; and it is with its mighty voice of misery that it cries out. Gracious God, do not reject the prayer of this earth's exiles! O Lord, Goodness beyond our understanding, Who are acquainted with our misery through and through, and know that by our own power we cannot ascend to You, we implore You: anticipate us with Your grace and keep on increasing Your mercy in us, that we may faithfully do Your holy will all through our life and at death's hour. Let the omnipotence of Your mercy shield us from the darts of our salvation's enemies, that we may with confidence, as Your children, await Your [Son's] final coming — that day known to You alone. And we expect to obtain everything promised us by Jesus in spite of all our wretchedness. For Jesus is our Hope: through His merciful Heart, as through an open gate, we pass through to heaven (*Diary*, 1570).

Chaplet of the Ten Evangelical Virtues

After making the Sign of the Cross, you pray one Our Father, and then ten Hail Mary's. In each Hail Mary, after saying, "Holy Mary, Mother of God," you add the virtue (e..g, most pure), before continuing "pray for us sinners, now and at the hour of our death. Amen."

Her ten evangelical virtues are:

Most Pure
Most Prudent
Most Humble
Most Faithful
Most Devout
Most Obedient
Most Poor
Most Patient
Most Merciful
Most Sorrowful

At the end of the 10 Hail Mary's, you recite the Glory Be, followed by unique prayers:

In your Conception, O Mary, you were immaculate,
Pray for us to the Father, whose Son, Jesus, you brought forth into the world.

O God, who, by the Immaculate Conception of the Blessed Virgin, prepared a worthy dwelling for Your Son, grant, we pray, that as You preserved her from every stain, by virtue of the death of Your Son, which You foresaw, so through her intercession, we, too, may be cleansed and admitted to Your presence. Through Christ, our Lord. Amen.

Immaculata Virginis Mariae Conceptio [May the Virgin Mary's Immaculate Conception],
Sit Nobis Salus et Protectio [Be our Health and our protection].[275]

The Chaplet of St. Michael

O God, come to my assistance. O Lord, make haste to help me. Glory be to the Father, etc.

[Say one Our Father and three Hail Marys after each of the following nine salutations in honor of the nine Choirs of Angels]

1. By the intercession of St. Michael and the celestial Choir of Seraphim, may the Lord make us worthy to burn with the fire of perfect charity. Amen.

2. By the intercession of St. Michael and the celestial Choir of Cherubim, may the Lord grant us the grace to leave the ways of sin and run in the paths of Christian perfection. Amen.

3. By the intercession of St. Michael and the celestial Choir of Thrones, may the Lord infuse into our hearts a true and sincere spirit of humility. Amen.

4. By the intercession of St. Michael and the celestial Choir of Dominions, may the Lord give us grace to govern our senses and overcome any unruly passions. Amen.

5. By the intercession of St. Michael and the celestial Choir of Powers, may the Lord protect our souls against the snares and temptations of the devil. Amen.

6. By the intercession of St. Michael and the celestial Choir of Virtues, may the Lord preserve us from evil and falling into temptation. Amen.

7. By the intercession of St. Michael and the celestial Choir of Principalities, may God fill our souls with a true spirit of obedience. Amen.

8. By the intercession of St. Michael and the celestial Choir of Archangels, may the Lord give us perseverance in faith and in all good works in order that we may attain the glory of Heaven. Amen.

9. By the intercession of St. Michael and the celestial Choir of Angels, may the Lord grant us to be protected by them in this mortal life and conducted in the life to come to Heaven. Amen.

Say one Our Father in honor of each of the following leading Angels: St. Michael, St. Gabriel, St. Raphael and our Guardian Angel.

Concluding prayers:

O glorious prince St. Michael, chief and commander of the heavenly hosts, guardian of souls, vanquisher of rebel spirits, servant in the house of the Divine King and our admirable conductor, you who shine with excellence and superhuman virtue deliver us from all evil, who turn to you with confidence and enable us by your gracious protection to serve God more and more faithfully every day.

Pray for us, O glorious St. Michael, Prince of the Church of Jesus Christ, that we may be made worthy of His promises.

Almighty and Everlasting God, Who, by a prodigy of goodness and a merciful desire for the salvation of all men, has appointed the most glorious Archangel St. Michael Prince of Your Church, make us worthy, we ask You, to be delivered from all our enemies, that none of them may harass us at the hour of death, but that we may be conducted by him into Your Presence. This we ask through the merits of Jesus Christ our Lord. Amen.

NOTES

[1] Rev. Tadeusz Rogalewski, *Stanislaus Papczyński (1631-1701): Founder of the Order of Marians and Inspirer of the Marian School of Spirituality*. (Marian Press: Stockbridge, MA, 2001), p. 364.

[2] Stanislaus Papczyński, *Historical Writings* (Marian Press, Stockbridge, MA, 2007), p. 64-65: "After all, the Divine vision ... was imprinted upon my soul in respect to the founding of the Congregation of the Immaculate Conception of the B.V.M."

[3] *Ratio Formationis Marianorum*, General Chapter — Rome 2005 (General Curia of the Congregation of Marian Fathers, Rome, 2008), n. 19. Hereafter *Ratio Formationis.*

[4] Cf. International Commission on English in the Liturgy (ICEL), *The Liturgy of the Hours: According to the Roman Rite* (Catholic Book Publishing, New York, 2009), Vol. II (Lent-Easter), Tuesday of the Fifth Week of Lent, Evening Prayer. In Latin, "Cæléstis Sponse, máculas ab Ecclésia tua diléeta exclúde."

[5] Donal Anthony Foley, *The Miraculous Medal — A Reminder to Ask with Confidence for Graces Needed*, https://www.bluearmy.com/the-miraculous-medal-a-reminder-to-ask-with-confidence-for-graces-needed/ (accessed December 2, 2021).

[6] Bl. George Matulaitis, *Journal* (Marian Press, Stockbridge, MA, 2003), p. 60.

[7] Saint Maximilian Kolbe, Conference, February 18, 1933. Quoted in Fr. Louis Maximilian Smith, FI, *The Era of the Immaculate*, https://saintmaximiliankolbe.com/the-era-of-the-immaculate (accessed March 14, 2023).

[8] Ibid.

[9] George Pollard, *The Revelation of the Immaculate Heart at Fatima in 1917*, www.ewtn.com/catholicism/library/revelation-of-the-immaculate-heart-at-fatima-in-1917-5465 (accessed March 14, 2023).

[10] "Dogmatic Constitution on the Sacred Liturgy: *Sacrosanctum Concilium*," (Vatican City: Libreria Editrice Vatican City, 2011), n. 13. Hereafter *Sacrosanctum Concilium.*

[11] Ibid., n. 11.

[12] John Paul II, "*Rosarium Virginis Mariae*: On the Most Holy Rosary," https://w2.vatican.va/content/john-paul-ii/en/apost_letters/2002/documents/hf_jp-ii_apl_20021016_rosarium-virginis-mariae.html (accessed March 14, 2023), n. 1, 3, 5, 14. Hereafter *Rosarium Virginis.*

[13] Andrzej Pakuła, MIC, PhD, *Spirituality of the Religious Life according to Saint Stanislaus Papczyński and the Early Tradition of the Congregation of Marian Fathers,* trans. Marina Batiuk and Joseph Roesch, MIC (Marian Heritage Press, Stockbridge, MA, 2022), p. 169.

[14] Ibid. See St. Stanislaus Papczyński, *Selected Writings* (Marian Heritage Press, Stockbridge, MA, 2022), p. 638.

[15] From *The Writings of St. Maximilian M. Kolbe,* Antonella di Piazza (ed.), (Nerbini International, Lugano, Switzerland, 2016), 1307. Hereafter *SK.* Quoted in Fr. Louis Maximilian Smith, FI, *The Immaculate: Mother and Teacher*, https://saintmaximiliankolbe.com/immaculate-mother-teacher (accessed on March 14, 2023).

[16] International Commission on English in the Liturgy (ICEL), *Order of Baptism of Children* (Catholic Book Publishing, New York, 2019), #99.

[17] "Dogmatic Constitution on the Church: *Lumen Gentium*," (Vatican City: Libreria Editrice Vaticana, 2011), n. 39. Hereafter *Lumen Gentium.*

[18] Janusz Kumala, MIC, *The Immaculate Conception as the Icon of the Mercy of the Triune God: Inspiration for the Spiritual Life and Apostolate.* Ephemerides Marianorum 6 (2017), pp. 165-193.

[19] Saint Thérèse of Lisieux, *Story of a Soul: The Autobiography of the Little Flower (*TAN Books, Charlotte, NC, 2010), p. 66.

[20] Conference 195 by St. Maximilian Kolbe given to the solemnly professed friars, Niepokalanów, Thursday, November 24, 1938; notes taken by Br. Caesarius Koperski. Quoted in Fr. Matthias Sasko, FI, *Silence and Recollection*, https://saintmaximiliankolbe.com/silence-and-recollection (accessed on March 23, 2023).

[21] Benedict XVI, *Deus Caritas Est* (Libreria Editrice Vaticana, Vatican City, 2005), n. 12. Hereafter *Deus Caritas Est.*

[22] Francis, *Amoris Laetita* (Libreria Editrice Vaticana, Vatican City, 2014), Chapter 4. "Love in Marriage."

[23] See *Catechism of the Catholic Church* (*CCC*), 2822: "His commandment is 'that you love one another; even as I have loved you, that you also love one another' (Jn 13:34; cf. 1 Jn 3:4; Lk 10:25-37). This commandment summarizes all the others and expresses his entire will."

[24] See John Paul II, Encyclical Letter *Dominum et Vivificantem* (Libreria Editrice Vaticana, Vatican City, 1986), n. 10. Hereafter *Dominum et Vivificantem.*

[25] Jonathan Fleischmann, *Who Are You, O Immaculate Conception?* Accessed on 15 March 2023. https://saintmaximiliankolbe.com/who-are-you-o-immaculate-conception/

[26] Father Louis Maximilian Smith, FI, *The Immaculate: Mediatrix of Divine love*, https://saintmaximiliankolbe.com/the-immaculate-mediatrix-of-divine-love/ (accessed on March 15, 2023).

[27] Benedict XVI, "Homily for Canonization Mass of St. Anthony Galvão," https://www.ewtn.com/catholicism/library/homily-at-mass-and-canonization-of-blessed-frei-galvo-pope-benedict-xvi-6216 (accessed on April 22, 2023).

[28] *TouchofArt.* Icon of Our Lady of Pneumatofora, https://www.touchofart.eu/en/Anna-Kloza-Rozwadowska/aklo46-Icon-of-Our-Lady-of-PNEUMATOFORA/ (accessed 15 March 2023).

[29] Gilles Emery, OP. *The Trinitarian Theology of St. Thomas Aquinas* (Oxford University Press, New York, 2007), p. 258: "He is also, in this sense, the divine person 'closest to us,' so to speak, the one who is most intimate with us, because he is given to us." See Emery's footnote 161: "III Sent. D. 2, q. 2, a. 2, qla 2, ad 3: 'The Holy Spirit is closest to us, because it is through him that all gifts are given.'"

[30] Saint Seraphim of Sarov, *On Acquisition of the Holy Spirit*, ed. S.A. Nilus (Kindle Books). https://www.britannica.com/topic/Protocols-of-the-Elders-of-Zion#ref1259012

[31] John Lisman and Nonna A. Otmakhova, *Storage, Recall, and Novelty Detection of Sequences by the Hippocampus: Elaborating on the SOCRATIC Model to Account for Normal and Aberrant Effects of Dopamine*, https://citeseerx.ist.psu.edu/document?repid=rep1&type=pdf&doi=9ae3280ebf70dacc53807fd9217af632b16b7372 (accessed June 18, 2023).

[32] Janusz Kumala, MIC, *The Immaculate Conception as the Icon of the Mercy of the Triune God.*

[33] *Lumen Gentium*, n. 65.

[34] A. Rodrigues, *Perfection.* In: *The Lexham Theological Wordbook*, ed. Douglas Magnum (Lexham Press, Bellinham, WA, 2014). Song 4:7 is taken up by the Latin hymn to Our Lady, "Tota Pulchra Es." Hereafter *The Lexham Theological Wordbook.*

[35] *Dominum et Vivificantem*, n. 39.

[36] *Comforter* comes from the Latin *to strengthen much*. Taken in this way, the Holy Spirit, as *Comforter*, is not concerned about making us *comfortable*, but rather, *strong* in our weaknesses, after the example of St. Paul, who experienced this power and strength of the Spirit in his weaknesses in 2 Corinthians 12:7-10. See *Online Etymology Dictionary*: www.etymonline.com.

[37] *The Collected Works of St. John of the Cross*, trans. Kerian Kavanaugh, OCD, and Otilio Rodriguez, OCD (ICS Publications, Washington DC, 1991), pp. 776ff.

[38] Saint Ignatius of Loyola, *The Spiritual Exercises of St. Ignatius of Loyola*, trans. Elder Mullan (P. J. Kenedy and Sons, New York, 1914), pp.169ff. These are commonly known as the "rules of discernment" for the first week. Hereafter *Spiritual Exercises.*

[39] Pope Francis compares the Church to a field hospital. See Deborah Castellano Lubov, "Pope Francis: Church a 'field hospital for vulnerable'," https://www.vaticannews.va/en/pope/news/2022-05/pope-francis-audience-village-of-francis.html (accessed May 25, 2023).

[40] Stanislaus of Jesus Mary Papczyński, *Mystical Temple of God* (Marians of the Immaculate Conception, Marian Press, Stockbridge, MA, 2005), p. 115: "Next, it is the greatest charity to pray earnestly to God for the freedom of the souls remaining in purgatory, or to assist them by merciful alms as by various other means."

[41] Cf. Benedict XVI, *Spe Salvi* (Libreria Editrice Vaticana, Vatican City, 2007), n. 45ff, for a discussion on Purgatory. Hereafter *Spe Salvi.*

[42] *Online Etymology Dictionary*, https://www.etymonline.com/word/pure (accessed October 17, 2020). Hereafter *Online Etymology Dictionary.*

[43] Julian of Norwich, *Revelations of Divine Love,* trans. Fr. John-Julian, OJN (Paraclete Press, Brewster, MA, 2011), p. 89: "By these remedies it would be fitting for every soul to be healed. And even though the soul is healed, its wounds are seen before God, not as wounds, but as awards… and in this way all shame be transformed to honor and more joy."

[44] For a biography of St. Joan of Arc, see Mark Twain, *Joan of Arc* (Ignatius Press, San Francisco, 1989).

[45] *Our Sunday Visitor,* "The Life of St. Mark Ji Tianxiang: Persevering in faith despite addiction," https://www.oursundayvisitor.com/the-life-of-st-mark-ji-tianxiang-persevering-in-faith-despite-addiction/ (accessed June 12, 2023).

[46] Pakuła, *Spirituality of the Religious Life*, p. 167.

[47] Cf. *CCC*, 493: "The Fathers of the Eastern tradition call the Mother of God 'the All-Holy' (*Panagia*), and celebrate her as 'free from any stain of sin, as though fashioned by the Holy Spirit and formed as a new creature' [*Lumen Gentium*, n. 65]." Cf. *CCC*, 492.

[48] *Collins Latin Dictionary* (HarperCollins Publishers, Glasgow, 1997), s.v. "salus."

[49] Blessed John Duns Scotus, *Lectura III Sent.*, 123: "Christ was the most perfect mediator. Therefore he exercised the highest degree of mediation in favour of another person. Now he could not be a most perfect mediator and could not repair the effects of sin to the highest degree if he did not preserve his Mother from original sin (as we shall prove). Therefore, since he was the most perfect mediator regarding the person of his Mother, from this it follows that he preserved her from original sin." In Noel Muscat, OFM. *John Duns Scotus and His Defense of the Immaculate Conception*, http://www.christendom-awake.org/pages/marian/scotus&immac.htm (accessed March 27, 2020).

[50] Joseph Ratzinger, *Daughter Zion: Meditations on the Church's Marian Belief,* trans. John McDermott, SJ (Ignatius Press, San Francisco, 1983), pp. 62–70. Cf. Łukasz Żak, "Niepokalane poczęcie Najświętszej Maryi Panny w mariologiczną myśli kard. Josepha Ratzingera," *Salvatoris Mater* (October 2, 2008), pp. 345-355.

[51] Cf. *Lumen Gentium*, n. 65: "But while in the most holy Virgin the Church has already reached that perfection whereby she is without spot or wrinkle, the followers of Christ still strive to increase in holiness by conquering sin."

[52] *Constitutions and Directory of the Congregation of Marian Fathers of the Immaculate Conception of the Most Blessed Virgin Mary* (General Curia of the Marian Fathers, Rome, 2018), p. 77, n. 7. Hereafter *Constitutions and Directory.*

[53] Chris Byrley, "Healing," in *The Lexham Theological Wordbook.*

[54] Gabrielle Bossis, *He and I* (Pauline Books, Boston, 2012), p. 26 (November 3, 1936): "Believe that in My blood there is infinite power to purify." Cf. Mt 8:26 on the lack of faith.

[55] *Online Etymology Dictionary*, https://www.etymonline.com/word/Holy (accessed March 22, 2023).

[56] Saint Thérèse of Lisieux, *Letters of St. Thérèse of Lisieux, Volume II: General Correspondence 1890-1897* (ICS Publications, Washington, DC, 1982).

[57] Cf. Lois Lowry, *The Giver* (Laurel Leaf, Boston/New York, 2002) regarding how one cannot eliminate only the bad parts of life; in so doing, one diminishes the good parts as well. For a secular but enlightening psychological evaluation of this, see Steven Hayes, Kirk Strosahl, and Kelly Wilson, *Acceptance and Commitment Therapy: The Process and Practice of Mindful Change* (The Guilford Press, New York, 2012).

[58] *Merriam-Webster's Collegiate Dictionary*, 11th ed. (Thomson Press, Faridabad, India, 2019), s.v. "restoration."

[59] Thomas Aquinas, *Summa Theologica*, trans. Fathers of the English Dominican Province (Benziger Bros., New York, 1947-1948), III, 1, 3, ad 3. Hereafter, *Summa Theologiae.*

[60] *Dominum et Vivificantem,* n. 24.

[61] See Dr. Matthew Breuninger, *Finding Freedom in Christ: Healing Life's Hurts* (Emmaus Road Publishing, Steubenville, OH 2022).

[62] Rodrigues, *Perfection*. "The Hebrew terms רהֹטָ (ṭāhōr, 'pure') and ץחַרָ (rāḥaṣ, 'to wash') are used to express the idea of perfection in terms of purity. The term καθαρός (katharos, 'pure') expresses perfection as physical or moral purity."

[63] Ibid. "רהֹטָ (ṭāhōr)., adj. clean, pure, genuine. Describes things, animals, or people as ritually, physically, or morally clean or pure."

[64] Cf. Benedict XVI, *Jesus of Nazareth, Holy Week* (Ignatius Press, San Francisco, 2011), pp. 58-59.

[65] Ibid., p. 59.

[66] *Summa Theologiae,* I, q. 43, a. 5, ad. 2: "Whereas the Son is the Word, not any sort of word, but one Who breathes forth love."

[67] Francis, *Lumen Fidei* (Libreria Editrice Vaticana, Vatican City, 2013), n. 20.

[68] Benedict XVI, "Mass, Imposition of the Pallium and Conferral of the Fisherman's Ring for the Beginning of the Petrine Ministry of the Bishop of Rome. Homily of His Holiness Benedict XVI," https://w2.vatican.va/content/benedict-xvi/en/homilies/2005/documents/hf_benxvi_hom_20050424_inizio-pontificato.html (accessed July 7, 2017).

[69] Saint Augustine, *Confessions* (Lib. 10, 26. 37-29, 40: CSEL 33, 255-256), in: Crossroads Initiative, *Late Have I loved You, Beauty So Ancient and So New!*, https://www.crossroadsinitiative.com/media/articles/late-have-i-loved-you-beauty-augustine_feast_august-28/ (accessed on March 22, 2023).

[70] Attributed to G.K. Chesterton in *Living Truth: Experiencing Christ in You, Completely Satisfied,* https://livingtruth.ca/blogs/devotionals/completely-satisfied (accessed May 12, 2023).

[71] *Online Etymology Dictionary.*

[72] *Spe Salvi*, n. 47.

[73] Letter of the Holy Father Francis to His Eminence Cardinal Reinhard Marx, https://www.vatican.va/content/francesco/en/letters/2021/documents/20210610-cardinale-marx.html (accessed March 22, 2023). "Then we will feel that salutary shame which will open the doors to that compassion and tenderness of the Lord which is always close to us. As a Church we need to ask for the grace of shame so that the Lord will keep us from being the shameless harlot of Ezekiel 16."

[74] *Online Etymology Dictionary.*

[75] Cf. St. Paul's distinction between worldly and spiritual sorrow or sadness in 2 Corinthians 7:10. One (what we call today *toxic shame*) leads to death, another (what we call *guilt*) to repentance and new life. Whereas toxic shame states, "I am bad," authentic guilt recognizes, "What I did is bad."

[76] There are several resources available that can facilitate this process. Bob Schuchts, *Be Healed: A Guide to Encountering the Powerful Love of Jesus in Your Life* (Ave Maria Press, Notre Dame, IN, 2014). Bob Schuchts, *Be Transformed: The Healing Power of the Sacraments* (Ave Maria Press, Notre Dame, IN, 2017). Adam Young, *The Place We Find Ourselves,* https://adamyoungcounseling.com/get-the-app/ (accessed April 27, 2023).

[77] Blaise Pascal, *Pensées*, Section III: Of the Necessity of the Wager, https://ccel.org/ccel/pascal/pensees/pensees.iv.html (accessed May 12, 2023), "277. The heart has its reasons, which reason does not know."

[78] Saint Augustine, *Homily on the First Letter of John, 4, 6. New Advent,* https://www.newadvent.org/fathers/170204.htm (accessed March 22, 2023).

[79] From the writings of St. Maximilian M. Kolbe, KW 486, quoted in Fr. Louis Maximilian Smith, FI. *The Era of the Immaculate*, https://saintmaximiliankolbe.com/the-era-of-the-immaculate/ (accessed March 22, 2023).

[80] See Paul VI, *Paenitaemini* (Libreria Editrice Vaticana, Vatican City, 1966).

[81] For an excellent examination of what living the Gospel entails as regards economic well-being and voluntary poverty, see Thomas Dubay, *Happy Are You Poor: The Simple Life and Spiritual Freedom* (Ignatius Press, San Francisco, 1981).

[82] Cf. Thomas Dubay, *Fire Within: St. Teresa of Avila, St. John of the Cross and the Gospel — on Prayer* (Ignatius Press, San Francisco, 1989), pp. 186ff. "St. John is of the opinion that 'this state [of definitive union] never occurs without the soul's being confirmed in grace.'" Cf. John of the Cross, *Spiritual Canticle*, st. 11, no. 3, in *The Collected Works of St. John of the Cross*, p. 497.

[83] I hope to explore this further in a future book.

[84] Excerpts from his letters, https://www.matulaitis-matulewicz.org/excerpts-from-his-letters/ (accessed on March 22, 2023). See also: "Strive, therefore, to become ever more perfect and to rise ever higher. Do not be so worried about how far you still have to go. God rewards us for effort and good will. As you observe your weaknesses and imperfections, therefore, abase yourself the more before God. The Lord, seeing your humble heart, will not spurn you. But you must never despair on account of your defects and failings. The weaker we feel ourselves to be, the more should we confide in God. He is our strength and salvation. Valiantly cry out in the words of St. Paul: 'I can do all things in him, who strengthens me.' And fight. God will not abandon you."

[85] For an integrative vision of the psychological and spiritual aspects of this, see Adam Young, *The Place We Find Ourselves*, episodes 34, 41-43, 45-47. See also Jake Khyme and Bob Schuchts, *Restore the Glory Podcast,* https://www.restoretheglorypodcast.com, (accessed May 12, 2023).

[86] *Online Etymology Dictionary*. See Paul VI, *Paenitaemini,* "Therefore, the following is declared and established: I. 1. By divine law all the faithful are required to do penance."

[87] Saint John of the Cross, *Collected Works*, p. 839.

[88] Cf. N.T. Wright, *Surprised by Hope: Rethinking Heaven, the Resurrection and the Mission of the Church* (HarperCollins, New York, 2008), on the distinction between Platonic and Christian understanding of *redemption* through *resurrection of the flesh.*

[89] Cf. *Thomas Merton on Desert Spirituality* (Audiobook, Learn 25, 2022). In these recorded conferences, Thomas Merton describes the various movements of early monasticism that emphasized harsh penances of the flesh. See also Francis, *Gaudete et Exsultate* (Libreria Editrice Vaticana, Vatican City, 2018), n. 37.

[90] *The Dialogue of the Seraphic Virgin Catherine of Siena,* trans. Algar Thorold (Kegan Paul, Trench, Trubner & Co., London, 1896), p. 209.

[91] *The Collected Works of St. John of the Cross,* p. 152.

[92] Cardinal Robert Sarah, *The Power of Silence: Against the Dictatorship of Noise* (Ignatius Press, San Francisco, 2017).

[93] *The Collected Works of St. John of the Cross*, p. 150.

[94] Saint Maximilian Kolbe, Conference 195, quoted in Fr. Matthias Sasko, *Silence and Recollection.*

[95] See Jonathan Fleischmann, *Transubstantiation into the Immaculate*, https://saintmaximiliankolbe.com/transubstantiation-into-the-immaculate/ (accessed March 22, 2023).

[96] Edward Leen, *Progress Through Mental Prayer,* (Sheed & Ward, New York, 1937) p. 275. Quoted in Fr. Matthias M. Sasko, FI. Silence and Recollection. https://saintmaximiliankolbe.com/silence-and-recollection/ (accessed March 22, 2023).

[97] Conference 195 by St. Maximilian Kolbe, quoted in: Fr. Matthias M. Sasko, FI. *Silence and Recollection.* Accessed on March 22, 2023. https://saintmaximiliankolbe.com/silence-and-recollection/ (accessed March 22, 2023).

[98] *The Practice of the Presence of God* (Martino Publishing, Mansfield Center, CT, 2016).

[99] See Ewa Czaczkowska, *Faustina: The Mystic and Her Message* (Marian Press, Stockbridge, MA, 2014).

[100] See Fr. Thaddaeus Lancton, MIC, *Stepping on the Serpent: The Journey of Trust with Mary* (Marian Press, Stockbridge, MA, 2017).

[101] Maximilian Kolbe, KW 21. Quoted in: Fr. Louis Maximilian Smith, FI. *The Era of the Immaculate.* Accessed on March 22, 2023. https://saintmaximiliankolbe.com/the-era-of-the-immaculate/.

[102] See Peter S. Williamson, *Catholic Commentary on Sacred Scripture: Revelation (*Baker Academic, Grand Rapids, MI, 2015), pp. 207ff.

[103] At a moment unknown to us, God created all the angels. However, some freely and permanently decided to turn away from serving God. These became demons. See *CCC,* 391-395.

[104] Footnote in the NABRE for Revelation 12:17.

[105] Maximilian Kolbe, Conference, September 4, 1937, quoted in Smith, *The Era of the Immaculate.*

[106] *Online Etymology Dictionary.*

[107] *The Collected Works of St. John of the Cross*, p. 210.

[108] For an excellent examination of these matters, together with the "seven deadly wounds," see Bob Schuchts, *Be Healed,* Part II: Facing Our Brokenness. See also the PDF resource of the John Paul II Healing Center, http://franklinhardincatholic.org/wp-content/uploads/Seven-Deadly-Wounds.pdf (accessed May 27, 2023).

[109] *Spiritual Exercises,* p. 179. This is the sixth rule for the second set of rules for discernment.

[110] Bob Schuchts, *Be Healed,* chapter 5.

[111] See Fr. Angelo Geiger, FI, *St. Maximilian's "Secret" to Holiness*, https://saintmaximiliankolbe.com/st-maximilians-secret-to-holiness/ (accessed March 22, 2023).

[112] From Saint Catherine of Siena, *The Dialogue, trans. Susan Noffke* (Paulist Press, Mahwah, NJ, 1980), quoted in: Houston Catholic Worker, *Saint Catherine of Siena: Do for Your Neighbor What you Cannot Do for Me* (October 1, 1995), https://cjd.org/1995/10/01/saint-catherine-of-siena-do-for-your-neighbor-what-you-cannot-do-for-me/ (accessed May 27, 2023).

[113] *Rosarium Virginis,* n. 15.

[114] Rev. Tadeusz Rogalewski, *Stanislaus Papczyński (1631-1701): Founder of the Order of Marians and Inspirer of the Marian School of Spirituality*, p. 240.

[115] Raniero Cantalamessa, *Come, Creator Spirit: Meditations on the Veni Creator* (Liturgical Press, Collegeville, MN, 2003), p. 477. He quotes William of Thierry: "The Holy Spirit is substantively the will of God, and when the Spirit enters into a soul, 'he shows himself as the very will of God for the one in whom he dwells.'" William of St. Thierry, *The Mirror of Faith,* 61 (*Sources Chretiennes* 301, p. 128).

[116] *Roman Missal*, p. 869, Collect for the Mass of the Immaculate Heart of Mary: "O God, who prepared a fit dwelling place for the Holy Spirit in the Heart of the Blessed Virgin Mary, graciously grant that through her intercession we may be a worthy temple of your glory."

[117] Cf. *Dominum et Vivificantem*, n. 46-48.

[118] See Lancton, *Stepping on the Serpent: The Journey of Trust with Mary*, pp. 64ff.

[119] In this regard, *mortal sin* can be seen as firm, consistent opposition to the purifying and sanctifying work of the Holy Spirit within the heart of each person. Unto death, this opposition becomes the *unforgivable sin*, since by its very nature such a person blocks the forgiveness of God given in the Holy Spirit. Cf. *CCC*, 1817, 1864, 2092, and esp. 1430–1433; *Dominum et Vivificantem*, n. 46.

[120] Benedict XVI, *Jesus of Nazareth: From the Baptism in the Jordan to the Transfiguration*, trans. Adrian J. Walker (Doubleday, New York, 2007), chapter 5: The Lord's Prayer, Kindle Position 2217.

[121] Cf. Joseph Ratzinger, "Theological Commentary to the Third Secret of Fatima," http://www.vatican.va/roman_curia/congregations/cfaith/documents/rc_con_cfaith_doc_20000626_message-fatima_en.html (accessed March 31, 2020).

[122] See St. Gregory of Nyssa, *Commentary on the Song of Songs* (Homily 15: Jaeger VI, 466-468), quoted in Crossroads Initiative, *Glory of the Holy Spirit* — Gregory of Nyssa, https://www.crossroadsinitiative.com/media/articles/glory-of-the-holy-spirit-gregory-of-nyssa/ (accessed May 12, 2023).

[123] *Confessions* III, 6, 11, quoted in Benedict XVI, *Angelus* (December 11, 2011), https://www.vatican.va/content/benedict-xvi/en/angelus/2011/documents/hf_ben-xvi_ang_20111211.html (accessed May 12, 2023).

[124] Letter of St. Maximilian Kolbe to Br. Mateusz Spolitakiewicz (October 10, 19235), quoted in: Fr. Matthias M Sasko, FI, *The Essence of Marian Devotion*, https://saintmaximiliankolbe.com/the-essence-of-marian-devotion/ (accessed May 29, 2023).

[125] *Summa Theologiae*, q. 93, a. 6, ad. 1.

[126] Quoted in Sr. Fidelity Grace SV, *12 Ways to Overcome Discouragement*, https://aleteia.org/2022/08/13/12-ways-to-overcome-discouragement/ (accessed May 12, 2023).

[127] Worry derives from the Old English wyrgan, which is akin to the Old High German *wurgen*, meaning "to strangle"; and Lithuanian *veržti*, "to constrict." *Merriam-Webster's Collegiate Dictionary* (Springfield, MA: Merriam-Webster, 2003), s.v. "Worry."

[128] See Matthew Walker, *Why We Sleep: Unlocking the Power of Sleep and Dreams* (Scribner, New York, 2018)

[129] Charles Péguy, *The Portal of the Mystery of Hope*, trans. David Louis Schindler, Jr. (Eerdmans Publishing, Grand Rapids, MI, 1996), pp. 124-125.

[130] Saint Augustine, *De civitate Dei* 19, 19: *Patrologia Latina* 41, 647, (hereafter PL) quoted in *CCC*, 2185.

[131] See John Paul II, *Dies Domini* (Libreria Editrice Vaticana, Vatican City, 1998) https://www.vatican.va/content/john-paul-ii/en/apost_letters/1998/documents/hf_jp-ii_apl_05071998_dies-domini.html (accessed June 6, 2023).

[132] See Dubay, *Fire Within*, chapter 7 ("Conditions for Growth: St. Teresa").

[133] Thomas a Kempis, *The Imitation of Christ*, Book I, Chapter 19.

[134] See St. John of the Cross, *Collected Works*, pp. 506ff.

[135] Cf. *Inspectio Cordis*, on Lk 18:35-43, 29r, quoted in Michał Kozak, MIC, Conference IX: *Prayer, in And That Your Fruit Would Remain* (Rome, 2007) pp. 121–125.

[136] Cf. John Paul II, *Starting Afresh from Christ*, n. 25, https://www.vatican.va/roman_curia/congregations/ccscrlife/documents/rc_con_ccscrlife_doc_20020614_ripartire-da-cristo_

en.html (accessed March 22, 2023). Cf. John Paul II, *Novo Millennio Ineunte*, n. 32, https://www.vatican.va/content/john-paul-ii/en/apost_letters/2001/documents/hf_jp-ii_apl_20010106_novo-millennio-ineunte.html, n. 32-34 (accessed March 22, 2023).

[137] *Summa Theologiae*, I-II, q. 93, a. 6, ad. 1.

[138] Cf. Dubay, *Fire Within: St. Teresa of Avila, St. John of the Cross, and the Gospel — on Prayer*, chapter 11 ("The Universal Call"), pp. 199ff.

[139] Cf. Marian Pisarzak, MIC, *Saint Paul, the Apostle in Marian Spirituality: Study of the Patronage*, Ephemerides Marianorum 4(2015), pp. 281–298.

[140] Francis, Apostolic Exhortation *Gaudete et Exsultate*, n. 47–62, https://www.vatican.va/content/francesco/en/apost_exhortations/documents/papa-francesco_esortazione-ap_20180319_gaudete-et-exsultate.html (accessed on March 22, 2023).

[141] Cf. Wilfred Stinissen, *The Holy Spirit, Fire of Divine Love* (Ignatius Press, San Francisco, 2017), pp. 54ff.

[142] See *Lumen Gentium, n. 55.*

[143] Saint John of the Cross, *Collected Works*, p. 364.

[144] Blessed George Matulaitis, *Journal*, pp. 36-37 (October 24, 1910).

[145] John Paul II, *Novo Millennio Ineunte*, n. 15.

[146] Ibid., n. 38.

[147] John Paul II, Encyclical *Laborem Exercens*, n. 6, https://www.vatican.va/content/john-paul-ii/en/encyclicals/documents/hf_jp-ii_enc_14091981_laborem-exercens.html (accessed March 22, 2023): "… the basis for determining the value of human work is not primarily the kind of work being done but the fact that the one who is doing it is a person. The sources of the dignity of work are to be sought primarily in the subjective dimension, not in the objective one."

[148] A. Cencini, *La verità della vita. Formazione continua della mente credente* (San Paolo Edizioni, Milan, 2007), p. 286ff, footnote 11: "According to St. Bernard, the many occupations lead often to the 'hardness of heart which is nothing other than suffering of the spirit, confusion of the intellect, and the dispersion of grace' (*De Consideratione* II 3).

[149] Scott Hahn, *Catholic Bible Dictionary* (Image, New York, 2009), "Mystery," p. 633.

[150] Francis Martin and William Wright, *The Gospel of John (Catholic Commentary on Sacred Scripture)* (Baker Publishing, Grand Rapids, MI, 2015), p. 95.

[151] Smith, *The Immaculate: Mother and Teacher*, https://saintmaximiliankolbe.com/immaculate-mother-teacher/ (accessed March 22, 2023).

[152] *Online Etymology Dictionary*, accessed March 22, 2023.

[153] Cf. *Roman Missal*, "The Solemnity of the Immaculate Conception" (December 8).

[154] Blessed Columba Marmion, *Christ in His Mysteries*, 7th ed. (London: Sands, 1939), 22–24.

[155] Blessed Isaac of Stella, "Sermon 51," in the Office of Readings for Saturday of the II Week of Advent. Cf. *PL* 194, pp. 1862-1863, 1865.

[156] From the writings of St. Maximilian M. Kolbe, KW 1326. Quoted in Fr. Louis Maximilian Smith, FI. *"A Global Form of Catholic Life,"* https://saintmaximiliankolbe.com/a-global-form-of-catholic-life/ (accessed March 22, 2023).

[157] Smith, *The Era of the Immaculate*, https://saintmaximiliankolbe.com/the-era-of-the-immaculate (accessed March 22, 2023).

[158] Here, we have not only *per Mariam ad Jesum* but *per Iesum ad Mariam*. Cf. M. Bilniewicz, *Mariology of John Paul II: An Overview*, p. 90, particularly footnote 64, where John Paul II used this at the closing of the 20th International Mariological Conference in Rome, September 24, 2000. In Kevin Wagner and M. Isabel Neumann, *Mariology at the Beginning of the Third Millenium* (Pickwick Publications, Eugene, OR, 2017). Cf. S. Napiórkowski, *Per Iesum ad*

Mariam. Interpretacja Wypowiedzi Jana Pawła II. http://ptm.rel.pl/files/bi_ma/bm04/bm04_03napiorkowski.pdf (accessed March 26, 2020).

[159] Hahn, *Catholic Bible Dictionary*, p. 634.

[160] Ibid., p. 634.

[161] Pavel Florensky, *The Comforter*, quoted in: E. Rogers, *The Holy Spirit: Classic and Contemporary Readings* (Wiley-Blackwell, West Sussex, 2009), p. 231. Cf. Gregory of Nyssa, *Against Apolinarios*, 52; *Patrologia Greca*, vol. 45, col. 1249 D-1251 A.

[162] Raniero Cantalamessa, *The Gaze of Mercy: A Commentary on Divine and Human Mercy*, trans. Marsha Daigle-Williamson (Word Among Us Press, Frederick, MD, 2015), p. 165. See also *Roman Missal*, Tuesday after Pentecost.

[163] Blessed John Duns Scotus, *Lectura III Sent.*, 138: "It is more noble to forgive one's guilt by preserving that person from it, than by permitting that same person to fall into guilt and then to remit that person's guilt." Quoted in Noel Muscat, OFM, *John Duns Scotus and His Defence of the Immaculate Conception*, https://franciscanstudies.files.wordpress.com/2018/10/john_dunsimma.pdf (accessed May 12, 2023).

[164] John Paul II, *Dives in Misericordia* (Libreria Editrice Vaticana, Vatican City, 1980), n. 9.

[165] Saint Maximilian Kolbe, *Who Then Are You, O Immaculate Conception?*
https://www.piercedhearts.org/hearts_jesus_mary/heart_mary/max_kolbe_immaculate_conception.htm (accessed March 22, 2023).

[166] Saint John Henry Newman, *The Mission of My Life*,
https://www.johnhenrynewmancatholiccollege.org.uk/saint-john-henry-newman/ (accessed March 22, 2023).

[167] See Luke Bergis and Joshua Miller, *Unrepeatable* (Emmaus Road Publishing, Steubenville, OH, 2018).

[168] John Paul II, Encyclical *Evangelium Vitae* (Libreria Editrice Vaticana, Vatican City, 1995), n. 86.

[169] Kolbe, *Who Then Are You, O Immaculate Conception?*

[170] The title *Sponsa Spiritus Sancti,* "Spouse of the Holy Spirit," is applied to the Blessed Virgin Mary by St. Francis of Assisi in the Antiphon "Sancta Maria Virgo," within his Office of the Passion. Cf. J. Schneider, OFM, *Virgo Ecclesia Facta: The Presence of Mary in the Crucifix of San Damiano and in the Office of the Passion of St. Francis of Assisi* (Academy of the Immaculate, New Bedford, MA, 2004), p. 105.

[171] Christian Bergman, *Who is the real Immaculate Conception?* (Catholic Archdiocese of Melbourne) https://melbournecatholic.org/news/who-is-the-real-immaculate-conception (accessed on March 22, 2023).

[172] Saint Maximilian Kolbe, *SK 1318.* Quoted in: Jonathan Fleischmann, *Who Are You, O Immaculate Conception?*

[173] Saint Maximilian Kolbe, "Sketches for a Book," February 17, 1941, quoted in David Armstrong, *The Catholic Mary: Quite Contrary to the Bible?* (Verbum), p. 149.

[174] Cf. Rodrigues, *Perfection*: "In Hebrew, the concept of perfection is usually expressed with words derived from the root תמם (tmm), particularly the adjectives תָּמִים (*tāmîm*, 'complete, perfect') and תָּם (*tām*, 'complete, perfect') and the verb תָּמַם (*tāmam*, 'to be completed, be perfect')." See also *Theological Dictionary of the New Testament [TDNT]*, ed. Gerard Kittel and Gerard Friedrich (Grand Rapids, MI: Eerdmans, 1964), Vol. 4, p. 831.

[175] *The Message: Catholic/Ecumenical Edition; The Bible in Contemporary Language*, trans. Eugene H. Peterson and William Griffin (Tyndale House Publishers, Inc., Carol Stream, IL, 2013), Ephesians 1:4.

[176] Rodrigues, *Perfection.* cf. 2Sa 22:31, 33; Job 36:4; 37:16; Ps 18:31, 33; 19:8.

[177] Ibid.

[178] *Online Etymology Dictionary* (accessed March 22, 2023).

[179] Cf. John Paul II, Encyclical Letter *Redemptoris Mater* (Libreria Editrice Vaticana, Vatican City, 1987), n. 8.

[180] Karl Keating, *Catholicism and Fundamentalism, The Attack on "Romanism" by "Bible Christians,"* (Ignatius Press, San Francisco, 1998), p. 268-272: "Both theologically and philologically, he says, the word indicates 'a transformation of the subject.' The sense is not just 'to look upon with favor, but to transform by this favor or grace.' *Kecharitomene*, then, signifies a plenitude of favor or grace." Cf. Rene Laurentin, *The Truth of Christmas beyond the Myths* (St. Bed's Publications, Petersham, MA, 1986), pp. 18–19.

[181] Cf. Dave Armstrong, *A Biblical Defense of Catholicism* (Sophia Institute Press, Manchester, NH, 2003), p. 175-187.

[182] See Irenaeus of Lyons, *Adversus Haereses,* 4.20.1.

[183] Cf. NABRE comment on Ps 139:15, *The New American Bible, Revised Edition* (Our Sunday Visitor Publishing Division, Huntington, IN, 2012)..

[184] Cf. St. John of the Cross, *The Dark Night of the Soul,* in *The Collected Works of St. John of the Cross.*

[185] Cf. St. Ignatius of Loyola, *Spiritual Exercises,* "rules of discernment," pp. 169-179.

[186] Saint Augustine, *Sermo* 169, 13 (PL 38,923), quoted in *CCC,* 1847.

[187] See Timothy Gallagher, *The Examen Prayer: Ignatian Wisdom for Our Lives Today (*Crossroad Publishing Company, New York, 2006).

[188] Kumala, *The Immaculate Conception as the Icon of the Mercy of the Triune God.*

[189] *Roman Missal,* Preface for the Immaculate Conception, p. 1015. In fact, all the prefaces for the Blessed Virgin begin with praise of God. "It is truly right and just, our duty and our salvation, always and everywhere to give you thanks, Lord, holy Father, almighty and eternal God, and to praise, bless, and glorify your name [on the solemnity] of the Blessed ever-Virgin Mary," *(Preface I of the BVM; cf Preface II of the BVM).*

[190] Maximilian Kolbe, KW 1310, quoted in Smith, *The Immaculate: Mediatrix of Divine love.* https://saintmaximiliankolbe.com/the-immaculate-mediatrix-of-divine-love/ (accessed March 22, 2023).

[191] *Roman Missal,* Common Preface IV.

[192] Quoted in St. Alphonsus Liguori, *The Practice of the Love of Jesus Christ,* chapter 9 ("Charity thinketh no evil"), http://www.catholictradition.org/Christ/christ7-9a.htm (accessed June 6, 2023).

[193] Ignatius Loyola in *The Letters of St. Ignatius of Loyola*, translated by William J. Young, SJ, Chicago, 1959, n. 55.

[194] Saint Ambrose, *Commentary on the Gospel of Luke*, 2, 26-27. Quoted in Fr. Louis Smith, *"Deign to Tell Me Who You Are."*

[195] Benedict XVI, *Jesus of Nazareth,* p. 64.

[196] *Ratio Formationis*, n. 19.

[197] See Zygmunt Bauman, *Liquid Modernity* (Blackwell Publishers, Ltd, Malden, MA, 2000).

[198] John Paul II, Encyclical Letter *Redemptor Hominis* (Libreria Editrice Vaticana, 1979), n. 10.

[199] *Gaudium et Spes*, n. 24.

[200] John Paul II, *Dominum et Vivificantem*, nn. 23, 37, 39.

[201] Saint John of the Cross, *Collected Works*, p. 605.

[202] For an in-depth description of how to engage one's sorrow and pain so as to encounter the joy

of the resurrection, see Adam Young, "The Place We Find Ourselves," Episodes 24-26 (Podcast). See also the aforementioned book by Bob Schuchts, *Be Healed.*

[203] *Summa Theologiae*, I-II, q. 3, a. 1, ad 1.

[204] Cf. Ralph Martin, *The Fulfillment of All Desire: A Guidebook to God Based on the Wisdom of the Saints* (Emmaus Road, Steubenville, OH, 2006), p. 7ff.

[205] See the tenth and eleventh rules of the rules for the first week in Ignatius of Loyola, *Spiritual Exercises*, p. 171.

[206] Cf. Fr. Timothy Gallagher, *The Discernment of Spirits: An Ignatian Guide for Everyday living* (Crossroad, New York, 2005).

[207] Saint John of the Cross, *Spiritual Canticle*, in *Collected Works*, p. 65.

[208] *Daily Roman Missal* (Midwest Theological Forum, Inc, Woodbridge, IL, 2012), p. 701.

[209] See the Second Reading from St. Augustine in the Office of Readings for St. Philip Neri (May 26), Sermo 171,103,5; PL 38, 933-935.

[210] Cf. Jean-Charles Nault, *Noonday Devil: Acedia, the Unnamed Evil of Our Times*, trans. Michael J. Miller (Ignatius Press, San Francisco, 2015).

[211] Saint Maximilian Kolbe, *Sketch* from February 17, 1941, https://www.piercedhearts.org/hearts_jesus_mary/heart_mary/max_kolbe_immaculate_conception.htm (accessed June 7, 2023).

[212] Smith, *The Immaculate: Mediatrix of Divine Love.*

[213] St. Maximilian Kolbe, KW 991/Q. Quoted in: Fr. Louis Maximilian Smith, FI. *The Immaculate: Mediatrix of Divine love.* Accessed on March 22, 2023.

[214] Father Louis Smith, "A Global Form of Catholic Life."

[215] Saint Maximilian Kolbe, KW 643. Quoted in Father Louis Smith, *"A Global Form of Catholic Life."*

[216] *Dominum et Vivificantem*, n. 41.

[217] John Paul II, *Dominum et Vivificantem*, n. 38.

[218] Saint Stanislaus of Jesus and Mary Papczyński, *The Rule of Life*, https://padrimariani.org/en/mic-library/ (accessed May 5, 2023), n. 4, p. 15.

[219] Bogusław Gil, *Misterium Niepokalanego Poczęcia inspiracją i siłą Zgromadzenia Marianów*, Ephemerides Marianorum 3(2014), pp. 275-292.

[220] Saint John of the Cross, *Collected Works*, p. 882.

[221] *Online Etymology Dictionary*, (accessed July 11, 2017): "the sin of pretending to virtue or goodness" from the Attic Greek *hypokrisis* "acting on the stage; pretense."

[222] Cf. Henri de Lubac, *The Mystery of the Supernatural* (Herder & Herder, New York, 1998).

[223] *Constitutions and Directory*, n. 7.

[224] Cf. Thomas Merton, *New Seeds of Contemplation*, p. 74ff, as quoted in: Cencini, *La Verita della Vita*, p. 72ff.

[225] St. Maximilian Kolbe, SK 556, quoted in: Jonathan Fleischmann, *Transubstantiation into the Immaculate.*

[226] Ibid., SK 508.

[227] Ibid.

[228] Jonathan Fleischmann. *Who Are You, O Immaculate Conception?*

[229] Smith. *The Immaculate: Mediatrix of Divine Love.*

[230] From the writings of St. Maximilian M. Kolbe, KW 486, quoted in: Smith. *The Era of the Immaculate.*

[231] Blessed George Matulaitis, *Journal*, p. 45.

[232] Benedict XVI, Encyclical Letter *Caritas in Veritate* (Libreria Editrice Vaticana, Vatican City, 2009), n. 8ff.

[233] Bl. George Matulaitis, *Journal*, p. 60 (January 13, 1911).

[234] Ibid.

[235] See Donald H. Calloway, MIC, *The Immaculate Conception in the Life of the Church* (Marian Press, Stockbridge, MA 2004), pp. 121ff.

[236] Cf. *Marians in Prayer* (Marian Press, Rome — Stockbridge, MA, 2021), Prayer for Fidelity to Our Charism (Prayer for Friday Morning), p. 9.

[237] Cf. Francis, Apostolic Exhortation *Evangelii Gaudium* (Libreria Editrice Vaticana, Vatican City, 2013), n. 1.

[238] Cf. A. Cencini, *La Gioia* (Edizioni San Paolo, Milan, 2012).

[239] An example of this harmony between deep contemplation and activity is St. John Paul II, whose spirituality was profoundly influenced by St. John of the Cross.

[240] Benedict XVI, *Jesus of Nazareth*, Vol. II, p. 63.

[241] From the writings of St. Maximilian M. Kolbe, KW 508, quoted in Smith, *"A Global Form of Catholic Life."*

[242] P. D. Fehlner, "Mariae Advocatae Causa: The Marian Issue in the Church Today," in *Mary: Unique Cooperator in the Redemption* (Academy of the Immaculate, New Bedford, MA, 2005), pp. 538-539. Quoted in Smith, *The Immaculate: Mother and Teacher,* https://saintmaximiliankolbe.com/immaculate-mother-teacher/ (accessed March 23, 2023).

[243] KW 991/O, April 14, 1933, quoted in Smith, *The Era of the Immaculate*. Accessed on March 23, 2023.

[244] From the writings of St. Maximilian M. Kolbe, KW 382, quoted in Fr. Louis Maximilian Smith, FI, *Deign to Tell Me Who You Are*, https://saintmaximiliankolbe.com/deign-to-tell-me-who-you-are/ (accessed March 23, 2023).

[245] Ibid.

[246] *SK* 1307, quoted in ibid.

[247] Albert VanHoye, *A Different Priest. The Letter to the Hebrews* (Convivium Press, Miami, 2011), p. 287.

[248] *Roman Missal*, Eucharistic Prayer I: "hostiam immaculatam."

[249] Cf. Fulton Sheen, *The Priest Is Not His Own* (Mockingbird Press, Augusta, GA, 2022). Albert VanHoye, *A Different Priest: The Letter to the Hebrews,* p. 266ff on Heb 9:14: "The qualifying description given to Christ, who 'offered himself immaculate,' corresponds to the prescription laid down in Leviticus concerning animals offered in sacrifice (Lev 1:3, 10; 3:1, 6, 9; etc.), but the meaning is obviously different. For the animals, it was about the absence of physical blemish; for Christ, it is about moral and spiritual integrity."

[250] Benedict XVI, *Jesus of Nazareth, Holy Week*, p. 60.

[251] *Summa Theologiae*, III q. 66, a. 2. *Roman Missal*, Solemnity of the Immaculate Conception (December 8), Collect: "you preserved her from every stain by virtue of the Death of your Son, which you foresaw."

[252] Servais Pinckaers, *The Spirituality of Martyrdom: To the Limits of Love* (CUA Press, Washington, DC, 2016).

[253] Blessed George Matulaitis, *His Life*, https://www.matulaitis-matulewicz.org/hislife.php (accessed April 1, 2020).

[254] *Merriam-Webster's Collegiate Dictionary*, s.v. "oblation."

[255] Quoted in Fr. Stefano Manelli, FI, *"Only Love Creates,"* https://saintmaximiliankolbe.com/only-love-creates/ (accessed May 8, 2023).

[256] Cf. John Paul II, Audience of November 23, 1988, "Behold Your Mother!" https://www.ewtn.com/catholicism/library/behold-your-mother-24191# (accessed March 23, 2023).

[257] For more consideration of this, see Edith Stein, *The Science of the Cross*, trans. Josephine Koeppel, OCD (ICS Publications, Washington, DC, 2002).

[258] Rafael Arnaiz Baron, *Obras Completas* (Editorial Monte Carmelo, Burgos, Spain, 2017), n. 1133, p. 935.

[259] Cf. *The Navarre Bible. Saint Paul's Letters to the Thessalonians, and Pastoral Letters* (Scepter Publishers, New York, 1999), Commentary on 1 Thess 4:1.

[260] Saint John Chrysostom, *Homily on 1 Thess*, 4:1, quoted in ibid.

[261] Cf. *Deus Caritas Est* n. 7.

[262] Cf. Jn 14:23; 1 Cor 3:16, 6:19; 2 Cor 6:16.

[263] *Sacrosanctum Concilium*, n. 47.

[264] Cf. *CCC* 1368.

[265] Philo, *Sacr.* AC., 51: "But Moses says that he will 'sacrifice the abominations of the Egyptians to God,' namely the virtues which are faultless and most becoming victims..." Quoted in: *Theological Dictionary of the New Testament*, Vol. 4, p. 831.

[266] Cf. Jose Arias, *The Morning Star*, trans. Ven. Casimir Wyszyński (Marian Heritage Press, Stockbridge, MA, 2019), p. 17. Cf. *Lumen Gentium*, n. 65; John Paul II, General Audience of Sept. 3, 1997; *Constitutions and Directory*, n. 13, 18, 24; Paul VI, Apostolic Exhortation *Marialis Cultus* (Libreria Editrice Vaticana, Vatican City, 1974), n. 35.

[267] *Prayer of Consecration to the Immaculate Conception*, http://www.all-about-the-virgin-mary.com/prayer-of-consecration-to-mary.html (accessed May 23, 2023).

[268] *Litany to the Holy Spirit*, https://www.ewtn.com/catholicism/devotions/litany-to-the-holy-spirit-266 (accessed May 23, 2023).

[269] *Litany of the Holy Spirit*, https://hozana.org/en/prayer/litany-of-the-saints/holy-spirit (accessed May 23, 2023).

[270] *Litany of the Holy Spirit*, https://sacredheartsisters.com/wp-content/uploads/2020/05/Litany_of_the_Holy_Spirit.pdf (accessed May 23, 2023).

[271] From *Marians at Prayer*, a private prayer book used by the Marians, pp. 67-68.

[272] Litany to the Immaculate Conception in Benjamin Francis Musser, OFM, *Kyrie Eleison — Two Hundred Litanies* (Magnificat Press, Westminster, MD, 1944). Quoted in Litany to the Immaculate Conception, https://www.catholicculture.org/culture/liturgicalyear/prayers/view.cfm?id=1127 (accessed May 23, 2023).

[273] Litany of the Immaculate Conception of Mary, Mother of God, https://magnificat.ca/odm/en/litany-of-the-immaculate-conception-of-mary-mother-of-god/ (Accessed May 23, 2023).

[274] *Litany to the Immaculate Conception*, https://fatima.org/wp-content/uploads/2021/06/Litany-12-Immaculate-Conception.pdf (accessed May 23, 2023).

[275] *Marians at Prayer*, p. 43-44.

About the Author

Father Thaddaeus Lancton was born as the youngest son to a Catholic family of five on February 22, 1987, in Houston, TX. He had two childhood dreams: becoming an Air Force pilot and an astronaut, and becoming a priest. Having lost grandparents and parents during his youth, he learned from a young age to pray for the Holy Souls in Purgatory.

After attending Strake Jesuit for high school, Fr. Thaddaeus entered the Jesuit novitiate for one year in 2005. After leaving, he entered the Marian Fathers of the Immaculate Conception in 2007.

He has obtained a B.A. in philosophy at Franciscan University of Steubenville, a Master of Science in psychology from the Divine Mercy University, and a doctorate in sacred theology from the John Paul II Catholic University in Lublin, Poland. He is the author of *Stepping on the Serpent: The Journey of Trust with Mary* (Marian Press, 2017).

Since Fr. Thaddaeus has learned and speaks various languages, he has lived and worked in the Philippines, Poland, Bolivia, and Argentina. He is currently assigned to the Marian house in Steubenville, Ohio as formator for the seminarians.

Father Thaddaeus is inspired by the mystery of the Immaculate Conception to live and proclaim the free gift of the mercy of God, which accompanies, protects, and guides us from conception until death.